AT THE HEART OF THE UNITED STATES AIR FORCE ARE ITS PEOPLE. THE PILOTS AND AIR CREW, THE GROUND TECHNICIANS, SERVICING TECHNICIANS, LOGISTICAL SUPPORT STAFF AND ALL THE SUNDRY JOBS REQUIRED TO OPERATE THE WORLD'S LARGEST GLOBAL AIR POWER COME TOGETHER IN PERFORMANCE AND A CONSTANT STATE OF READINESS, EPITOMISED HERE BY THE CREW OF AN F-15E STRIKE EAGLE AS VIEWED FROM THE AFT WINDOW OF A KC-135A REFUELING TANKER. *USAF*

Contents

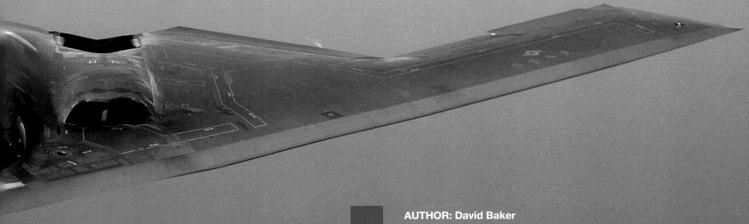

AUTHOR: David Baker
DESIGN: atg-media.com
PUBLISHER: Steve O'Hara
PUBLISHING DIRECTOR: Dan Savage
REPROGRAPHICS: Jonathan Schofield and Paul Fincham
PRODUCTION EDITOR: Dan Sharp
ADVERTISING MANAGER: Sue Keily, skeily@mortons.co.uk
MARKETING MANAGER: Charlotte Park
COMMERCIAL DIRECTOR: Nigel Hole

PUBLISHED BY: Mortons Media Group Ltd, Media Centre,
Morton Way, Horncastle, Lincolnshire LN9 6JR.
Tel: 01507 529529

ACKNOWLEDGEMENTS: The author would like to thank the
United States Air Force for help and assistance over 50 years
of a close working cooperation in research and associated
activities in many locations around the world, the sum total of
which has formed the basis for some of the material used in this
publication. Secondarily, the assistance of the US Department
of Defense over a similar period has contributed greatly to
gathering historical material which has also contributed to the
information on these pages. In particular to Bettie Sprigg at the
Pentagon so many years ago and who opened so many doors.
Thanks are also due to Steve O'Hara at Mortons for having
published this book, suffering the vagaries of the author along
the way, and to the production editor, Dan Sharp, with whom it
has been a pleasure to work.

PRINTED BY: William Gibbons and Sons, Wolverhampton

ISBN: 978-1-911276-32-6

Uncertain Prelude

The call for Americans to take to the skies over future battlefields came in 1783 when Benjamin Franklin observed a hot-air balloon ascending over the rooftops of Paris. Impressed by their free-floating disregard for boundaries and borders, he foresaw invading armies using balloons to cross land dominated by enemies to place troops at the rear of combat units.

That capability achieved plausibility when Jean-Pierre Blanchard crossed the English Channel in a balloon less than two years later.

The French concurred with Franklin and set up the world's first military air unit – the Aerostatic Corps – in 1794 but Napoleon disregarded the balloon as an observation post, disbanded the Corps and some say, lost the battle of Waterloo as a result.

A year earlier, in 1793 Blanchard had taken his balloon to the United States from where he made the first ascent from North American soil watched by George Washington, who disagreed with Napoleon and encouraged development of the unpredictable devices. But the Army apparently sided with Napoleon and thought them a frivolous distraction, avoiding requests for their use during the war with the Seminole Indians in 1840 and against the Mexicans at Vera Cruz in 1846. Just 15 years later they came into their own when hydrogen balloons were deployed first by the North in the American Civil War, and then by the South, from 1861. But it was a short-lived romance with lighter-than-air flight; by the following year both sides regarded them as superfluous.

In 1892 Brigadier General Adolphus W. Greely, Chief Signal Officer, set up a balloon section and shipped one to Cuba for the war against the Spanish. Operating from the region around Santiago, it directed artillery fire at the famous Battle of San Juan Hill. This came to an inglorious halt when bullets riddled the envelope and brought it down near to enemy lines.

But the potential for balloons had been emphatically set down when besieged Parisian dignitaries during the Franco-Prussian war of 1870-71 sought a means of evacuation across encircling enemy lines by making good their escape by air. Unfortunately the plan went askew when the prevailing winds lifted them up only to deposit them in the ranks of enemy troops laying siege to the capital!

Undaunted by such embarrassing episodes, the British took balloon troops to Africa during the campaign in the Sudan during 1885 where they were used at Mafeking among other places. They subsequently played a major role in the Boer War where they were handled and exploited with military precision and great success, enabling drawings of enemy positions sent to the ground in message bags sliding down the retaining cable. It was all a bit Heath Robinson but it worked and the Army quickly gained respect for its 'balloonatics'.

Waves of change were on the way, however. What was really required was a lighter-than-air craft capable of liberated flight but in a controlled direction. That became possible with the advent of the airship during the 1890s, placing propellers powered by reciprocating engines on gas envelopes and directing them through the air at will using rudders and elevators. Most notable were the dirigibles of Count von Zeppelin and the Brazilian Alberto Santos Dumont shortly after the dawn of a new century. The Brazilian would be the first to make significant contributions to both lighter-than-air and heavier-then-air flight but not before two Americans had become the first to take a flying machine into the air.

Inspired by the logic of scientific principles, Wilbur and Orville Wright had thought through the engineering necessary to use a lightweight reciprocating engine to provide the forward motion and accelerate the passage of air across a lifting surface. That would, in turn allow an aircraft to ascend from the ground and fly at will, devoid of the complexity of a large gas bag. They built their Wright Flyer No. 1 and powered it into the air for the first time on December 17, 1903.

But the brothers were difficult to work with, reclusive and suspicious that the secrets of their aeroplane would be stolen by competitors. In fact the majority of Americans would not discover this

TRAVERSÉE EN BALLON DU PAS-DE-CALAIS PAR BLANCHARD ET JEFFERIES 1785

Monument élevé à la mémoire de Blanchard au lieu de sa descente près de Calais.
COLLECTION. 476.   1ʳᵉ Série(N°2)   ROMANET & Cⁱᵉ IMP. EDITᴬ PARIS.

ABOVE: One of the most notable early balloonists was Pierre Henri Blanchard who made his first ascent in a hydrogen balloon from Paris in March 1784, heralding a new age of flight and a potential military use of the new science of aeronautics. *DAVID BAKER*

ABOVE: US troops inflating the balloon Intrepid in 1862 during the American Civil War. Aerial reconnaissance and gun laying was a new use for balloons and served to demonstrate the many ways in which both they and aeroplanes would be valuable for future military applications. DAVID BAKER

LEFT: Blanchard signalled the end of England's isolation from the European continent when he became the first person to cross the English Channel in a balloon in 1785, making his first balloon flight in America in 1793. DAVID BAKER

ABOVE: The world's first 'aircraft carrier', the George Washington Parke Custis was acquired by the Union Navy during the Civil War of 1861-65 as a platform from which to spy on Confederate forces. US ARMY

ABOVE: In the Franco-Prussian war of 1870-71, Parisians besieged by Prussian forces sought a way of escape by taking to balloons, most of which came down in the ranks of the encircling army with some being swept out to sea! DAVID BAKER

world-changing feat, which had been achieved by Americans on US soil, until several years later. At the time of his graduation from West Point in 1907, Henry H. Arnold, the future commander of US Army Air Forces had no knowledge that aircraft existed. Two years earlier the Wrights had offered the Flyer to the Army Board of Ordnance of Fortification which all but questioned the very existence of an aeroplane.

With justifiable reason, for the US government and the informed citizenry were sceptical about powered heavier-than-air flight after the exploits of Samuel Pierpont Langley, an astronomer and inventor who built models of flying machines. Langley sent them successfully down the Potomac River at a height of 80ft, powered by a flash boiler using steam. But attempts to get a man in the air with bigger aircraft were unsuccessful, despite getting the attention of the US Navy who set up a board to study the concept using funds appropriated by the War Department. On two attempts, at the end of 1903 and in early 1904, the Langley contraption got

fouled by its launch catapult and collapsed into the river.

By 1905 the Wrights had responded to overtures from the British to buy Wright flying machines by offering the design to the US Army, so as to keep the invention in America, they said. But when asked by the Wrights to present their requirements, the Board of Ordnance and Fortification refused to issue a specification. By the end of the year the Wrights had been approached by the French too and on hearing about the overseas interest aroused by the Wright Flyer, President Theodore Roosevelt intervened. He had already heard about the invention from the Aero Club of America, from whence things moved quickly.

On August 1, 1907, the Signal Corps set up its Aeronautical Division to govern "all matters pertaining to military ballooning, air machines

and all kindred subjects" with Captain Charles de F. Chandler in charge together with two enlisted men. They were to examine the advancing science of 'aeronautics' as well as radio-telephony for communications to and from the ground. Finally, in December, and in response to President Roosevelt's directive, Secretary of War William H. Taft requested bids for a flying machine capable of carrying two people at 40mph for 125 miles. Only the Wright brothers responded by producing an aeroplane.

Suddenly, almost overnight it seemed, the Army was talking about aviation. The industrialists, businessmen and sportsmen who populated the Aero Club, founded in 1905 to promote all forms of flying, encouraged debate about the uses of flying machines. One Captain William 'Billy' Mitchell lectured on the uses of aeroplanes for reconnaissance and for dropping

ABOVE: Samuel Pierpont Langley made heroic attempts to propel a powered flying machine into the air but failed, his name immortalised in one of the first aeronautical laboratories in America. *NACA*

ABOVE: The world's first heavier than air powered flight took place at Kill Devil Hills, North Carolina, on December 17, 1903, when Orville Wright flew a distance of 120ft in 12 seconds at an average speed of 6.8mph in a freezing wind gusting to 27mph. *NACA*

ABOVE: Orville Wright prepares to demonstrate the vicissitudes of the Wright A flying machine as the reclusive Wright brothers seek a contract with the US Army. *US ARMY*

LEFT: The Wright A Flyer at Fort Myer near Washington, DC, on September 9, 1908, where the Army Signal Corps would make its first purchase of a powered flying machine. *US ARMY*

bombs. As part of his examination and portfolio of submissions for the rank of captain, Mitchell had studied aeronautical theory at Fort Myer, greatly influenced by the enthusiasm for such applications from General Greely.

Despite the growing interest in heavier-than-air machines, there was still discussion about the higher weight-lifting capabilities of airships and the Army decided to offer $25,000 for a winning dirigible. Seeking backing for his airship, Thomas Baldwin offered to sell his design for a mere $6750, hoping to secure sales and recoup his money on volume deliveries. His airship was accepted and made some impressive appearances throughout 1908.

But it was the Wright Brothers who benefitted most from this new interest in flying, which would soon gather popular support as American citizens got a glimpse, for the first time, of what aircraft really were and how they could perform. Rejected a year before and dismissed by Army traditionalists, the order for a Wright flying machine, the first government contract for an American aeroplane, was placed on February 10, 1908.

THE WRIGHT STUFF

Wilbur and Orville Wright had made considerable progress since making their first flight in December 1903, their improved designs retaining the tried and tested pusher layout with chain-drive between the engine and the propellers set across a biplane configuration with a foreplane stabiliser in front and twin vertical rudders aft.

The machine they brought to Fort Myer, Virginia (named after the man who disbanded the balloon section after the Civil War!), across the Potomac from Washington for initial trials on August 20, 1908, had a wingspan of 40ft. It was slightly modified over the Wrights' standard A-model airframe powered by a four-cylinder Wright engine of 25hp set on the lower wing to the right of the centreline. The pilot sat in the centre, with the passenger to his right on cushioned seats next to the engine. The cylindrical fuel tank was above the lower wing to the left of the engine with a thin narrow, vertical radiator set to fill the space between upper and lower wings.

Skids were provided to satisfy an Army requirement for the aircraft to be capable of flying from rough ground but the method of getting it

into the air was still by catapult along a prepared rail, a heavy falling weight pulling a running cable to launch the aircraft. In a favourable headwind it could get into the air under its own power, however. Once in the air, the pilot used levers to his left to control the aircraft. Forwards and backwards movements operated the elevator for pitch control and the wings were warped to go left or right.

The first flight demonstration took place on September 2 and over the following two weeks various flights were conducted including some with a passenger. On what was supposed to be the final preliminary demonstration flight on September 17, 1908, Orville Wright took to the air carrying Lt Thomas Etholen Selfridge. The propeller cracked, snagged a flying wire and the aircraft crashed to the ground from a height of 125ft. Orville was severely injured, but survived, while Selfridge died a few hours later, the first casualty to flying. On impact his head hit a strut, fracturing his skull. From then on, Army pilots wore head protection.

It had fallen to Lt Selfridge to be the first US Army officer to fly solo, when he had flown the *White Wing*, designed and put together by Alexander Graham Bell's Aerial Experiment Association (AEA). Sponsored by Baldwin, *White*

Wright B

A development of the Wright Flyer which could trace its origin to the aircraft in which Wilbur and Orville Wright first flew, the Wright B was purchased by the US government and attached to the Aeronautical Division of the Signal Corp in 1911. The aircraft was also built by Burgess under license and a modified version became the first aircraft to cross the United States. The flight began on September 17, 1911, from Brooklyn, New York, and ended at Long Beach on December 10 after a total flying time of 84 hours. Another version of the Wright B was built under licence by Curtiss as the Model F.

LENGTH	26ft
WINGSPAN	39ft
HEIGHT	8.75ft
GROSS WEIGHT	1250lb
MAXIMUM SPEED	45mph
CRUISING SPEED	40mph
RANGE	110 miles

Wing was the second aircraft developed by the AEA with considerable contributions, including engine, from Glenn Curtiss, who would very quickly achieve fame for his progressive aircraft designs. Selfridge had been assigned by the government to work with the AEA and helped design *Red Wing*, the AEA's first aeroplane, which flew for the first time on March 12, 1908, but was destroyed on its second flight.

An improved aircraft was brought to Fort Myer in June 1909 with observers assigned by the Army to record and to evaluate its performance. On July 27, Orville Wright kept his machine and his passenger, Lt Frank Latham, aloft for one hour, 12 minutes and 40 seconds, achieving a record in the process. Three days later an ebullient crowd of 7000 spectators at Alexandria, Virginia, watched President Taft welcome Orville Wright and Lt Benjamin D. Foulois, back from a 10-mile cross-country flight at an average speed of 42.5mph. This achievement gave the Wrights a bonus of $5000 on top of the $25,000 contract price.

The Army formally accepted the Wright Model A on August 2, 1909, with the historic number '1' in the list of aircraft serials that began a sequence which today runs into the several hundred thousand. Aeroplane No 1 was used extensively and by 1911 was in seriously poor condition through many landing accidents and repair cycles. It was finally retired on May 4, 1911, but is now in the custody of the Smithsonian Institution in Washington, DC.

Military aircraft serial numbers ran consecutively until a complete revision of the system in 1921 which awarded numbers contained within the financial year of the contract award. Starting each fiscal year at 1 and running to conclusion at the end of that fiscal year, it was prefixed with the last two digits of the financial year. The highest number reached by the date of transition (June 30, 1921) at the start of fiscal year 1922, was 68,592, the accumulated number of aircraft ordered by the Army to that date. The system exists to the present day.

Part of the contract awarded to the Wrights was that they should train two Army officers to be pilots and in October 1909 Wilbur trained Lieutenants Lahm and Frederick E. Humphreys at a field adjacent to College Park, Maryland. Both men soloed and with only three hours flying time apiece were officially inducted as the first Army pilots on October 26. Because an Army regulation restricted the amount of time an officer could be called to 'special duties', Lahm returned to his cavalry unit and Humphreys rejoined the Engineers, leaving the Army without pilots. Neither did it have a serviceable aeroplane, No 1 having been damaged in a crash landing on November 5.

While No 1 was in repair, because the wood, canvas and wire-braced aeroplanes of the day were unsuitable for the wintry weather of DC, the Army moved operations to Fort Sam Houston, Texas, and received No 1 in February 1910. The only candidate for pilot duty was Lt Foulois. On March 2 he took to the air to teach himself to fly, of necessity each ascent being a solo on instructions by letter from the Wrights! Eventually someone from the Wrights turned up to give practical advice and Foulois made 61 flights between March and September but still the Army had only one pilot and one aeroplane.

RIGHT: *American publishing magnate William Randolph Hearst offered a $50,000 prize to the first man to fly across the US coast-to-coast. The most flamboyant flight attempt was made by Calbraith Perry Rogers who named his Wright EX after a sponsor, the manufacturer of the grape drink* **Vin Fiz.** *DAVID BAKER*

BELOW: *A contrast of flying devices as the Wright 'Military Flyer' is moved at Fort Myer alongside a gas balloon used for reconnaissance.US ARMY*

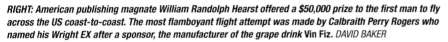

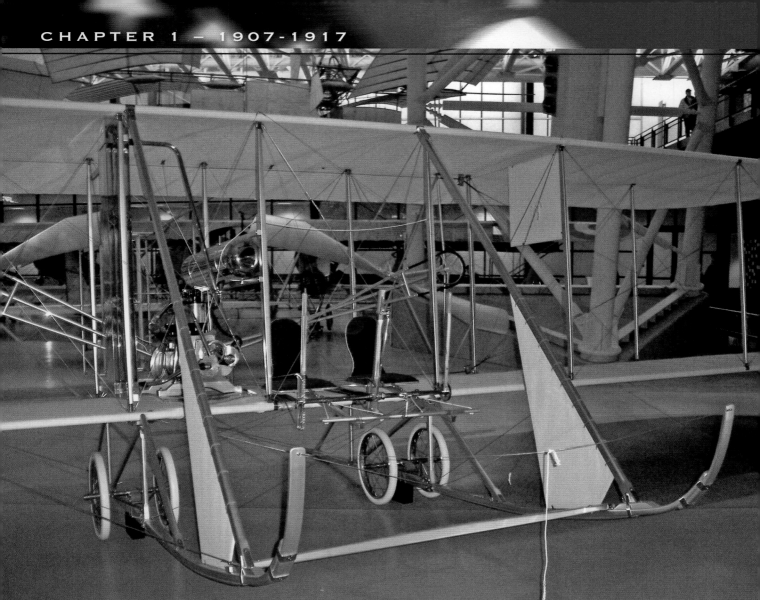

ABOVE: A progressive development of the early Wright aeroplanes, the Wright B, seen here as a replica at the National Air and Space Museum, Washington, DC, incorporated a wheeled undercarriage and modified controls, a considerable improvement on the Wright A. DAVID BAKER

When Aeroplane No 1 was retired in May 1911 and delivered up to the Smithsonian in October it went in parallel with the first funding awarded by Congress for Army aviation, the Signal Corps having previously awarded contracts from its experimental fund and from readjusting payments from other sectors. During 1910, Fort Sam Houston had a meagre $150 for fuel, oil and repairs, while Foulois had funded himself through pilot 'training'. That all changed on March 13, 1911, when Congress appropriated $125,000, whereupon Chief Signal Officer James Allen ordered five new aircraft at about $5000 apiece. In April a Wright B and a single-seat Curtiss Model D arrived with a 60hp engine, the latter being Army Aeroplane No. 2.

After a brief period away from heading up the Aeronautical Division, Captain Chandler resumed his position in June 1911 and presided over an expansion of the inventory and the facilities. Long

duration flights of 42 miles were accomplished, achieving altitudes of more than 4000ft and investigations began into the use of aerial photography and new bombsights, the latter developed by Riley E. Scott. But when the Army had no money to develop it further, Scott took his invention to Europe and returned richer by $5000. To avoid the winter weather, activities moved to Augusta, Georgia, returning to College Park in April 1912.

During the year a further dozen pilots were trained up and visits were made to manufacturing plants for shop and flying courses, their training now expanding to the mechanics of flight and the more sophisticated nuances of flying. In August 1912 Foulois took two aeroplanes to Connecticut to determine the advantages of reconnaissance from a prescribed altitude of 2000ft during exercises. By the end of the year College Park had 14 flying officers, 39 enlisted men and nine

aeroplanes, including one hydroplane from the Burgess Company, the first tractor biplane bought by the Army.

For winter the Wright aeroplanes went to Georgia while the Curtiss machines were taken to San Diego, California, where Glenn Curtiss had a facility. This would become the Army's first permanent aviation school. In February 1913 the group at Augusta were ordered south to join the 2nd Army Division in Texas City where they prepared to support military operations against General Victoriano Huerta, who had seized power in Mexico on February 23. While he was there, Chandler organised his men into the 1st Aero Squadron which began the formal recognition of an active military aviation unit.

A STRUGGLE FOR INDEPENDENCE

The crisis in Mexico never did develop into a war with the US but considerable time was spent in the air exploring how flying could best assist an army in the field. There was deep dissatisfaction among the aviators however, who were becoming increasingly frustrated by what they saw as the heavy-handed leadership of ground-hugging staff officers at the top in Washington – oblivious to the unique nature of this new adjunct to the Signal Corps. The aviators became vocal, writing with their complaints to senior military figures in the

COMMANDERS 1914-1917

• Captain Charles deForest Chandler	*Aug 1, 1907 – June 30, 1910*
• Captain Arthur S. Cowan	*July 1, 1910 – June 19, 1911*
• Captain Charles deForest Chandler	*June 20, 1911 – September 9, 1914*
• Major Samuel Reber	*September 10, 1913 – July 17, 1914*
• Lieutenant Colonel Samuel Reber	*July 18, 1914 – May 5, 1916*
• Lieutenant Colonel George O. Squier	*May 6, 1916 – February 19, 1917*

ABOVE: One of the greatest challenges in the first decade of aeronautical flight was the low power of aircraft engines, maintenance being frequent and repairs common. This engine is undergoing attention at the Curtiss hangar at San Diego in 1914. US ARMY

ABOVE: Henry H. Arnold graduated from West Point in 1907, when he had never heard of aeroplanes, and would progress through the ranks of the US Army and command the largest assembly of combat aircraft of all time during the Second World War. US ARMY

nation's capital. The seeds of autonomy had been sown and were enshrined within those letters, which had the desired effect and began a process of change that would take 34 years to complete.

By 1913 the San Diego school, fast becoming the core facility for Army aviation, was supplemented by two other schools, one in the Philippines and another in Hawaii, which was not yet a State of the Union. Gradually aviation slipped away from College Park and the home of Army aviation was returned to more conventional forms of military training amid idyllic surroundings, a welcome respite for those seeking to escape the summer humidity of Washington.

In 1912 qualified military pilots had first been awarded badges denoting their affiliation as Army aviators and the following year, with 30 regularly assigned to flying duties, there was an appeal for volunteers to join the new group of elite young men who made up their ranks. Some were of the opinion that their organisation should be separated from the Army, to become an independent force in its own right, but not everyone agreed. Among the pilots, few thought they had the established credentials, or the necessary experience for full independence.

A bill was presented in Congress calling for separation but it failed to pass. Even so, special legislation enacted on July 18, 1914, afforded special recognition to Army aviation, an act which changed the name of the Aeronautical Section, US Signal Corps, to the Aviation Section of the Signal Corps – with an authorised strength of 60 officers and 260 enlisted men to take charge of all military aircraft, balloons and related flying equipment. But it also limited officers to unmarried lieutenants of the line and most of the volunteers would come from branches other than the Signal Corps. Despite this new sense of heightened recognition, the Aviation Section remained a very small component of an Army that now boasted 98,544 officers and men.

By 1914 the Signal Corps had five years of reasonable experience with both pusher and tractor configurations but the Signal Corps condemned the pusher types since they had accounted for almost all fatalities experienced up to that point. When pusher types crashed nose down, as they usually did, the engine was rammed forward into the pilot and his passenger, often resulting in fatal injuries. Aircraft design was moving away from the Wright Flyer generation to a new breed of aeroplane that was faster, more powerful and with much improved performance. Flying was becoming an all-weather pursuit too, and was developing capabilities that would see the emergence of flying fighting forces.

Just as war was breaking out on eastern and western fronts in Europe, in September 1914 the 1st Aero Squadron was reorganised on a more formal basis at the order of the War Department. Now consisting of 16 officers and 75 enlisted men with eight aeroplanes, the squadron was under the command of Captain Foulois. As the sole tactical strength of the Aviation Section, it would form the cornerstone of expansive growth when America entered the First World War in April 1917. Before then, there were other battles to fight.

Trouble with Mexico broke out again in 1915 when Francisco 'Pancho' Villa threatened to send attacking bandits across the border and on March 9, 1916, he raided Columbus, New Mexico. President Woodrow Wilson asked Brigadier General John J. Pershing to assign 15,000 troops to suppressing the Mexican revolutionaries and the 1st Aero Squadron arrived at Columbus on March 15. Four days later they began flying operations but struggled to make the overland flight to the forward position at Casas Grandes, Mexico. One aircraft had to turn back, one was damaged on a forced landing and the remaining six had to make a night landing. Moreover, they were unable to climb over the 12,000ft mountains. ▶

ABOVE: Alexander Graham Bell played a significant role in the development of aviation, seen here (bearded) with Lieutenant Thomas Selfridge who became the first fatal casualty to an air crash on September 17, 1908. US ARMY

ABOVE: Captain Charles deForest Chandler holds a Lewis gun in a Wright B with pilot Lieutenant Roy C. Kirtland. Chandler fired the gun in flight for the first time on June 7, 1912, a portent of air-to-air dogfights to come. US ARMY

Curtiss JN

ABOVE: *While aviation was taking leaps into the future during the war of 1914-18, American aircraft were adopting the latest design trends, evidenced by the Curtiss Jenny. This JN-4 is on display at the Museum of Aviation, Robins Air Force Base, Georgia.*

In a series of almost comical episodes, Foulois was forced to land, taken prisoner, jailed, then set free when the recognised Mexican authorities came to his rescue, while other aircraft were set upon by over-enthusiastic supporters of the rebel cause, stealing bits of aircraft which then proceeded to shed various parts as they attempted to fly! By April 20, six of the eight aeroplanes had been condemned as unusable while replacements fared no better, unable to cope with the extreme temperature and altitude conditions prevalent.

While US Army aviation progressed on a series of stuttering steps, the US aviation industry was falling behind its European counterparts and manufacturers looked across the Atlantic to the technical developments which were already dramatically outpacing anything available in the United States. The aircraft taken to Mexico included Curtiss JN types, designed by B. Douglas Thomas, formerly an engineer with Avro in Britain. He had been commissioned by Curtiss to come up with a tractor biplane using the established techniques then becoming standard practice in European design and layout.

The JN types – very quickly dubbed the 'Jennies' – were designed as trainers and orders were soon being taken from Britain as the demand there outstripped production capacity. Curtiss had turned a pre-war flying boat, the America (designed by another Englishman, John C. Porte), into a successful export to Britain

where the Royal Navy put them to good use as maritime patrol aircraft. They sponsored development in Britain into the even more successful Felixstowe flying boats, originating from the basic Curtiss design.

Orders from the UK underpinned a major growth in US manufacturing capability but it was a demand-based industry responding to requirements from foreign buyers and did little to produce the kind of equipment the Aviation Section called for. The Jennies were ideal for training, stable and easy to control. But they lacked the power performance, agility and adaptability that characterised most European aircraft built for fighting or for protracted aerial reconnaissance duties.

While the industry was experiencing a modest upsurge in demand, subsidising the building of new factories, Congress recognised the need for more direct access to aircraft being produced for overseas orders and in March 1916 gave the Aviation Section a budget of $500,000 for the year – twice what it had before. By this date the JN-4 was being introduced on the Mexican campaign and there was some improvement in overall performance. Deals were being done with European engine builders, Wright developing an engine with Hispano Suiza which powered some of the JN-4 types, aircraft which now had a top speed of 75mph and a range of 250 miles.

Despite progress, there was better news to come. With war in Europe and the Middle East

Designed by Englishman Benjamin Douglas Thomas, the Curtiss Jenny series aeroplanes appeared in 1915. The type was bought by the Aeronautical Division as a trainer for new pilots. Several versions and variants were produced for the Army and the Jenny became popular after the war for 'barnstorming' displays at fetes and air shows across America. The 1st Aero Squadron received its first JN-2 in July 1915. The aircraft became so popular that it was eventually manufactured by six different companies and continued to be flown regularly into the 1930s.

LENGTH	27.3ft
WING SPAN	43.6ft
HEIGHT	9.9ft
GROSS WEIGHT	1920lb
MAXIMUM SPEED	75mph
CRUISING SPEED	60mph
RANGE	120 miles

taking on a new technological dimension the US Congress recognised the need for action and the National Defense Act of June 1916 significantly increased the size and manpower invested in the Aviation Section and provided, through a budget act of August 29, the unimaginable sum of $13 million for military aeronautics in the Signal Corps and the National Guard. General Pershing took a personal interest in the potential of aviation and recognised the extraordinary growth in aircraft applications for military purposes on the Western Front in the war in Europe. ✪

Chapter 2: War! 1917-1918

ABOVE: Even before the 1914-18 war, large aircraft produced by other nations were flying between distant places, far outstripping the performance of any indigenous American designs. Russia's Sikorsky S-22 Il'ya Muromets made a number of lengthy flights soon after it appeared in 1913 as the world's first four-engine aircraft. This example is displayed in the Monino museum. *DAVID BAKER*

By the time Woodrow Wilson took the United States to war with the approval of Congress on April 6, 1917, the Aviation Section had expanded beyond its meagre strength during the onset of the Mexican war. And on that day it received another name change, to the Aeronautical Division of the US Signal Corps. But the equipment it used still lagged far behind the standard set by current front-line aircraft in Europe, where speeds in excess of 100mph were common and engines of 160hp were standard for large aeroplanes.

Giant Russian aircraft with four engines were flying several hundred miles on a single sortie, heavily armed 'scouts' were being transformed into highly manoeuvrable fighters with forward-firing machine guns, and bombers capable of

delivering several hundred pounds of bombs were being designed. In Britain, airfields were being set up to test new aircraft and the ballistics of bomb dropping were being researched in remote locations on the coast of East Anglia. Nothing comparable existed in the United States.

Only modest progress had been made in standing up units within the Aviation Section which were still largely committed to supporting ground operations, assisting cavalry units and providing reconnaissance, which, it has to be said, still occupied the majority of sorties carried out by aircraft of both sides along the Western Front. The 1st Aero had been joined by the 3rd, 4th and 5th squadrons in the continental United States, with the 2nd deployed to the Philippines and the 6th in Hawaii with the 7th stationed in

Panama. But only the 1st was up to strength and several of the other squadrons were still awaiting men and equipment, including aeroplanes. As 1917 wore on, enough planes were in hand to raise the total strength to 20 squadrons.

When America declared war with the Central Powers in Europe, the Aviation Section had 131 officers, mostly pilots and students, and 1087 enlisted men but fewer than 250 aeroplanes. Added to these were five balloons in varying states of operational readiness. Of a total 366 aeroplanes ordered by the government, only 66 had been delivered but their performance was low and the engines were less reliable than their counterparts in Europe.

Nowhere was there any plan by the War Department to employ these resources, albeit ➤

meagre, in a war-ready situation. There were no structural organisation plans, no means of deploying them overseas and little idea as to how they could be used – effectively or otherwise. Due to censorship brought about by war, the Allied powers had prevented the Americans from getting any detailed technical information about the latest developments in engine and airframe design and construction and for their part the Americans had not sent a single observer to discover the latest tactical or strategic use of air power.

While the government expected to mobilise a million men under arms, nobody had any real sense of the reality of modern warfare. If the Aeronautical Division was ill-equipped to fight, the Army was even less so. Fifty years of peace since the American Civil War had given the country a sense of isolation from the trauma of conflict with a complete lack of will to fight on foreign land. As recently as 1916 President Wilson expressed outrage that the War Department should have made plans about how to fight a war, not that those plans bore any relationship to how modern war was actually fought.

EXPANSION

The need for more aircraft and manpower for the Aviation Section resulted in an appropriation of $10.8 million in May and a further $43.4 million in June, with six new squadrons of aircraft and two of balloons planned. Already, contingents from Britain and France were in the United States discussing how best the Americans could contribute, one priority being to send a large and powerful air force to Europe. But the European allies also wanted to tap into the American capacity for large-scale production. Prime Minister Alexandre Ribot of France sent President

Wilson a telegram on May 26, 1917, asking for a fleet of 4500 aircraft, 5000 pilots and 50,000 mechanics in France by 1918. The proposal required a production peak of 16,500 aircraft delivered during the first six months of 1918.

Stunned and incapable of understanding how such quotas could be provided, the US government turned for advice to the National Advisory Committee for Aeronautics (NACA). The NACA had been set up on March 3, 1915, modelled on the British Advisory Committee for Aeronautics which had been in existence since April 30, 1909. Following Britain's example, the French and the Russians established their own independent organs to conduct scientific study of aerodynamics and marry that to engineering principles as they pertained to industries designing and producing aircraft. But in America there had been reluctance on the part of the government to get involved in this new-fangled 'sport' of flying, which was until the outbreak of war still seen as nothing to do with the government.

The NACA wanted a laboratory where its engineers could carry out scientific investigations into aerofoil shapes, work out the mathematical models on which flight was based and perform tests using wind tunnels and various rigs for examining loads and stresses experienced by an aircraft in flight. In essence, it was a direct descendent to the work carried out by the Wright brothers, which had been mathematical, scientific and methodical. To do that, the NACA set up the Langley Aeronautical Laboratory, named after Pierpont Langley of less than distinctive fame! Over the next several decades the laboratory would make very many original contributions to the science of flight, until it

was renamed the National Aeronautics and Space Administration (NASA) in 1958.

Meanwhile, something needed to be done to put the aircraft industry, vital for feeding the Army's Aeronautical Division, into a more productive mode of operation and to achieve that the president turned to Howard E. Coffin of the Hudson Motor Car Corporation. Known as the Coffin Board, the organisation he set up quickly discovered that the aero industry was not amenable to the mass production techniques of the Ford Motor Company that could assemble a kit-box of Ford parts into 10,000 identical cars each year. About all that linked the two industries was the common use of a gasoline engine.

To enhance production, Coffin worked out that the optimum way to produce aircraft was to agree a standard design for each category the Army required (pursuit, observation, bombing, etc.) and then provide manufacturing facilities for sets of wings, tailplanes, cockpits, engines, and deliver those to a single facility where the separate components could be put together. The recommendations went some way toward rationalising the way the military could be served in a time-efficient manner and mobilised for war in a way the country never had been before. Not since the Confederate Army was assembled at the end of the 18th century had Americans prepared for a war with an off-shore enemy.

The Aeronautical Division now realised that it needed to direct industry with specifications and requirements for new aircraft. Only on that basis could a professional air force decide for itself what it required rather than make do with what industry wanted it to buy. It also needed the capability to carry out its own research and development to decide what those

ABOVE: The first meeting of the National Advisory Committee for Aeronautics in 1915, a government body set up to advance the science and engineering of aeronautics to catch up to global developments with powered aircraft. NASA

ABOVE: Howard E. Coffin (1873-1937) was an American industrialist who played a significant role in improving aircraft production as the United States geared up for war, building aircraft for Britain and France from their own existing designs. LIBRARY OF CONGRESS

ABOVE: *Observation balloons played a vital role in the war in Europe and American forces used them on the Western Front for a while to carry out gun-laying and spotting duties, tasks which would be quickly superseded by aeroplanes.* DAVID BAKER

ABOVE: *Balloons like this one, here carrying an American air observer, were vulnerable to attack from pursuit aircraft and some American pilots became adept at shooting them down. These victories were considered just as valuable when added to their 'score'.* US ARMY

specifications and requirements should be.

To this end, an industrial city was chosen where military aviation could build a technical research facility; bureaucracy and prolonged deliberation kept the NACA in slow motion and, in any event, as an independent government body it was not charged with carrying out the research specifically required by the Army.

McCook Field at Dayton, Ohio, was chosen to build upon an existing group of civilians, regular officers, technicians and engineering types. War dragooned into uniform several highly placed production elites from the burgeoning motor industry and here their technical expertise was invaluable.

When specific aircraft types were chosen, drawings were made of the required sectional elements, factory space was leased or acquired

and a work force was mobilised that transformed the social demographic of the United States. Unlike cars, aircraft were built primarily from wood, fabric and sundry materials such as leather, requiring workers already skilled in dealing with those materials. As a result, women

began flowing into the new aircraft factories along with men drawn from other industries.

The need for specialised raw materials saw the establishment of new supply lines. A Spruce Production Division was set up, in which 27,000 officers and enlisted men were employed in locating, cutting and transporting by rail the vast quantity of spruce and fir needed to build the airframes. Special long-fibre cotton cloth for aircraft covering, a replacement for the traditional linen usually imported from Europe, was developed by a research team working with the manufacturers and suppliers to deliver the material to seamstresses who sewed and stitched the panels to cover the wings and fuselage frames.

Engines were a vital element in the overall production chain – there were always more units needed than the equivalent number of airframes due to faults, breakdowns, servicing and simply because some aircraft had multiple motors. The decision to build a powerful in-line engine in the United States took the efforts of several companies and resulted in the Liberty, produced in eight-cylinder and twelve-cylinder versions. The US Bureau of Standards helped develop the Liberty engine, along with engineers from a range of companies. Before that, the Americans had no engines of light weight and sufficient horsepower to equip the aircraft coming of the supply lines.

AMERICAN AIR ACES 1917-1918

• Rickenbacker, Captain Edward V.	26
• Luke, 2nd Lieutenant Frank Jr.	18
• Vaughan, 1st Lieutenant George A.	13
• Kindley, 1st Lieutenant Field E.	12
• Springs, 1st Lieutenant Elliott W.	12
• Landis, 1st Lieutenant Reed G.	10
• Swaab, 1st Lieutenant Jacques M.	10

Jesse G. Vincent of Packard and Elbert Hall of Hall-Scott left Fageol Motors to design the Liberty, which they did in five days during late May 1917, economising on development by adopting the single overhead camshaft and rocker box of the German Mercedes D.IIIa engine. During the fall of 1917 the War Department ordered 22,500 Liberty engines and awarded contracts for it to be manufactured by several leading engine producers and car manufacturers, including Buick, Cadillac, Lincoln, Marman and Packard. But throughout the war period, two domestic engines from Curtiss and Hall-Scott were produced while several European motors such as those from Hispano-Suiza, Gnome and LeRhone were purchased and built under license to make up the shortfall.

As part of the essential need to acquire technical information about combat aircraft design and engineering, Major Raynal C. Bolling took a large mission to Europe in June 1917. Known as the Bolling Commission, it returned with a recommendation for US production facilities, now beginning to get into their stride, to concentrate on training types. The fast-changing pace of combat aircraft design in Europe was happening so quickly that it seemed unwise to manufacture aircraft of that type in the United States for delivery to the front.

The urgent need for aircraft to equip the expanding requirements of the Aeronautical Division could not be met by the evolving American manufacturing plants for at least a year. To accommodate the shortfall, in August 1917 the French agreed to supply the Americans with 5875 aircraft and 8500 engines by July 1, 1918. Most of those were Spads, Nieuports and Bréguets, manufactured with raw materials provided by the United States. But the desire to select specific types for particular purposes, and manufacture those using mass construction techniques – assembling aeroplanes from separately manufactured elements – required the Americans to choose a specific type.

The Bolling Commission was made aware of several Allied types which could be used for quantity production in the United States but the one which looked the most attractive was the de Havilland DH.4, an all-wood two-seater employed for observation and light bombing. A truly exceptional aircraft, the DH.4 had been designed to use the 160hp Beardmore engine but it could also be fitted with the 200hp B.H.P., the 230hp Siddeley Puma or the 250-p Rolls-Royce Eagle engine. In service it proved its worth in a variety of roles, including that of a two-seat fighter, and did yeoman service in several theatres.

The Americans liked it for its robust construction, rugged reliability and consistent performance – and liked it too because it

ABOVE: Henry H. Arnold with a Liberty 12 engine, the first mass-produced aero engine produced in the United States and used widely in a range of aircraft. US ARMY

ABOVE: This production batch of S.E.5a aircraft at the Wolsey Motors plant in Birmingham epitomises the hand-built crafting of aircraft, a very different form of manufacturing industry to that created for automobiles, despite initial expectations to the contrary. This type was also manufactured in America. BRUCE ROBERTSON

ABOVE: Designated SE-5 in American service, the British S.E.5a was a strong and reliable fighter – easy to fly, liked by British and American pilots alike and favoured by some of the leading fighter pilots during the later stages of the war. US ARMY

would suffice as an ideal mount for the Liberty engine. A sample airframe arrived at McCook Field in August 1917 and a new 400hp Liberty engine was immediately installed. First flown in that configuration on October 29, 1917, it was subjected to several changes to fit American production lines and immediately dubbed the 'Liberty Plane'. It was initially put into production with the Standard Aircraft Corporation of Patterson, New Jersey, the Dayton-Wright Company, and the Fisher Body Division of General Motors. Altogether, these companies built 4846 Liberty Planes by the end of hostilities.

The first sortie flown by the American Expeditionary Force with the Liberty Plane took place on August 2, 1918, but it quickly became clear that the modifications had rendered the aircraft less effective than the original British design. Moreover, the position of the fuel tank behind the pilot made it difficult for the occupant to survive a crash landing and a review board found it bizarre that the observer was sometimes required to climb on top of the rear fuselage to compensate for the nose-heavy attitude in flight! Sadly, by the time it arrived back at the front the assembled Liberty Planes were already outclassed, by which time the Americanised version of the DH.9A was already in production.

Production had been slow gearing up and the deliveries from French factories were the only means of equipping the Aeronautical Division, which on May 21, 1918, was renamed (yet again) as the Division of Military Aeronautics, United States Army, free at last of its attachment to the Signal Corps. But here too there were disappointments and it was not only American factories that were failing to match anticipated quotas. Instead of the 5875 airframes from France due by July 1, 1918, French factories produced only one-quarter that number and the Americans cancelled the contract before it ran out.

One factor in not supplying anticipated aircraft to the front was the shortfall in shipping which, with the urgent priority to move men and vehicles, was always a problem. There were simply too few ships available and what there were gave priority to the military equipment. But as the pendulum swung from manufacture

of training types such as the Jenny to combat types like the Liberty Plane, the industry began to mature along with accelerating capabilities of manufacture and delivery. But it was all too late to take realistic effect. While the Americans produced more than 3000 DH-4s (as they re-designated them), only 1200 had reached the front by the end of hostilities.

OVER THERE

The fighting airmen of the American Expeditionary Forces (AEF) arrived in France with no experience of combat and only basic training in how to approach the enemy in the air. It took a year to get the first squadrons ready to support the American forces on the ground. Training was supported by a programme which followed the example of Canada, which had been recruiting for the war effort since August 1914. There, training was divided into ground, primary and advanced phases. The man chosen to take charge of a similar system in

America was Hiram Bingham, who, as a former explorer and Yale University history professor, had no formal association with aviation but who had, at the age of 41, learned to fly.

Bingham set up a series of flying schools at eight universities, which is where his professional affiliation was supremely helpful for what appeared, to a cosseted set of high-end academics, to be an irrelevant preoccupation for adventurous youth escaping the serious business of study and preparation for a stable profession! But the call to arms swept away the contempt that still existed in some quarters for noisy and hazardous pursuits. The war changed those entrenched attitudes and gave America a new set of heroes as it swept on to the world stage, already the wealthiest and most productive nation on Earth.

The training programme was delayed for some time while appropriate flying fields and associated facilities were built and Canada provided airfields and barracks there while the Americans prepared ground. Eventually, 27 flying fields were set up in the United States, mostly in the southern States to get reasonable year-round weather, with a further 16 in Europe, where the weather was often not so good. Training began with passing a test which included cross-country flying, map reading and the use of a compass. This usually lasted six to eight weeks, involving 40-50 hours in the air, during which time the trainees received 25% of rated flying pay.

The training fields in France were very different to those in America. At Issoudun, the biggest, the field was built on clay which turned to mud in wet weather making flying almost impossible. On arrival, with pay of a spectacular $100 a month, recruits were set to work making duck

ABOVE: Brigadier General Benjamin D. Foulois (left) with Major General James E. Fechet and Brigadier General H. C. Pratt. In November 1917 Foulois was placed in command of Army air operations in France. US ARMY

ABOVE: Raynal Cawthorn Bolling (1877-1918) was tasked with taking a group of specialists and engineers to Europe in 1917 to study European aircraft designs and return with recommendations as to which should be placed in production in America. His group was known as the Bolling Commission.
US LIBRARY OF CONGRESS

LEFT: Issoudun airfield in France, seen from the air, was the largest American training field in France and became the base from which recruits were shown how to fight in the air. US ARMY

boards, erecting tents, cleaning, cooking and doing guard duty until they began flying training.

Most had to wait several months, performing menial chores at Issoudun, Tours and St Maixent, while the backlog of trainees were processed with flying instruction. Usually assigned to JN-4 aircraft, and rated as Reserve Military Aviators, some 15,000 cadets reported to flying schools and by the end of the war 8688 had received RMA rating from US flying schools, which added to those trained abroad, resulted in 10,000 pilots trained by the end of the war.

The advantage in foreign flying schools was to give the recruits an experience of flying aeroplanes which could not be had in the US, providing realistic training under conditions closer to those they would experience in flying against an enemy. Training too was required for the mechanics, as any hope of recruiting from the motor industry and other trades was quickly dashed with the increased sophistication and specialisation of contemporary aircraft. Special schools for them were set up to provide courses on armament, aeroplane engines, armor, propellers and rigging requirements, together with instruction on ignition sets, welding, instruments, sail-making, vulcanising and copper work.

By the beginning of 1918, specialised courses were bolted on to existing technical training institutions to specialise in the new industry

and by June almost all were concentrated at large schools in St Paul, Minnesota, and Kelly Field, Texas. By the end of the year, 7600 technicians had been processed through these two schools. Elsewhere, the British and the French took in trainee mechanics, teaching these men skills many would find useful in the development of postwar aviation; but after the

war the majority would find very little application for their focused trade and were forced to return to jobs on the farm or in the motor industry.

By April 1918 the air arm of the US Army was ready to begin operations and they wanted to form up into a unified, all-American force, attached to a specific sector with their own commanders and their own operational responsibilities. The British and the French wanted them integrated, to learn how to fly and fight on the front line and to acquire experience first. General Pershing resisted vehemently and got his way.

No one doubted the Americans would fight well – volunteers had been crossing the Atlantic since 1915 to join the Lafayette Escadrille, where of the 267 who volunteered, 180 served at the front shooting down 199 German aircraft for the loss of 51 killed, 19 wounded and 15 taken prisoner. One of their group was the black volunteer Eugene Jacques Bullard, who was descended from slaves and who had become a professional boxer. He was the first black pilot to score a verified victory when he shot down a Fokker Triplane in November 1917.

General Pershing refused to accept him for transfer to the US Army, at a time when blacks were prohibited from applying for aviation duty but 93 did transfer and another 26 became aviators with the US Navy. The Army transferees formed the nucleus of the 103rd Pursuit Squadron, which became the first air unit to fly in action but they served with the French forces as no other US squadrons were ready. The 1st Aero Squadron got to France on September 3, 1917, the build-up continuing with the 95th in February and the 94th on March 5. Despite having no guns to install on their Nieuport fighters, the 94th flew scouting missions over the front 10 days after their arrival. But when the guns did arrive, operations had to stand down as none of the pilots had received training in how to fire them!

But it fell to the 94th – the famous 'Hat-in-the-Ring' squadron – to fly and fight over enemy lines for the first time on April 3, 1918. Later commanded by American air ace Edward V. 'Eddie' Rickenbacker, the 94th became famous and drew in pilots who would become household names in America. Initially, to British pilots in the Royal Flying Corps and to pilots in the German Air Service, the sobriquet 'air ace' was granted after 10 confirmed aerial victories but this changed to five and that is the standard used today.

Not all aces had been equally challenged, however, since downing a balloon was considered a 'kill' because an aerial device had been taken out of action just as effectively as an aircraft destroyed. Invariably, observers in a basket suspended beneath the gas bag were unable to survive a flamed balloon, although the Germans did employ parachutes which were usually effective. It

ABOVE: *Members of the 1st Aero Squadron in their war with the Mexican bandits in 1916 were soon to be placed on a much higher profile with the advent of America into the war in Europe.* US ARMY

ABOVE: *The oldest US military flying unit, members of the 1st Aero Squadron present themselves at North Island, California in front of a Burgess Model H on which they had learned to fly.* US ARMY

ABOVE: *Crewmembers of the 1st Aero Squadron pose in front of their French built Salmson 2A2, one of several European types used by the Aeronautical Division of the US Signal Corps.* US ARMY

ABOVE: Members of the Lafayette Escadrille in July 1917, volunteers who had gone to France to fight before America declared war on Germany. Standing (left to right) are Soubiron, Doolittle, Campbell, Persons, Bridgman, Dugan, MacMonagle, Lowell, Willis, Jones, Peterson and de Maison-Rouge. Seated (left to right) are Hill, Masson with 'Soda' their pet lion, Thaw, Thénault, Lufbery with lioness 'Whiskey', Johnson, Bigelow and Rockwell. US ARMY

ABOVE: This Lafayette pin belonged to Charles Heave Dolan, Jr, the 31st member of the Escadrille, which carries the swastika, from very early times a symbol of good luck long before its interpretation was sullied when the Nazi party adopted it as their badge in the 1920s. US ARMY

Lafayette Escadrille

A group of Americans volunteered to fight for France on the Western Front long before America entered the war, joining a special squadron administered by the French Air Service. Eventually, 38 Americans joined the unit and the majority transferred to the United States Army Aeronautical Division on February 18, 1918, becoming the 103rd Aero Squadron. The origin of the group lies with Dr Edmund L. Gros, founder of the American Hospital in Paris and with Norman Prince, an American expatriate flying with the French Air Service, who sought to persuade the French government of the value in allowing American volunteers to fight. They formed the Escadrille Américaine which became operational on April 20, 1916. In December the name was changed to Lafayette Escadrille to avoid the implication that America officially supported the French.

Two lion cub mascots, Whiskey and Soda, provided light relief and alarm to new arrivals! The first aerial victory was recorded by Kiffin Rockwell on May 18, 1916. Wounded in the leg during an air fight on May 26, he refused hospitalisation, went back into the air and was killed on September 23, 1916. Nine of the 38 were killed or died of wounds received in combat either with this unit or after they became the 103rd Aero Squadron. They are remembered in a memorial outside Paris, erected in 1928.

was possible to walk away from a crashed aeroplane brought down by enemy fighters but never from a balloon set alight in the air.

Because of this it becomes difficult to rate the success of American pilots such as Frank Luke, who achieved 18 credited victories – of which only four were fixed-wing aircraft – against the 26 credited victories of Eddie Rickenbacker of which only five were balloons. Conversely, victories scored high above the range of ground fire were free from the concentrated screen of protective anti-aircraft artillery surrounding an observation balloon, for all its exposure. Nevertheless, just as the rising score cards of leading fighter pilots in all the combatant countries attracted public attention, so too did these individual American airmen receive a wider acclaim than the ordinary soldier down in the mud of the trenches. And they had added recruiting value too.

To middle-Americans, in their dispersed towns and rural locations, on farms and in homesteads far from the cities and burgeoning urban sprawl of the Eastern Seaboard, the exploits of these brave young men created purpose out of a confused disconnection with the political decisions over war and peace debated in the marble buildings of the nation's capital. A renewed connection with the bigger world was engaging Americans through the tales of derring-do, of their sons and brothers now in far off lands, carrying the flag and fighting for the freedom their fathers and grandfathers had sought to find in the United States. For others, it was time to bring them home.

General Pershing responded to the call for integration into Allied units by refusing to do anything of the sort and for administrative purposes he set up a Zone of Interior in similar fashion to the way in which he had created the American Expeditionary Force. The Zone of Interior would be an assembly point for logistical supplies coming in from convoys and from gifted materiel from French and British armies. Bolling was put in charge of the Zone of Interior while Mitchell was placed in charge of air operations in the Zone of Advance, which was abolished as expansion made it apparent that a massed air contingent could be attached to 1st Army. Mitchell was assigned to its headquarters as an operational commander.

In July 1918 the air service joined the Aisne-Marne offensive and came up against crack German fighter units which were superior in aircraft and experience while US observation squadrons were desperate to get scout escorts to help protect them. When Pershing's 1st Army attacked the German-held St Mihiel salient, that part of the front which had been occupied by the enemy for a couple of years, the air service was better prepared and maintained a relentless pressure day and night. For the first time an American officer had control over a section of the front which involved 1481 aircraft including 701 pursuit types, 323 day bombers and 91 night bombers. Although fewer than half were flown by Americans, the entire operation was led by General Pershing.

Some of the bombers were part of Hugh Trenchard's Independent Force, now a part of the Royal Air Force, which on April 1, 1918, had become the world's first independent air force through the amalgamation of the Royal Flying Corps and the Royal Naval Air Service. Some of Trenchard's bombers were redirected to support the assault on St Mihiel and Mitchell began to understand the value of an offensive against strategic targets such as marshalling yards, factories and power stations, even the seat of government and cities packed with munitions workers. Mitchell would never forget that and make mischief later over an argument with the navy.

Under the Meuse-Argonne campaign that began on September 26, Mitchell made better use of his aircraft and while the fighting on the ground would see 110,000 Americans dead or wounded over the following seven weeks, the airmen had better weather than previously and flew massed formations of up to 100 aircraft at a time across the front. It was also an opportunity to engage in night pursuit, of German bombers attacking airfields and supply dumps under the veil of darkness, but to no avail. Effective night fighting was still a long way off. On October 9, Mitchell sent 200 bombers and 100 fighters to attack German troop concentrations, the most effective being against Bayonville on October 18 where aircraft flown by American pilots killed 250 enemy soldiers and wounded 750.

When the armistice of November 11, 1918, brought a halt to more than four years of conflict, the contribution of the American air service had been notable, with 776 enemy aircraft and 72 balloons destroyed, 130 tons of bombs dropped on 150 raids and 18,000 photographs taken on reconnaissance missions. In return the air service had lost 569 airmen killed or wounded, 654 dead from disease or accidents, and 290 aeroplanes and 37 balloons. But the real accomplishment had been the creation of a new air fighting force from very meagre and inadequate beginnings, of the establishment of an aircraft industry where none existed before, and in the forging of a new group of air leaders who would be the backbone for preserving US military air capabilities until another war transformed it into a truly global force.

ABOVE: A replica Nieuport 23 sesquiplane of the lineage which was so popular among American airmen for its light handling, nimble to fly and effective operational use. TOM SMITH

Before the end of hostilities, responding to the outstanding success being achieved in the air and troubled by the loss of life on such a colossal scale, General Pershing gave much thought to the development of unmanned aerial fighting machines and in these deliberations posited the concept of the cruise missile. Very little technical progress was made but throughout the period of hostilities key individuals promoted the possibility of a remotely controlled flying bomb or even an autonomous type of cruise missile.

These possibilities centred on work carried out by Elmer Sperry of the Sperry Gyroscope Company and Peter C. Hewitt who together approached the Signal Corps about the possibility of installing gyroscopes in conventional airframes connected to an automatic control system. Once launched they would fly a pre-set course to carry explosives, contained within the body of the projectile, to an enemy target such as a munitions dump or a town or city. The Navy was the first to show interest and five Curtiss N-9 seaplanes were bought by the government to conduct

a series of tests. These brought moderate success when Carl L. Norden (later famous for his Second World War bombsight) demonstrated a few successful flights of very limited range.

In parallel the Army finally took an interest and supported Charles Kettering, already famous for inventing the electric starter motor for automobiles, filed a suitable report and got a contract to form an evaluation team. This gathered some of the giants of industry and aviation, including Orville Wright, and produced what became known as the Kettering Bug, of which the Army ordered 25 on January 25, 1918. Over the next several months tests were carried out and some modest success was achieved, but all too quickly the limitations of extant technology showed the concept to be ahead of its time.

Most of these trials were held in great secrecy, their inventors believing them to be the technology of the future – which in some prescient way they were – and the Army was paranoid about German spies infiltrating the United States and stealing military secrets. So

Nieuport 28

Founded by Edouard Nieuport, the Nieuport company made spark plugs and magnetos for automobiles until it provided some of the electrical equipment for the Antoinette engine fitted to Henri Farman's Voisin biplane, which flew on January 13, 1908. With the help of his brother Charles and Jacques Schneider, Nieuport built his own aeroplane in 1909. He exploited the sesquiplane design, where the lower wing has less than half the surface area of the upper wing and developed a series of biplanes on this concept at the beginning from the beginning of the war.

Designed by Gustav Delage, the Nieuport 28 was built and flown in June 1917 although it was not to become available until early 1918 when it was enthusiastically adopted by the French and American air services, the type being used to increase the victory scores of several leading aces. With a single Gnome rotary engine delivering 160hp, the aircraft no longer sported the familiar sesquiplane layout but had wings of almost equal span, characterised by a slight dihedral on the upper mainplane. Just over 300 were built.

LENGTH	21.3ft
WING SPAN	26.75ft
HEIGHT	8ft
GROSS WEIGHT	1635lb
MAXIMUM SPEED	123mph
CEILING	17,390ft
RANGE	180 miles

it was that elaborate stories were concocted to explain to civilians who came upon downed test planes without a pilot that he had got concussion and had wandered off. By getting the local inhabitants to spill out and search for him, they effectively got rid of keen-eyed spectators puzzled by the complex arrangement of radio equipment inside the pilotless biplanes. One curious farmer was even told that the missing pilot was 'Hap' Arnold himself!

As a less well-known aspect of the American involvement in the war, and responding to the frantic concerns of the American government that the fighting involving American lives appeared to be escalating without pointing toward a

ABOVE: The Americans bought 189 SPAD XVII biplanes, used for training prior to moving pilots across to the more potent SPAD S.XIII. This particular aircraft was built by Mann, Egerton & Company, delivered to the RAF and then sent to the United States. DAVID BAKER

United States. With elections to both houses of Congress coming up in November 1918, and the Democratic President in his second term where he had won only 42% of the popular vote, Woodrow Wilson was trying to avert a threatened Republican takeover of Congress and urged his military chefs to minimise the escalating conflict.

The Army responded by seeking any way possible to reduce the number of its airmen being killed during bombing and reconnaissance missions and protagonists of the pilotless device thought the Kettering Bug afforded such an opportunity. In October a further 75 were ordered for concentrated trials in the general belief that the war would go on well into 1919. Enthusiastic military officers dreamed up a plan to build 10,000-100,000 at a cost of $400-$500 apiece and to replace all piloted aircraft with these weapons by the end of the following year. The device they imagined could win the war had a speed of 50mph and a range of 75 miles carrying a 180lb warhead. It was to have been the first iteration of a design concept proponents imagined could automate the modern battlefield. Eventually, it would.

Nobody knew that Wilson had another solution up his sleeve and had already held secret discussions with the German government – agreeing to an armistice if the Kaiser departed in exile to Holland, thus avoiding explaining to his electorate why American troops had died to shore-up a European monarch. In return,

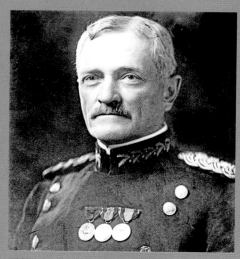

ABOVE: General John Joseph Pershing led American troops in France during 1917 and 1918 but harboured deep concerns for the loss of life and worked to try and find ways to prevent unnecessary casualties. US ARMY

America would agree to an armistice and give the French and British an ultimatum that if they failed to comply they would themselves become the belligerent forces. Wilson just missed the election day of November 1918 and in opposition to the war the public put Republicans in charge of both houses of Congress, six days before the armistice. But the violence was over. ✪

BELOW: A replica SPAD S. XIII in the colours of the 94th Aero Squadron, the famous 'Hat-in-the-Ring' unit which saw so many American air aces achieve fame in this type. USAF

Spad S.XIII

A year after it had been formed as Aéroplanes Deperdussin, the company became the Société de Production des Aéroplanes Deperdussin (SPAD) in 1912. It produced a highly successful range of aircraft types, the SPAD S.XIII making its first flight on April 4, 1917, as an improved version of the Spade S.VII. The Bolling Commission favoured the type for construction in the USA but all 893 acquired during the war came from Britain or France. Always preferred by the Americans, it was substituted for the Nieuport 28 only when there were insufficient SPAD S.XIIIs. It was the favoured choice of the US air service and pilots alike, its strong and solid performance making it an ideal mount for dogfighting as well as for ground-attack. Fitted with a powerful eight-cylinder 220hp Hispano-Suiza 8Be-8 engine, it was acquired by 15 countries and saw extensive use after the war. Nearly every French fighting unit was equipped with the type during 1918, more than 7300 being built before production ended after the war.

LENGTH	20.5ft
WING SPAN	27.1ft
HEIGHT	8.5ft
GROSS WEIGHT	1888lb
MAXIMUM SPEED	135mph
CEILING	21,800ft
RANGE	171 miles

Chapter 3: Rebirth 1919-1935

ABOVE: First flown on December 17, 1915, the Handley Page O/400 had pioneered the concept of the strategic bomber, sustained by Britain's Royal Air Force after the war, but the idea took root with several leaders of American air power in the years after the First World War. BRUCE ROBERTSON

ABOVE: The development of air power as a strategic weapon of war was pursued in the US by men such as Lieutenant Colonel Edgar S. Gorrell (right), here with Lieutenant Herbert A. Dargue and the 1st Aero Squadron during the Mexican war of 1916. US ARMY

BELOW: Military aviation went into the doldrums after the war, although air shows and exhibitions exploited the technology developed by the combatant powers and sustained an industry on civilian applications, such as the aeroplanes on display here at the 1922 Paris Salon. MUSEE DE L'AIR

The conflict ended long before the US Army could deliver on its promises but long enough to show the mettle of the American air-fighting soldier and to ensure that Army air power would survive. Growth within the service had been strong, from an air arm of 1200 officers and men to a force of 200,000 in 19 months, one quarter of whom were serving overseas.

In the early months of the war some 38,000 young men had volunteered to serve the air arm. The surge of interest in the exploits of American aviators fuelled a public familiarity with the air heroes of all sides, including the Frenchmen Roland Garros, René Fonck and Georges Guynemer, the British flyers Mick Mannock, James Byford McCudden and Albert Ball, and of the German fighter pilots Max Immelmann, Oswald Boelcke and Manfred von Richthofen. And there was one fast rising new ace, Hermann Göring, whose name they would come to know again.

To the list of wartime aces were also added American names such as Eddie Rickenbacker, Frank Luke, Elliott White Springs and Reed Landis, names which would inspire a new generation of Americans for another war yet to come, and cloak the exploits of these air combat pioneers in a romantic association with adventure, freedom of the air and excitement – surely the most powerful recruiting sergeant of all. The legacy was strong.

The development of aviation in America had been stimulated by the war and would

not have occurred at the rate it did had the United States remained neutral or a non-combatant. It established an industrial base from which the Army would receive at least some of the aircraft it sought and provided a military aviation cadre which would form the basis for development of global air power within 25 years, stimulated by another war, this time

involving US forces fighting around the globe.

When the European war broke out in 1914, the American aircraft industry had 16 manufacturers with a combined output of 49 aeroplanes. By November 1918 it employed 175,000 workers in 300 plants with the potential to produce 21,000 aircraft a year. During the 19 months America had been at war, this young industry had delivered

ABOVE: A veteran of the First World War and a strong advocate of an independent air force, Major General Mason Patrick was appointed Chief of the Air Staff in October 1921 and pushed for experimental research facilities at Wright Field, learning to fly in 1922 at the age of 59. US ARMY

ABOVE: When the US Navy discounted claims that bombers could sink battleships, Brigadier General William 'Billy' Mitchell challenged that and began a vigorous debate which would anger opponents of air power. Here, Mitchell poses for the camera beside his Vought VE-7 at the Bolling Field Air Tournament in May 1920. US ARMY

COMMANDERS 1918-1935

• **Major General Charles E. Menoher**	*June 4, 1920-October 4, 1921*
• **Major General Mason M. Patrick**	*October 5, 1921-December 13, 1927*
• **Major General James E. Fechet**	*December 14, 1927-December 19, 1931*
• **Major General Benjamin D. Foulois**	*December 20, 1931-December 21, 1935*

13,844 aircraft and 41,953 engines – yet every aeroplane that flew the flag had been designed in another country and not one US-designed aircraft had seen combat. But the fact remained that only 1200 American-built combat aircraft reached the war front and of the total produced about half were trainers of a type not dissimilar to those the Army had taken to war against 'Pancho' Villa.

And there was very little sign of things getting better, as the government turned its back on Army aviation and aircraft production in particular. The very day that the armistice took effect, the US government cancelled $100 million worth of orders for the Army's Division of Military Aeronautics involving 13,000 airframes and 20,000 engines, eliminating 90% of its wartime potential and reducing actual production of 14,000 aircraft in 1918 to a low of 263 in 1922.

Like the European victors in that war, the US government turned its back on the opportunity to subsidise the nascent industry, which suffered savage cuts to orders in peacetime and to an industry which had helped win the war, through the equipment used on the Western Front and elsewhere. It would be several years before supporters of a beleaguered industry won battles to get government grants for mail contracts and the like. For the most part, despite the proud boast in government history books, the aircraft industry and the caucus of military aviation they served, pulled themselves up without very much assistance.

Advocates for air power were committed to resurrecting a strong force to help deter aggressors and defend the United States and offensive bombing operations had sold the concept to air service leaders before hostilities ceased. A month before the Armistice, at the suggestion of the RAF's Hugh Trenchard, an Inter-Allied Independent

Air Force had been established, involving US airmen contributing to "the breakdown of the Germany army, its government and the crippling of its sources of supply".

The Americans planned to use Handley Page O/100 and O/400 bombers and had their eyes on the massive V/1500, which had a bomb load of 7500lb, a range of 1300 miles with an endurance of 17 hours. When the armistice was signed three V/1500 aircraft of No. 166 Squadron were standing by at Bircham Newton to carry out raids on Berlin. The flights never happened but the scale of the RAF's intent greatly impressed the Americans, not least Mitchell who became an advocate of strategic bombing and turned the effectiveness of the application into a personal crusade.

The origin of strategic bombing as a doctrinal policy in the purest sense began with Lieutenant Colonel Edgar S. Gorrell, chief of the US Strategical Aviation Branch in France. In December 1917 he proposed bombing German commercial centres to strangle the German army of supplies and thereby render it unable to fight. He campaigned quietly, behind the scenes, advocating a bombing-first policy seeing the continued pouring of resources into trying to win battles on the ground through increasing intensity in aerial reconnaissance and observation as counter-productive. He was persuaded that the only way to halt aggression was to destroy the enemy's ability to wage a sustained war.

Some of this thinking certainly influenced the move made in parallel to develop autonomous flying machines but the notion of a strategic bombing offensive was ahead of its time and had not been realistically espoused, or practised, by any air arm to that date. Even the bombing campaign waged by Trenchard had at its core

Aircraft designations

In a system devised in 1919, US military aircraft were identified in 15 basic categories, with a symbol of two letters identifying role. These covered various groups of pursuit aircraft, bombers, etc., and were further defined by a second letter which qualified the type within the group, so that Pursuit aircraft (P) were further divided into Pursuit, Watercooled (PW), etc. In addition to pursuit types the 15 categories included ground-attack, liaison, observation, bombing and training.

In May 1924 the system was revised so that new aircraft were given a single letter which has continued in modified form, with various additions, deletions and changes to the present. Most notable were the categories for bomber (B), cargo (C), heavy bomber (HB), light bomber (LB), observation amphibious (OA), pursuit (P) and primary trainer (PT). In the 1930s, several additions were made, such as photographic (F), gyroplane (G), and two-seat fighter (PB – Pursuit Biplace).

From 1924 a status prefix letter, or letters, was attached to the designation system to show experimental or development status. A prefix 'X' was added to show that the aircraft was a prototype or that it was a specific aeroplane which had been withdrawn from service to carry out some test or be used for evaluation of a new piece of equipment, on completion of which it would be returned to service and the 'X' withdrawn.

The prefix 'Y' was adopted in 1928 to signify a pre-production aircraft and it gradually became adopted as the standard norm for aircraft about to go into service but pre-production rather than prototype. During the first half of the 1930s, a number 1 would follow the prefix Y to indicate a budgetary source of financing for the type. It has become common to retrospectively apply these X or Y prefixes, even to aircraft that never carried them.

ABOVE: A Dreadnought-era warship, the USS Alabama, is hit by a white phosphorous bomb from a DH-4 during Army tests in September 1921, a series mounted by Brigadier General Mitchell to prove his case. US NAVY

While the British all but disbanded their Royal Air Force, despite the wholesale cancellation of wartime orders, in America there was little inclination to do away with what was still officially known as the Division of Military Aeronautics but which everybody referred to as the air service. Issues over bombing, whether strategic or tactical, and fighters, either as escorts for bombers or as intercepting pursuit planes, was placed on hold while the Army reorganised across its wide spectrum of activities.

A NEW START

In January 1919 the General Staff set out a plan for a peacetime air arm and proposed a structure composed of 24,000 officers and men but Congress disagreed, cut the requested budget by two-thirds and slashed the personnel to half that number. Moreover it was openly stated that there was "not a dollar available for the purchase of new aircraft". Secretary of War Newton D. Baker was not opposed to air power for the service but was set against the clamour for an independent air force for the United States, believing that the aeroplane was so new as to need the nurturing umbrella of the Army. Congress agreed with Baker, supported by Pershing when the hearings began to settle the fate of military aviation in America.

In the Army Reorganization Act of June 4, 1920, the Division of Military Aeronautics formally became the United States Army Air Service (USAAS) and was funded to a complement of 1516 officers and 16,000 enlisted men including a maximum 2500 cadets. The whole Army was to be limited to a strength of 280,000 men. The hopes of Mitchell and Foulois for an independent air force would have to wait a further 27 years and only Foulois would live to see it.

But there was hope for future expansion. The AAS alone in the Army structure, had control of its own research and development, procurement opportunities and supply of equipment including decisions over its own personnel and training functions. It also secured enhanced flying pay for its pilots and was allowed to place flyers in control of tactical units while the Chief of the Air Service was given the rank of major general and

a determination to strike the enemy's civilian population, sow panic and erode morale. The RAF's Independent Force was about just that and not as a result of some determined analysis of enemy resources and a calculated decimation of raw materials used to forge weapons.

Gorrell went so far as to advocate round-the-clock bombing by day and by night, with the British flying night missions and the Americans daylight raids. In 1915 the Allies had looked vaguely at such possibilities and decided that the limited capacity of aeroplanes to carry loads would dilute their primary value in serving as observation platforms and tools for reconnaissance. As the ground war intensified and became increasingly entrenched, the direction had already been selected by

circumstance and not before 1917 did the British begin terror raids on German population centres with aircraft which were only then practicable.

Some senior military figures were opposed to the entire concept of strategic bombing on moral grounds, believing the specific targeting of civilians unacceptable. The German air raids on Britain by airship and aeroplane had so incensed the British that the government found it wholly acceptable to agree to the formation of Trenchard's Independent Force but the moral arguments would not go away and persist to this day. During the 1914-18 war, however, all possibilities were new and their practical application untested so that the value or otherwise of destroying enemy infrastructure was largely theoretical.

BELOW: The Martin Company would play a major role in providing the Air Service with bombers during the decade after the war, beginning with the MB-2 first flown in September 1920 and quickly adopted by Brigadier General Mitchell for his bombing tests. US ARMY

ABOVE: *A Martin MB-2 drops a phosphor bomb on the Alabama in a follow-up to the attack by the DH-4.* US NAVY

ABOVE: *A major debate raged throughout the 1920s as to the effectiveness of strategic bombing and the preference for fighters or bombers, epitomised here by a pursuit aeroplane 'attacking' a Martin MB-2.* US ARMY

Martin MB-2

With a wooden fuselage and tail unit and wings from its predecessor, the MB-1 of 1918, this aircraft had a bomb load of up to 3000lb and a defensive armament of twin 0.303in Lewis guns on Scarff rings in the nose and aft cockpits, with a single downward-firing Lewis gun above an aperture in the underside of the fuselage. Manufacture began in 1920 and the type equipped four squadrons of the 2nd Bombardment Group in the continental United States, the Canal Zone, Hawaii and the Philippines.

Martin delivered 130 MB-2 aircraft and the last of the production lot had turbo-superchargers fitted to their 420hp Liberty 12 engines. The designation MB denoted 'Martin Bomber' and predated the later production lots which adopted the new designation system introduced in 1919, the type becoming the NBS-1, for 'Night Bomber Short-distance', earlier aircraft retaining their original designation.

LENGTH	42.7ft
WING SPAN	74.2ft
HEIGHT	14.6ft
GROSS WEIGHT	12,027lb
MAXIMUM SPEED	99mph
CRUISING SPEED	91mph
CEILING	8500ft
RANGE	558 miles

the Assistant Chief that of brigadier general.

There were to be 27 squadrons in seven groups under two wings. The 15 observation and four surveillance squadrons emphasised the Army support role, with four pursuit and four bombardment squadrons. One unit was to be equipped with the Martin MB-2 and was labelled a heavy bomber squadron and there were to be 32 balloon companies. Tactical air units were set up under the commanders of the nine Army corps areas that had been organised under the 1920 Act and each would have air officers on their staff as advisers.

At the centre of it all was Billy Mitchell, as strong an advocate as ever for air supremacy and the primacy of the bomber. As Assistant Chief of the Air Staff between 1920 and 1925, Mitchell was a vocal advocate of the flying aviator and a constant thorn in the side of the Army. Crusader and martyr, he exceeded the mandate of his office and was punished for it – hero to

many but villain to the establishment core of the Army senior staff in a series of undisciplined acts of disobedience that championed the aviator and his cause but outraged the leadership.

The stand-off began when Mitchell opposed the universal mood in America, and many in the armed services, that total war was immoral and that the military existed to protect the higher value of moral dignity and to use minimum force to quell aggression, not to wage war on civilians by using indiscriminate bombing methods. But Mitchell went further, asserting that air power could win wars and sign the death warrant on sea power as well. In a feud that boiled over into the public gaze, Mitchell challenged the Navy to prove its ships were invulnerable to attack from bombers and that aircraft could never threaten the survival of warships at sea.

The matter became more heated when defence secretary Baker spoke out against indiscriminate bombing but the government

acquiesced and allowed a demonstration to take place in Chesapeake Bay beginning on July 20, 1921. It was strongly contested by the Navy, who turned up only under protest. The ex-German warship Ostfriesland, exposed to bomb attacks by the Air Service, the Navy and the Marine Corps took damage and began to settle at the stern, listing to port, taking on water. Additional bombing runs were held up while the Navy inspectors went aboard to carry out a damage assessment. As Mitchell's aircraft circled they were running out of fuel and by the time the Navy inspectors had left the ship, the bombers had only time to drop half their load and none of the larger bombs.

Next day a carefully orchestrated sequence of attacks were carried out involving five NBS-1 (MB-2) bombers with Lieutenant Colonel Clayton Bissell in the lead plane. Each aircraft dropped a single 1100lb bomb with three scoring direct hits. But with nine bombs to go the Navy stopped further bombing runs and went aboard to assess the damage. By midday the Ostfriesland had sunk a further 2ft and by 1ft at the bow. As the Navy inspectors departed, Mitchell readied his main force of six NBS-1 aircraft and two Handley Page O/400s, each carrying a single 2000lb bomb. One of the O/400s had to return with technical problems but the NBS-1s dropped six bombs in 13 minutes starting at 12.18pm.

The objective had been to have the bombs detonate on the surface close to the ship so that the pressure wave from the explosion would be amplified through the water to the hull of the warship. With each blow the ship rose up to 10ft and sank back, her plates ripped apart by the concussion causing it to sink 22 minutes after the first detonation. But the reason why the warship sank is questioned

ABOVE: Designed very soon after the war, and relying on experience from the Martin MB-1 of 1918, this close-up view of the MB-2 shows its high quality finish and detailed inset panel fixtures. *US ARMY*

on an inspection tour in Europe during 1924 he met with the Italian advocate of strategic bombing, Giulio Douhet and returned recharged once more to take on the Army hierarchy.

The final blow to Mitchell's military career came after outspoken comments following the tragic loss of the American airship Shenandoah, which crashed during a storm on September 5, 1925, accusing the leadership of incompetence

to this day, both Air Service and Navy raising credible argument as to why it succumbed to this staged demonstration. For Mitchell it was vindication of a long held belief that air power could be decisive on land and at sea. Further tests, against the old US battleship Arizona in

1921 and the American battleships Virginia and New Jersey in 1923 supported Mitchell's case.

Altercations with his own superiors, with the War Department and with the Navy worsened Mitchell's reputation, the armed services painting him as a rebellious troublemaker. While

Curtiss B-2

Marking a low point in the inventory of the Army Air Corps, the Curtiss B-2 was the only bomber in service between 1929 and the early 1930s. The Curtiss Model 52 carried two geared V-1570 Conqueror engines but the 12 production aircraft had two 600hp Curtiss GV-1570 engines. Uniquely, the aircraft had a gunner's cockpit inside the two rear engine nacelles attached to the lower wing. Welded steel tube truss wing spars with riveted aluminium ribs replaced the wood structure of earlier Curtiss types, largely as a result of Curtiss' association with Charles Ward Hall, an advocate of metal fabrication.

Two production aircraft were ordered in 1928 and the rest the following year while one was employed testing an early form of automatic pilot in 1930. A single B-2A was fitted with dual controls. The B-2 could carry 2508lb of bombs and had six 0.303in machine guns in defensive positions. The last B-2 was retired in 1936.

LENGTH	47.3ft
WING SPAN	90ft
HEIGHT	16.5ft
GROSS WEIGHT	16,591lb
MAXIMUM SPEED	132mph
CRUISING SPEED	105.5mph
CEILING	17,100ft
RANGE	805 miles

ABOVE: Introduced in 1929, a flight of Curtiss B-2 Condor bombers from the 11th Bombardment Squadron, 7th Bombardment Group, based at Rockwell Field, California, over Atlantic City. *USAF*

ABOVE: *The ability of aircraft to remain in the air for long periods, and carry out raids over great distances, encouraged the concept of mid-air refuelling, the first instance of which had been conducted on June 27, 1923, by Captain Lowell H. Smith and Lieutenant John P. Richter taking on fuel from an aeroplane flown by 1st Lieutenants Virgil Hine and Frank W. Seifert.* US ARMY

ABOVE: *From 1923 Huff-Daland produced a family of bombers, also known as Keystone when the company changed its name, including this B-4A with the 28th Bombardment Squadron seen over the Philippines. Keystone bombers would dominate the Air Corps from the late 1920s to the early 1930s.* US ARMY

ABOVE: *The transition from biplane to monoplane bomber was gradual. First flown in 1931, characterised by its high wing with inverted braced-gull configuration and a fully retractable landing gear, the Douglas Y1B-7, later B-7, was the first USAAC aircraft given the new 'B' designation for bomber category.* USAF

and 'treasonable' behaviour. But it was Mitchell who was court-martialled. One of the judges was Major General Douglas MacArthur, who described the requirement to sit on Mitchell's trial as one of the more distasteful acts he had been ordered to do. The trial had been pressed upon the Army by President Calvin Coolidge, who could not abide dissent among senior officers. Mitchell was suspended for five years without pay, although Coolidge later modified the verdict and awarded him half-pay. Mitchell resigned on February 1, 1926.

The case of Billy Mitchell was a seminal period when the trial itself served as a public airing of contested interpretations on the value and the application of air power and it has resonated on several occasions down the decades. Most notably it would reappear again as a contest between air and naval power immediately after the Second World War and the consequences of that debate, and its resolution, would have profound implications for both services. But in 1921, when Mitchell conducted his tests, the Air Service was in no state to flex its muscle. The service had little strength to boast about.

The serviceable aircraft on hand and in storage amounted to 1500 Jennies for training purposes, 1100 DH-4Bs for observation duties, 179 SE-5 pursuit planes (the US designation for the British S.E.5a), and 12 Martin MB-2 bombers. The Handley Page bombers had been built by Standard Aircraft but were not on the list of aircraft on strength. The MB-2 was a product of the bid by Glenn L. Martin to replace foreign aircraft with US designs and developed quickly from the MB and the MB-01. The MB-2 had two 410hp Liberty 12A engines fixed to the top of the lower wing and outboard of the fuselage. In June 1920 the Army had ordered 20 and re-designated them NBS-1. They constituted the entire bombing inventory on strength.

Yet for all the lack of real momentum in assembling a strong, peacetime air service the development of better and more capable aircraft progressed. Aircraft such as the experimental Barling bomber, the XNBL-1, of 1923 revealed just how ambitious the industry could be. This giant triplane weighing 42,000lb and powered by six Liberty 12A engines failed to push the aircraft to reach 100mph or even to get over the Appalachians on a 100 mile flight. The two-engine NBS-4 Condor, however, came out as the best bomber of the decade, with a top speed of 100mph and a combat radius of 300 miles but lacked the potential for fulfilling the requirements sought by the Army.

The pursuit aircraft of the 1920s saw the emergence of the Curtiss Hawk, the PW-8 being capable of 178mph and an altitude of 22,000ft with a range of 335 miles and this clear disparity between the speed and the performance of the fighter and the lumbering vulnerability of the bomber steered policy toward the defensive pursuit aircraft, especially when cost was factored in and it avoided embarrassing debate over the morality of bombing. Nevertheless, for all the relative shortcomings in the performance of its aircraft, the air service was steadily expanding its capabilities as well as its infrastructure.

FEATS OF DARING
Not long after the end of the war, four JN-4H aircraft made a 4000 mile flight across the continent looking for safe and efficient air

ABOVE: *First flown on July 14, 1932, the Boeing Y1B-9A adopted many of the aerodynamic and structural details of the Boeing Monomail and was the first all-metal monoplane bomber built for the Army Air Corps. It is possible to see in this aircraft the progenitor of the B-17 Flying Fortress which evolved via the Model 247.* USAF

help of another DH-4 and a refuelling pipe.

While America went crazy for air shows and displays of aerial circus acts, even paying for some German pilots to come over from Europe and stun amazed spectators, air races and sporting events helped promote the coming age of air transport. The Air Service did a lot of the pioneering work, photographing extensive areas to help plan commercial air routes, using aircraft to support the Department of Agriculture by spraying crops to combat the boll weevil, and by flying aerial patrols over vast forests to alert the Forest Service to fires. Much of it was a public relations exercise designed to convince the American public of the benefits from a strong and capable air force, even in peacetime. But it provided useful practice, testing the abilities of both pilots and aircraft.

A striking feat of the period was the dawn-to-dusk flight by Lieutenant Russell L. Maughan from New York to San Francisco on June 23, 1924, in a Curtiss PW-8, an aircraft developed from the successful R-6 racer which took first prize in the Pulitzer Prize race of 1922. He flew the 2674 miles in 21 hours 48 minutes with five stops. In the same year eight aviators set off in four specially built Douglas World Cruisers to fly around the world. Two aircraft made it in 175 days having logged more than 26,000 miles between April 4 and September 28. In these achievements, the Air Service demonstrated an air-minded America which would stand it in good stead.

By the middle of the decade there was growing concern that planning for the practical application of air power was lagging behind requirements. Two key boards convened to determine a strategy for the Air Service and after a year of deliberations, in December 1925 they were found to support diametrically opposing

routes, searching for prime and emergency landing fields, building a comprehensive map of flight patterns linking major places where military aircraft operated. In 1919, two pilots and two mechanics took a Martin bomber around the continental rim of the USA, logging 9823 miles in an endurance flight to see how effective long range deployments could be achieved through a serious of small hops.

To demonstrate that aircraft could be made to reach out over great distance, in May 1923 Lieutenants G. Kelly Oakley and John A. Macready completed a 2520 mile flight from New York to San Diego in 26 hours 50 minutes in a T-2 transport aircraft. The T-2 was a Fokker C-IV, the first aircraft built by the Dutch aircraft designer after the war and the Army acquired seven, which in many aspects of its design reflected an evolution from the Fokker D-VII built for the German Air Service in 1918, with its tail and 'N' interplane struts. But the limited range of most aircraft prompted a search for solutions through aerial refuelling and in August 1923 Lieutenants Lowell H. Smith and John P. Richter remained aloft for 37 hours 15 minutes in a DH-4 over San Diego with the

ABOVE: *The first American pursuit aircraft built after the war were predominantly Curtiss and Boeing types, the former represented by this PW-8, first flown in January 1923 and ordered by the Army on April 27 that year. Developed from the successful R-6 racer, it was successively modified into an evolving family of Curtiss fighter aircraft.* USAF

ABOVE: *The Boeing P-12 was one of the best-known fighters of the inter-war period, originating in a private venture for the Navy. The first P-12 flew on April 11, 1929, and the type saw extensive service throughout the next decade.* USAF

Boeing P-12

Like many famous types, this aircraft began life as a private venture in the late 1920s and caught the attention of the Navy, for whom it was produced as the F4B-1, and also ordered by the Air Board for the Army on November 7, 1928. The prototype was fitted with a 450hp Pratt & Whitney R-1340-7 radial engine, breaking with the Army predilection for water-cooled, inline engines. Unusually the fuselage incorporated square-section bolted aluminium tubing instead of welded steel tubing. The fabric-covered wings were of wood with corrugated dural stressed skin over tailplane and ailerons.

In production variants different engines were installed, the most powerful being the 500hp R-1340-17 in the P-12E which had a top speed of 189mph. The P-12 began to enter service in 1930 and the engine was soon equipped with a ring cowl where previously there had been streamlined hats behind each cylinder. Some of the 586 aircraft built were used for experimental night flying and production orders continued to flow into 1932. All versions carried two 0.303in machine guns.

LENGTH	30ft
WING SPAN	20.1ft
HEIGHT	9.6ft
GROSS WEIGHT	2536lb
MAXIMUM SPEED	171mph
CRUISING SPEED	135mph
CEILING	28,200ft

views: one wanted a new military structure forged through a department of defence with an independent air force balanced with an equally separate army and navy; the other did not. Congress accepted the report which did not want an independent air force and in an Act passed on July 2, 1926 the US Army Air Service was renamed, the US Army Air Corps (USAAC).

The Air Corps Act, as it was known, authorised an increase from 996 officers, 8447 enlisted men, 153 aviation cadets and 1451 aircraft (of which only 1292 were fit for combat) to 1650 officers, 15,000 men, and 1800 aircraft. In 1926 the Corps had only 60 pursuit types and 169 observation planes but no bombers which could be considered modern or up to operational use in time of war, and only 125 training types were up to date, in a total aircraft inventory of around 1000.

But progress was going to be slow. The authorisations in the Air Corps Act were for a gradual increase to the newly specified levels by June 20, 1932, in a rolling five-year plan which anticipated further expansion at the end of that period. In fact, by that date, the Air Corps had 1305 officers, 13,400 enlisted men and 1709 aircraft. The 45 squadrons included four attack, 12 bombardment, 16 pursuit and 13 observation. Most of the gains had been with pursuit and bombardment units.

By the late 1920s a new generation of bomber advocates were expressing their determination to make the Corps strong in offensive capability. Major Hugh J. Knerr and Lieutenant Colonel Clarence C. Culver were persistent in their demand for modern bombers, not the all-purpose

aircraft of the present but aircraft specifically designed for bombing, with range and carrying capacity to match. In this move, a succession of technical developments transformed the design of combat aircraft from canvas covered wooden biplanes with open cockpits and fixed landing gear to metal skinned monoplanes with enclosed cockpits and retractable undercarriage.

Epitomising this shift, the Boeing B-9 and the Martin B-10 ushered in a new era in bomber design to satisfy Knerr and Culver who saw in these types the aircraft of the future. Developed as a private venture by Boeing, the B-9 was an evolution from the Model 200 Monomail and had two 575hp Pratt & Whitney radial engines, an internally braced cantilever wing with a monocoque fuselage and a retractable undercarriage. It had a maximum speed of 188mph and a range of 540 miles with 2260lb of bombs. But orders went to its competitor, the Martin B-10, which unlike the Boeing had internal bomb stowage.

The B-10 had an open cockpit but the first enclosed rotating gun turret of any US aircraft, mounted in the upper nose forward of the pilot and equipped with a 0.30in Browning machine gun. Powered by two 675hp radial engines it had a top speed of 213mph, a range of 1240 miles and a bomb load of 2260 lb. The Air Corps liked it and Martin grew the type into the B-12 and the B-14. This type would remain in service with the Air Corps until replaced by the B-17 Flying Fortress and the B-18 Bolo.

During the 1930s the mood was swinging positively in favour of an Air Corps equipped for offence and for carrying the fight to the enemy,

rather than in defence and the protection of forces and homeland. The extensive development of long range aircraft in this decade opened the possibility of attack from foreign powers. Where once it had been unthinkable to plan for attack from beyond the two great oceans that provided North America with a natural defence, the ability to cross oceans was being demonstrated by commercial airlines flying across the Pacific,

ABOVE: Not to be outdone, in 1928 Curtiss produced the P-6 Hawk with the powerful 600hp Conqueror engine producing a top speed of almost 200mph. *USAF*

The hope held by many was that this would lead to expansion and further pressure to craft an independent air force but progress was slow and hampered by the illogical division of responsibilities. Training was still under the control of General Staff, supply was under the Air Corps and general responsibilities were divided between the two. But these administrative conflicts failed to create division as both the Corps and the GHQ staffers worked together to maintain a coordinated support for what was now a technically more ambitious air force than it had ever been. Which was just as well, for the world was sliding inexorably toward a new war. ✪

albeit with intermediate staging fields on islands between the West Coast and the Philippines.

The emergence of the heavy bomber coincided with one of the more significant decisions of the inter-war period, the advent of the GHQ Air Force. Persistent calls for an independent air force coincided with the technical development of aircraft which made it more likely to be able to create a powerful force capable of influencing events on the ground far from the battlefront. There were also calls for the Air Corp to help protect America's vast shoreline and to carry out patrol duties on its borders.

In 1933 the Army decided to restructure its force into four field armies and examined how best the Air Corps could fit in to that. For its part, the Air Corps suggested a General Head Quarters air force with responsibility for bombardment, attack and pursuit aircraft for coastal defence – in effect, a national air defence force. During this debate national attention was focused on the Air Corps during the winter of 1934. At the beginning of that year, believing them to be

illegal, the postmaster-general had cancelled the commercial air mail contracts which for many years had subsidised private companies to deliver letters and packages for the US Post Office by air. The Air Corps was asked to take over that job.

In one of the worst episodes of Air Corps history, the new duties coincided with one of the worst winters on record, with blizzards, freezing rain and fog covering many states. In just three weeks, flying against appalling weather, nine airmen had been killed and numerous aircraft wrecked. Responding to public concern, two special investigating bodies were set up to determine the structure of the Air Corps and what it should be required to do. Relieved of its air mail duties in May, the GHQ Air Force concept was ordered into being on January 31, 1934, effective from March 1, 1935. With Brigadier General Frank M. Andrews in command it had headquarters at Langley Field with tactical units formed into three wings at Langley, Barksdale, Louisiana, and March, California.

Curtiss PW-8/P-1 ★

Carrying the company designation L-18-1, the PW-8 was a mixture of traditional and new designs, with metal fuselage and tail supporting wooden wings with wing-mounted radiators. The prototype flew as a company aeroplane in January 1923 and variants began to tumble out of the factory with significant modifications, the most visually evident being the tapered wings and tunnel radiator which had been inspired by the competing Boeing design, the XPW-9.

Under the new designation system the type became the P-1, the first Pursuit type, and has forever been known as the first of the famous line of Curtiss Hawks. As the P-1, the much modified PW-8 went into production, later development giving the type a rotary engine as the P-3. The P-1 carried two fixed forward-firing 0.303in machine guns.

LENGTH	31.6ft
WING SPAN	22.9ft
HEIGHT	8.5ft
GROSS WEIGHT	2866lb
MAXIMUM SPEED	160mph
CRUISING SPEED	128mph
CEILING	20,200ft

BELOW: The first Curtiss P-1 airframe was modified to carry the 480hp inline air-cooled Wright V-1640-3 Tornado engine which gave it a theoretical top speed of 161mph but the day of the biplane pursuit aircraft was over by the mid-1930s. *CURTISS*

Chapter 4: A Global Force 1935-1941

ABOVE: The appearance of the all-metal monoplane bomber with the Boeing B-9 still left some technological advances unexploited. These were embraced however by the Martin B-10, another private venture. Arguably one of the more ungainly combat aircraft of the period, it incorporated a fully-enclosed, manually-operated, gun turret in the nose. This example is seen over Hawaii. US ARMY

With war clouds gathering in Europe, rearmament became a focal point for discussion about the next equipment cycle and about the fundamental role of the Air Corps. Adolf Hitler, head of the Nazi party in Germany, had become chancellor in January 1933, Benito Mussolini was in charge of what amounted to a dictatorship in fascist Italy, and there were concerns that America might become embroiled in another European conflict, however distastefully that was regarded by most Americans.

Opponents of the long-range bomber reached the peak of their influence in 1938 and the chief of naval operations forced through an agreement that Air Corps operations should be restricted to no more than 100 miles beyond the American coastline. Then, secretary of war Harry H. Woodring confined bomber procurement to light, medium and attack types. But the trend was in the opposite direct as, by that time, the Air Corps was already testing some of the largest and most powerful aircraft in the world and was on its way to building a credible long-range bomber fleet.

By this time the Air Corps was already gearing up to re-equip with the Boeing B-17,

ABOVE: A flight of B-10B bombers, the primary service version, during a bombing exercise. The type remained dominant in the Air Corps throughout the second half of the 1930s. US ARMY

ABOVE: The Douglas B-18 Bolero was designed in response to a request for a successor to the B-10 and was a derivation of the commercial DC-2, itself the progenitor to the DC-3. By 1940 most bomber squadrons were equipped with this type. USAF

ABOVE: The layout of the B-18 cockpit was very similar to that of the DC-2, which was not uncommon for aircraft from Douglas, unlike Boeing where cockpits were uniquely designed for each type. MUSEUM OF THE US AIR FORCE

Douglas B-18

The Martin B-10 was the benchmark set by the US Army Air Corps when it went after better performance in a successor that it wanted to carry twice the bomb load and additional range. Hardly had the B-10 begun entering service than the Douglas DB-1 was demonstrated in direct competition with the Boeing 299 and the Martin 146, which was little more than a rework of the B-10 but with side-by-side seating.

Partly because the proposed B-18 was quoted as little more than half the cost of the Boeing aircraft, the Douglas bomber entered service, with a remote-controlled gun turret specially designed by automobile engineer Preston Tucker. Some 350 were built and many were sent to the Pacific theatre prior to the outbreak of war. But many were destroyed by the Japanese. Nevertheless, the B-10 carried a bomb load of 6500lb and defensive armament in nose, ventral and dorsal positions.

LENGTH	57.9ft
WING SPAN	89.5ft
HEIGHT	15.1ft
GROSS WEIGHT	27,673lb
MAXIMUM SPEED	215mph
CRUISING SPEED	167mph
CEILING	23,900ft
RANGE	900 miles

developed from a call to build a bomber capable of carrying a one ton bomb load and with a range of 5000 miles. Known as Project A, the requirement had been announced in May 1934 but the specification was totally unrealistic for the time. Nevertheless, compared to existing bombers the three proposals that came in were of heroic physical proportions and included the Boeing XB-15 and the Martin 146 (XB-16), the latter projected as a 52 ton, 173ft span monoplane powered by six 1000hp Allison V-1710-3 engines, four as tractor, six as pusher. Douglas also submitted their DB-1 derived from the increasingly popular DC-2 transport plane.

The Boeing Model 294 (XB-15) had a span of 149ft, a gross weight of 35 tons and carried a crew of 10, projecting a range of 5130 miles and a top speed of 200mph with four 2000lb bombs. Powered by four 14-cylinder Pratt & Whitney radial engines it had a colossal wing area of 2780sq ft. The Air Corps received only a single prototype of the Boeing Model 294 but the aircraft had some novel features for its day,

not least electrical power supplied by two 110V AC generators driven by petrol engines and it had sleeping and cooking facilities too. Boeing added a flight engineer station to relieve the crew of many sundry duties while the wing was so thick at the root that crewmembers could crawl into it in flight and service the engines.

Boeing's Model 294 had been put up as a contender for a slightly different requirement placed on April 14, 1934, but to compete against the Martin and Douglas proposals directly, the company wheeled out its Model 299 (XB-17), with a span of less than 104ft, a maximum weight of 19 tons and a crew of eight with heavy defensive armament and four 750hp Hornet engines. It had a projected cruising speed of 140mph (but the potential for more than 250mph), a range of 3100 miles and a 4800lb bomb load. After consultation with the Air Corps, the company had begun designing a refined alternative to the Model 294 on June 18, 1934.

Paradoxically, it adopted nothing from the XB-15 but a lot from the Model 247, a highly

ABOVE: The nose arrangement of the B-18 had a more functional layout than that of the B-10 and its derivatives, with heavy armament and a bomb load in excess of three tons. ARCTICEASHORSE

ABOVE: A Martin B-12 at March Field, California, in November 1935. A derivative of the B-10, this version had additional fuel tanks on the fuselage for long range duties. USAF

COMMANDERS 1935-1941

• **Major General Oscar Westover**	*December 22, 1935-September 21, 1938*
• **Major General Henry H. Arnold**	*September 29, 1938-June 20, 1941*

ABOVE: In the mid-1930s the Air Corps issued a requirement for a bomber with a range of 5000 miles and Boeing responded with their Module 294, ordered into prototype stage as the XB-15. A colossal aircraft for its day, it made its first flight on October 15, 1937, at the hands of Eddie Allen. BOEING

Martin MB-10B

The Martin Company owed its origin to Glenn Martin's separation from the Wright-Martin organisation of 1916 and achieved recognition as an independent aeroplane manufacturer with the MB-1 of 1918, powered by the ubiquitous Liberty engine. After providing the Air Service with the MB-2 bomber in the 1920s, the company delivered the B-10 for the Air Corps, a type which has gone down in history as the first to publicly demonstrate aerial bombing tests when 'Billy' Mitchell tried to sink old warships in a demonstration which attracted the ire of the US Navy.

The B-10 adopted a NACA-designed wing section and had three open cockpits, metal construction and a crew of three but the B-10B had closed cockpits. Ordered into service in 1933 it was significantly faster than the latest fighters and had a radio operator and a rear gunner in the aft cockpit. The B-10B carried a 2260lb bomb load and had 0.30in Browning guns in nose, ventral and rear turrets. Various developments, designated B-12 and B-14 brought further improvements before the type was retired in the late 1930s, although 189 were exported, some to the Dutch East Indies where they would become one of the first American aircraft to enter the war.

LENGTH	44.75ft
WING SPAN	70.5ft
HEIGHT	15.4ft
GROSS WEIGHT	16,400lb
MAXIMUM SPEED	213mph
CRUISING SPEED	193mph
CEILING	24,200ft
RANGE	1240 miles

ABOVE: The defensive armament of the XB-15 included six machine guns at nose (seen here), mid-upper, side-fuselage and ventral locations. BOEING

successful transport aeroplane with sleek lines and a top speed of 200mph, and it was impressive. Boeing knew that the Douglas DB-1 was looking likely to be the favourite competitor and sized the 299 to be midway between the Model 247 and the XB-15. Sizing meant a great deal and biggest was certainly not always the best. Larger aircraft cost more which meant fewer could be bought within the discretion of a fixed budget. Moreover, bigger aircraft were more expensive to operate and within the technical limits of reciprocating

engines they would probably be slower. The power-to-weight ratio was just too low.

There were other factors that the Air Corps had to consider too, balancing the cost/ vulnerability equation: bigger aircraft with their higher operating cost would be slower and therefore probably have less chance of surviving attack from the upcoming generation of fast fighters. The Corps recognised already that the last biplane fighter designs were significantly outpacing existing bombers. Future bombers had to close that gap. If they did not, mission attrition would be higher, fewer bombs would be placed on target and more expense would be incurred in buying costly replacements.

Balancing all those factors and by keeping close contact with the Air Corps, Boeing optimised all these parameters to produce an aircraft which was certainly smaller than could technically be developed, such as the XB-15, but one which would be faster, cheaper and easier to maintain and operate. And they chose a name which grabbed the attention of the public from the day it was publicly announced – Flying Fortress. And fortress it appeared to be, with defensive gun positions in dorsal, ventral, nose and fuselage side blister positions, all carrying 0.30in or 0.50in calibre guns manually swung.

The prototype flew for the first time on July 28, 1935, and flew 2000 miles to Wright Field, Ohio, at an average speed of 252mph. But on its first flight there on October 30 the XB-17 crashed when ground mechanics forgot to unlock the controls. This notwithstanding, the Air Corps was so impressed that an order for 13 YB-17s fitted with superchargers for high altitude flight was placed immediately and the type received the full service designation B-17.

What flight demonstrations there had been convinced the Air Corps of its worth but Congress greatly influenced government thinking and swung the long-term decision toward the B-18. But the Fortress had more speed, greater range, higher ceiling and carried a heavier bomb load. Nevertheless, while a protracted testing phase began, the Air Corps put the B-18 into immediate production with a contract for 133 signed in January 1936. For the time being, the Air Corps was not allowed to place the B-17 into quantity production and would conduct a sequence of evaluations with the 13 YB-17s it was allowed to receive.

Further opposition to the expanded Air Corps bomber programme again came from the Navy when it claimed it had the right to defend America's shores and resented the assumption on the part of the Army that its airmen should play any part in that role. Balancing arguments, the plan to deploy the B-17 was scaled back and the first contract for a limited number of just 39 fully developed and operationally configured aircraft was not made until 1938. That model, the B-17B, flew for the first time on June 27, 1939.

FIGHTERS TO THE FORE

By this time there was renewed concern about the crisis in Europe. Hitler had gained complete power over the state and its people, Mussolini was grabbing land in North Africa, Franco was fighting a war against socialist forces in Spain and everywhere there was a feeling of imminent conflict, all of which got the attention of the US government, representing an American population averse to further involvement overseas. Inaugurated in office first in 1933 and again in 1937, President Franklin D. Roosevelt was well briefed on the awesome power in Germany's Luftwaffe and was determined to rearm the Air Corps with modern weapons fit for the day America would again have to fight in a European war.

Since 1935, Germany and Britain had been developing fast monoplane fighters with closed cockpits and retractable landing gear, heavily armed with cannon and machine guns. Capable of speeds in excess of 350mph they were more than a match for existing American bombers. One idea to solve the problem of defending the bomber was the Boeing approach, a forest of defensive firepower carried by individual aircraft.

Some opinion in the Air Corps thought this necessary so that the bombers could defend themselves against swarms of attacking fighters.

Germany had developed the short-range Messerschmitt Bf 109 fighter to attack enemy

Boeing P-26

As the first all-metal American pursuit aircraft, the P-26 'Peashooter' was a visually colourful addition to the inventory when it entered service at the end of 1933, but that was largely due to the bright unit markings and national insignia which embellished the metal structure. It would remain with the Air Corps for eight years. Following a period of traditional biplane design, during which it had produced fighters for the Army for many years, Boeing took a break, and a gamble, with an aircraft which was neither impressive nor an appropriate response to foreign types. Variants of the P-26 would incorporate subtle refinements and there would be an increase in the performance of its single 600hp Pratt & Whitney R-1349-27. Armed with 0.30in and 0.50in machine guns, the P-26 could also carry two 100lb bombs or five 30lb bombs for a ground-attack role. Only 151 were built but the P-26 is one of the more visually delightful designs in a period when the monoplane was eclipsing the biplane in all roles and categories.

LENGTH	23.6ft
WING SPAN	28ft
HEIGHT	10ft
GROSS WEIGHT	3360lb
MAXIMUM SPEED	234mph
CRUISING SPEED	200mph
CEILING	27,400ft
RANGE	635 miles

ABOVE: The layout of gun positions in the various American bomber prototypes of the 1930s appears to have come out of a template, in reality it was the optimised arrangement for maximum all-round defensive fire. The XB-15 here is accompanied by a Boeing P-26. USAF

aircraft threatening its dive-bombers and medium bombers which would be supporting ground operations in the favoured 'blitzkrieg' method of assault. This strategy had become enshrined in German offensive procedure, whereby subjugation of an enemy would be violent and achieved with lightning speed.

For their part, the British had decided that defence was preferable to offence and had chosen to build an air-defence network involving fast Hawker Hurricanes and Supermarine Spitfires with an integrated early-warning radar system coordinating attacks on incoming bomber formations through separate sectors. While production of bombers outpaced fighters, in no way could it be said that in the late 1930s Britain had anything vaguely resembling a strategic bombing force.

The inadequacy of the American fighters, seemingly unable to provide a performance to match the new generation of fast, sleek bombers slipping into service during the early 1930s, frustrated many in the Air Corps. The inferior performance of fighters relative to bombers was made palpably apparent in 1933 when Air Corps manoeuvres failed to intercept a force of B-10s short of their target. Brigadier General Oscar Westover, who was commanding the operation while serving as Assistant Chief of the Air Corps, recommended the elimination of pursuit types altogether, claiming that "high speed and otherwise high performing bombardment aircraft, together with observation aircraft of superior speed and range and communications characteristics, will suffice for the adequate air defense of this country."

Further support for his view arose during 1934 at March Field, California, when a force of fighters was unable to reach one B-12 bomber on exercise after an alert. The B-12 was essentially a B-10 with more powerful engines which put it completely out of reach of the fighters of the day and nobody appeared to have the answer, even Hap Arnold asserting during Baker Board hearings in 1934 that the

inevitable future for pursuit types "is one of the mysteries nobody can answer right now".

In America, for a decade or more after the war Curtiss had supplied the majority of fighters bought by the Army but they were struggling to get out of the open cockpit biplane era. With the appearance of fast, streamlined bombers such as the B-10 appearing in the early 1930s, American fighters were outclassed and based on the assumption that potential enemies had the same sort of equipment (which they largely had) there was increasing concern over the ability of the Air Corps to intercept enemy bombers of the same class.

The first Boeing fighter delivered to the Army had been the PW-9 of the mid-1920s but the first real breakthrough for this manufacturer was the precursor to the P-12 which first flew in April 1929, an adaptation of the Navy's F4B-1. The P-12 was an open-cockpit biplane with fixed landing gear and with a top speed of around 170mph, equipped with two 0.30in machine guns they were succeeded by the Air Corp's first monoplane fighter, the Boeing P-26.

Dubbed 'Peashooter' by its pilots, the P-26 had an open cockpit with a fixed undercarriage and bracing wires which added further to drag which lowered the potential from the 500hp Pratt & Whitney R-1340 engine. With a top speed of barely 234mph and a ceiling of 27,000ft, it entered service in 1933 and would be deployed in the USA, Panama and Hawaii. An export model would fight Japanese forces in China in 1937 and American Peashooters would fight Japanese aircraft in the Philippines during December 1941.

In 1935, looking for a replacement for the P-26, the Matériel Division called for bids on a monoplane fighter with retractable undercarriage and closed cockpit – but only Curtiss put up its Model 75 as a contender so a second call went out in August, when Seversky provided the SEV. The Division then held off until April 15, 1936, when Consolidated and Vought submitted proposals with their P-30A and V-141, respectively. Hoping for a contract, Northrop

AIR FORCE PERSONNEL STRENGTH 1907-1940	
Year	Strength
1907	3
1908	13
1909	27
1910	11
1911	23
1912	51
1913	114
1914	122
1915	208
1916	311
1917	1218
1918	195,023
1919	25,603
1920	9050
1921	11,649
1922	9642
1923	9441
1924	10,547
1925	9670
1926	9674
1927	10,078
1928	10,549
1929	12,131
1930	13,531
1931	13,531
1932	15,028
1933	15,099
1934	15,861
1935	16,247
1936	17,233
1937	19,147
1938	19,147
1939	23,455
1940	51,165

ABOVE: Boeing's Model 299 bomber proposal was essentially a militarised evolution of the Boeing 247, a commercial transport aircraft with smooth lines and high performance. Ordered into prototype stage as the XB-17, the Model 299 had refinements lacking in earlier and contemporary bomber designs. USAF

brought along its own contender, the 3A. In extensive flight trials with prototypes submitted by these five candidates, the Consolidated prototype was disqualified when it was destroyed in a fatal crash, while the Northrop aircraft sped off across the Pacific Ocean and was never seen again.

Seversky turned out the winner of the first competition with the P-35, which had started out as a privately funded venture but which was the first truly modern fighter selected for the Air Corps. But the type still lacked the performance of its European contemporaries, boasting a maximum speed of 290mph, a ceiling of 31,400ft but a relatively short range of 950 miles. Similarly submitted as a private venture, the Curtiss Model 75 provided a second bridge between the biplane era and the monoplane age and was also ordered as the P-36. Deliveries of the P-35 began in May 1937 followed by the P-36 in April 1938.

By investing in the Seversky P-35 the Air Corps stimulated a development evolution which would lead directly to the famous Republic P-47 Thunderbolt, designed by Alexander Kartveli. The Seversky Aircraft Corporation had been founded in 1931 by the Russian nobleman and expatriate Alexander de Seversky, a pilot with the Imperial Air Service during the First World

ABOVE: The side blister for a lateral defensive position on the B-17 was complex and difficult to manufacture. It would be removed on later production variants in favour of an open area with machine gun mounted integrally or from a device suspended from the upper fuselage for a wider traverse of arc. BOEING

NOSE TURRET WITH GUN
MODEL 299
8195   7-24-35

ABOVE: Adopting the nose-position for the forward defensive gun, Boeing achieved a more streamlined front end with bomb aimer's position beneath it, more effectively blended into the contours of the forward fuselage than either the B-10 or the B-18. USAF

Boeing
B-17B/C/D/E

Carrying the civilian registration X-13372, the Boeing Model 299 made its first flight on July 28, 1935, the proposed B-17 bomber displaying four defensive gun positions and carrying a crew of eight. The amount of money invested by the manufacturer almost broke the company financially but 13 improved YB-17 types were ordered on January 17, 1936, all being delivered between January and August 1937. Improvements included a reshaping of the cluttered nose so that the bombardier also served as the nose gunner.

The B-17B was the first production model, having a revised rudder, larger flaps and belly bomb-aiming window. The 39 B-17Bs were delivered between June 1939 and March 1940. The B-17C eliminated the side-blisters and the ventral blister replaced by a 'bathtub' housing, the type also adopting self-sealing fuel tanks. All 38 were delivered by late 1940. The B-17D was different only in minor detail. When the first of 512 B-17E bombers appeared in September 1941 they had a redesigned vertical tail with a large dorsal fin and were delivered in camouflage paint. It also had a beefier defensive arrangement of up to 10 machine guns and a Bendix ball-turret in the under-fuselage position making it a true Flying Fortress. Forty-five B-17Es were delivered to Britain under Lend-Lease arrangement. The B-17E could carry a 4000lb bomb load.

LENGTH	73.9ft
WING SPAN	103.75ft
HEIGHT	19.2ft
GROSS WEIGHT	53,000lb
MAXIMUM SPEED	317mph
CEILING	36,600ft
RANGE	2000 miles

War who left Russia after the revolutions of 1917 and became a magnet for similar migrants from the aircraft industry. Seversky would lose control of the company in 1939, which would be renamed Republic Aviation Corporation.

PREPARING FOR WAR

With increasing concern over the situation in Europe, President Roosevelt believed that only substantial American rearmament could provide it with the armed forces it may very soon need to counter the expansionist policies of Nazi Germany. The perception was clear, that in the event of a German attack on France and the Low Countries they would quickly be overrun and that Britain would soon suffer the same fate. Several key American personalities had visited Germany, some such as Charles Lindbergh, famous for having made the first solo crossing of the Atlantic Ocean in 1927, who returned with dire warnings about German military power and about the possible development of a long range bomber force.

There was some justification for this, as initial moves in that direction had produced prototypes of aircraft which would have been quite capable of reaching America from European bases. But the death of arch strategic bombing advocate Generalleutnant Walther Wever in 1936 diverted attention from very long range bombers, although Hitler retained a fascination with seeing New York in flames, the major commercial centre of a nation he despised for its multi-racial population. But the clear impression existed that German long range bombing was a very real threat to America itself.

On the assumption that Britain would fall to German troops the president foresaw the need for an effective response from the continental US. For that, America would need a strike capability that could span oceans. During 1938 a series of classified meetings were held during which the strategic situation was analysed and judgments reached as to the requirement for Air Corps modernisation on a more ambitious scale. It was believed that after conquering Europe Hitler would turn to Greenland and to Africa, from where he

could deploy aircraft and troops to South America for an attack directly on the United States.

Senior leaders of the Air Corps were consulted and all agreed that a new level of capability was needed, one which could address air threats coming from South and Central America and for that the long range bombers would be essential for striking bases to the south of the country. At the beginning of 1938, the president had spoken of the need to keep the "potential enemy many hundred miles away from our continental limits". The Navy had proudly been considered as the bulwark against invasion and since the Monroe Doctrine of 1823 the British Royal Navy had been in tacit support of that.

The first step was taken with the Naval Expansion Act of May 1938 which approved a 20% increase in the strength of the US Navy, reacting specifically to the Japanese invasion of China and to Germany's annexation of Austria. Implicit within the Act was an expansion of US naval air power authorising a maximum complement of 3000 aircraft. This Act also authorised the building of an additional 105,000 tons of battleships, resulting directly in the laying down of the three Iowa-class battleships upon the deck of one of which, the USS Missouri, the surrender of Japan would be taken in September 1945.

With this expansion under way the Air Corps drafted plans during October 1938 for a force of up to 7000 aircraft and during a conference, President Roosevelt asked the War Department to plan for a programme of 10,000 aircraft of which 3750 would be combat types. Present at that meeting were Major General George C. Marshall, the new Army Deputy Chief of Staff, and Henry H. Arnold, who had become Chief of the Air Corps after the death of General Westover on September 21. While Marshall acquiesced, Arnold was more cautious and reminded the president that an air force was more than men and aeroplanes. It needed bases and properly trained personnel. That meant additional money.

It became apparent at the meeting that the president was wholeheartedly behind the

ABOVE: *The prototype XB-17 crashed during take-off on August 20, 1935. The flying controls had been inadvertently left in the locked position, but this did little to detract from the aircraft's technical superiority.* BOEING

ABOVE: *The XB-17 on flight tests bearing the USAAC markings, with the vertical blue stripe on the hinge line of the rudder and horizontal blue and white stripes, employed between 1919 and 1941.* USAF

ABOVE: *A drawing of the 'Flying Fortress' by Lieutenant Colonel Charles Ross Greening made in a prisoner-of-war camp epitomises the late-1930s assumption that the B-17 would be capable of defending itself in enemy skies.* CHARLES ROSS GREENING

proposed expansion of the Air Corps, believing that air power could do much more to win wars than the Army itself generally understood. For a while his enthusiasm ran away from the plausible, when the president spoke of a force of up to 20,000 aircraft and an industry capable of producing 24,000 aircraft a year. Major General Arnold came away from the meeting believing that in the history of the air force it was a 'Magna Carta' for air power.

President Roosevelt agreed to ask Congress for an additional $500 million to implement this expansion but later cut that to $300 million, of which $180 million should go to combat aircraft and the plan put before Congress was for a maximum force of 6000 aircraft. To support his rearmament plans, the president made an important speech before a Joint Session of Congress on January 12, 1939, stating unequivocally that "… our air forces are so utterly inadequate that they must be immediately strengthened".

Congress responded by approving the $300 million in legislation passed on April 3. In practical terms it gave the Air Corps a free hand to expand its strength to 5500 aircraft and 48,000 officers and men, which was the most they could get for that money. This allowed the Corps to purchase 3251 aircraft over the next two years which was almost exactly twice as many as it had on inventory at the beginning of the year. The long-term plan for the next two years gave the Air Corps an opportunity to expand both bomber and fighter inventories and these efforts were joined by the Air Board to determine how best to construct hemisphere defence.

These changes were instrumental in transforming the way the Army and the Navy regarded their own respective roles. With the Japanese pressing deep into China and using brutal force against military forces and civilians alike, discussion focused on the possibility of an attack by Japan on the United States. This led to discussion about the defence of North America itself, no longer just considered a continent from which to project opposing force to Nazi-occupied Europe but one which might itself come under siege.

In that regard, the role of the Air Corps extended to encompass a defensive responsibility for its new bomber force, aimed at supressing a potential invasion of the North American continent rather than itself being an instrument of propagating bombing attacks on foreign countries. This subtle change in the way the job of the bomber was seen quietened many voices which had spoken out against such uses of air power and cleared the way for a smoother ride through Congress.

And it was working too among the general public. When asked in a Gallup poll whether they favoured an immediate increase in America's air power, nine out of ten US citizens said they did. But this did not translate into an approval for pre-emptive action, or some declaration of war. The majority of Americans still favoured an isolationist approach and it was this internal battle within the country that President Roosevelt spent the next two years fighting, until involvement became unavoidable.

The Air Corps now began an intensive period during which several highly experienced officers joined Arnold in a major pooling of ideas determining how best to allocate resources and

ABOVE: *The first monoplane fighter produced for the Army Air Corps, the Boeing P-26 served with seven front-line pursuit groups until the late 1930s when it was replaced by the P-35 and P-36, this example in the markings of the 18th Pursuit Group at Wheeler Field, Hawaii.* USAF

make the most efficient use of the new money. Included within this group were Lieutenant Colonels Carl Spaatz, Joseph McNarney, and Ira Eaker, Major Muir Fairchild and Captain Laurance S. Kuter, all individuals who would play a vital role in the air war against Germany just four years hence. Arnold immediately implemented an intensive recruiting programme and began a series of tours of extended active duty to draw in reserve pilots. By September 1939 the Air Corps had grown to 2058 regular officers, 669 reserve officers and 23,779 enlisted men.

In the previous 20 years since the end of the 1914-18 war, the largest number of pilots graduating from flying school each year had been 246. Now there was a need to increase the number of schools to process the 1200 new pilots needed annually. While the Air Corps provided the aircraft, the facilities and the equipment, all the instructors were civilians, several of them ageing barnstormers who had lit up the skies across America after the war when they were made redundant to service. Now they were back, and receiving more pay than would have had they stayed in the service!

Trainees who completed the new 12-week primary course went to Randolph Field, Texas, for basic flight training and then along to Kelly Field, Texas, for advanced training. Yet not until 1941 did the Air Corps set up special courses for bombardiers and navigators, those jobs being learned at the GHQ Air Force units – on the job. To accommodate these new requirements the Corps changed the technical training programme. Previously all basic courses had been held at Scott Field, Illinois, before going on to Chanute or to Lowry Field, Colorado. In 1939 the Corps arranged for some enlisted men to go to civilian technical schools or to aircraft factories to

ABOVE: *The Seversky P-35 was put into production for the Air Corps in the mid-1930s, based on a low-mounted, elliptical wing with the main landing gear retracting backwards. It first saw action in the Philippines but in two days 40 of the 48 deployed were destroyed by the Japanese.* USAF

receive instruction in mechanical engineering. This diversification, adopted during the First World War, made better use of training facilities and worked very well, even expanding the range of courses and civilian centres employed.

NEW IDEAS
Airmen such as Andrews and Arnold began to plan the most effective use of the bomber, quietly debating how best to employ tactics and strategy against the day they would have to implement them. But they were not alone in

discussing these issues. On June 28, 1939, a report from the Kilner Board, which had been set up by the Air Corps to review the overall problems under the chairmanship of Brigadier General Walter G. Kilner, gave first priority to the development of liquid-cooled engines with a range in horsepower from 1500 to 2400, essential it said to universal improvement in performance of all types of aircraft.

There was also a need, it suggested, of engines delivering 3000hp, if very heavy long-range bombers were to be developed. The

ABOVE: The same design competition of 1935 which produced the P-35 also saw the appearance of the Curtiss P-36. In production for less than two years, deliveries began in April 1938. The type was significantly inferior to Japanese fighters of the period. USAF

second priority went to fire control apparatus and the third to the development of superior aircraft including single-engine fighters capable of speeds of up to 500mph and a tactical radius of up to 300 miles, a recommendation prompted by the Spitfire and the Bf 109. But it also proposed development of a bomber with a tactical radius of 3000 miles, available by 1944, with a maximum speed of 400mph above 20,000ft carrying a 4000lb bomb load, and three decreasing sizes of bomber down to the tactical ground support level.

In a tightening of objectives, and seeking to avoid ordering everything which industry was capable of developing, it focused specifically on projects which were technically achievable from the engineering capabilities of 1939. It did not want to get into research on guided missiles, jet engines, rockets or other exotic lines of scientific and engineering development which characterised the German effort from 1941 to the end of the war.

It is for this reason that the Air Corps focused specifically on acquiring weapons to fight today's war with today's needs, rather than divert resources into technology that might, but not with certainty, provide some future advantage. This is why the Americans initially made little progress with jet engines and sought help from Britain toward the end of the war when General Arnold secured the blueprints for Britain's jet engines. These had emerged from the single-handed pioneering work of Frank Whittle, almost all of which had begun before the start of the war in 1939.

But the Kilner report was crucial in setting up aircraft specifications for the latter stages of the war, with the Boeing B-29 appearing in time to bomb Japanese cities from the Marianas Islands beginning in 1944. It was also the stimulus for the six-engine B-36 which was ordered in 1941 but placed on a slow development track once the B-29 had demonstrated in flight tests that it would be adequate for the war effort and the defeat of Japan. Besides which, production facilities at Convair were needed for the B-24 Liberator and the B-32 Dominator. However, in 1943, before

ABOVE: In retrospect, a design ahead of its time, the Douglas XB-19 was designed in response to the Army's intervention into large bomber design as a secret requirement issued in 1935. The aircraft was an anachronism, slow, cumbersome and complex to maintain. It was never intended for volume production. USAF

access to the Marianas ensured forward staging bases for the B-29, a contract for 100 B-36s was awarded on July 23 that year. The first B-36 was rolled out on September 8, 1945, six days after the Japanese signed surrender terms on the deck of the USS Missouri in Tokyo Bay.

What also concerned the Kilner Board, which had the insight provided by some of the most informed men in the Air Corps, was the relative standing of American air power compared to that of European air forces. The degree of combat effectiveness was a crucial part of estimating how many resources the Air Corps could commit in wartime while balancing the levels of attrition and the rate of replacement deliveries. If the Air Corps had aircraft of equal survivability to those of the enemy, the levels of

attrition would be the same and the fight could be sustained on comparative rates of production.

The American production capacity was far greater than that of any of the belligerent powers it was likely to encounter and would gradually wear down the enemy though weight of numbers, subject to attrition rates being equal based on equal survivability. This would be seen in the forthcoming Battle of Britain during the summer months of 1940 when the Luftwaffe sought to destroy the RAF so that invasion forces could cross the Channel, albeit under intense bombardment from the Royal Navy.

The Luftwaffe was matched on equal terms with the quality of aircraft and airmen in the RAF and over the several months of Battle the Luftwaffe lost too many aircraft to sustain

ABOVE: Powered by four 2000hp Wright R-3350-5 radial engines, the XB-19 had a maximum bomb load of 37,100lb. With a maximum weight of 162,000lb and a cruising speed of 135mph it had a range of 7700 miles. With uprated engines, the sole example built saw service as a transport. *USAF*

ABOVE: The Stearman Kaydet, a name applied from 1941, was designed in 1934 as a private venture, modified into what would become the most recognised, and valued, US trainer in the inventory, bearing the prefix PT with a variety of type numbers. Boeing bought out the company in 1934. This example is the last of 10,346, used by Boeing in Wichita for publicity and bears the civilian registration. *BOEING*

the conflict, turning to morale-busting night bombing as an attempt to wear Britain down. The losses to the Luftwaffe were critical and it took many months for it to get back up to strength. Of course, none of this had happened when

members of the Kilner Board met but events would vindicate the rationale of their conclusions and this historical analogy is apposite.

What was depressingly evident from the recommendations was the inferior quality of US air power to the other forces in Europe. The US was outnumbered numerically by a wide margin, and outgunned in quality. The reality was that it would take two or three years to achieve a balance with forces the Air Corps were likely to come up against. But the pressure to upgrade the quality and the quantity of men and aircraft was challenged by expanding military responsibilities which the American government had unwittingly imposed, threatening to more than neutralise any additional funds or materiel authorised.

The solidarity of the western hemisphere – defined as the entire land mass of the North, Central and South American continents, had been guaranteed by the president at the Declaration of Lima on December 24, 1938, and committed the US to the defence of the entire hemisphere, embracing under its defence umbrella all the countries north and south of the equator. Less than a year later, on October 3, 1939, foreign ministers of all American countries met in Panama to sign a declaration of neutral rights to set a safe zone 300 miles off the cost encircling the entire hemisphere.

After it had been violated by Axis forces, in July 1940 they made the Monroe Doctrine multilateral and on August 18 Canada and the United States established the Permanent Joint Board on Defense, with equal representation from each nation. This allowed for the transfer of 50 ageing destroyers to Britain in defence of that agreement, since the Royal Navy had been the tacit protector of the international waters around North America. In return, on March 27, 1941, negotiations were completed giving the US a 99-year lease on Newfoundland, Bermuda, the Bahamas and several Caribbean islands.

This had both advantages and penalties for the Air Corps, which was now required to police a much larger area of land than had been envisaged before, or even when the Kilner report was issued. With German air raids on Iceland, only 400 miles from Greenland, in February 1941, US air power was required to look after the interests of both islands and this brought further pressure to add capability on an already stretched agenda.

Greenland had been cut off from its parent country when Denmark was overrun on April 9, 1940, and actively sought protection from America. Some 700 British troops had been on Iceland since May 10, 1940, when they invaded what was, de facto, a neutral country to deny it to Germany. By July 1941 American troops had occupied both Greenland and Iceland and the Air Corps was tasked with planning an audacious operation. On July 25 the 33rd Pursuit Squadron took its 30 Curtiss P-40s to Iceland to join RAF units and defend it against possible invasion.

Recognising that it would be some time before the full inventory of new aircraft was available, the flow of new bombers and fighters made it possible to plan construction of major air bases on Greenland and then Iceland, bringing into the range of current aircraft all of Great Britain and Norway. Scotland is less than 700 miles from Iceland, which is only 800 miles from Norway. The Air Corps was briefed by US government officials on a plan to provide facilities for the evacuation of British troops to American bases on Iceland, from which could flow a major quantity of material in the event of the Germans invading southern England.

Still classified are the details of that capability but six months before America entered the war, the Air Corps had a plan to strike at the heart of Germany from bases in Iceland, supported by logistics flown in to Greenland, both islands providing a secure location from which to attack by air German forces occupying the UK and Norway. On July 7, 1941, President Roosevelt confirmed to Congress that American troops, already in Greenland, were now "in possession" of Iceland. ✪

ABOVE: Boeing Stearman E75 (PT-13D) Kaydet bearing UK registration B-BSWC at Keevil, Wiltshire, preserving the deserved reputation of a true classic. *ADRIAN PINGSTONE*

Chapter 5: A taste of War 1941

Army Regulation 95-5 created the US Army Air Forces (USAAF) on June 20, 1941, with the Air Corps and the GHQ Air Force, which was renamed Air Force Combat Command, as its primary components. This move came about as a result of Secretary of War Henry L. Stimson seeking ways to place the air arm under a single commander. And the resulting reorganisation established the USAAF with General Arnold, Chief of the Army Air Forces, directly responsible to the Army Chief of Staff. In retrospect, this was a further move toward autonomy, but one which already created an independent Air Force in all but name.

On July 9, 1941, President Roosevelt asked the secretaries of war and the Navy to prepare recommendations for a major expansion of the rearmament programme. Forewarned, General Arnold tasked his Chief of Staff, Brigadier General Spaatz, to set up the Air War Plans Division (AWPD) to prevent the Army Air Force from being relegated to a supporting role for ground operations. Headed by Lieutenant Colonel Harold George, commanding officer of the 2nd Bombardment Group, the AWPD was to form up a general plan for air power required to defeat the Axis forces, should war break out, employing strategic, and not just tactical, air power.

Called AWPD-1, their plan was sent to the Army General Staff War Plans Division on August 12, 1941. It called for 24,500 combat aircraft of which 10,000 were to be four and six-engine bombers. On September 11, General George Marshall accepted the plan in full and authorised immediate implementation. The AAF could now begin to structure main objectives in time of war and decided that industrial targets should include electric power grids, transportation networks (including rail, inland water and highways) and the oil and petroleum industries.

Implicit in all of this was that the war would be fought against Germany. While Japanese aggression flourished unabated it was against China and was not yet threatening America, so the AAF focused all it's planning on Western Europe. On June 22, two days after the establishment of the Army Air Forces, the Wehrmacht unleashed Operation Barbarossa involving more than 3.5 million fighting men surging east across the 1800 mile border with Soviet territories, some of which the Russians had negotiated in a deal with Hitler during August two years previously. There was timely justification for the AAF planning on defeating Hitler.

Calculations on the required forces to carry out the mission made possible through AWPD-1, involved numbers of individual targets, disruptive explosives required to dislodge enemy possessions, bomb weights required

ABOVE: In Operation Barbarossa, four million German troops invade Russia on June 22, 1941, along a front that very soon was 1800 miles across. Within days the land and air forces of the Wehrmacht had all but destroyed the Soviet air force. VIA DAVID BAKER

ABOVE: Russian and German aircraft caught up in Operation Barbarossa. In the foreground is a Polikarpov UTI-4, a trainer for the I-16 Soviet fighter. In the background lies the wreckage of a German Henschel Hs 123. POLISH ARMY

for each target, bomb lift required, computed coefficients of aiming errors under combat conditions and the number of aircraft required. The results were revealing in that they displayed areas where gaps needed to be filled with equipment and additional aircraft types.

At this stage, immediately prior to direct American involvement, the requirements were for 10 groups of medium bombers such as the B-25 and B-26, 20 groups of heavy bombers such as the B-17 and the B-24, 24 groups of very heavy bombers typified by the B-29 and the B-32, and 44 groups of very-long-range (VLR) heavy bombers with a combat radius of 4000 miles. In all, this came to 98 bombardment groups with a total requirement for 6834 aircraft.

With Great Britain still holding out, it was assumed that these would operate from the UK and from the region of the Suez Canal. It was assumed that the VLR types would not be available before 1944 but raids from 1943 could be mounted on missions with heavy bombers using doubled-up crews. For their protection, 10 pursuit groups were to be stationed in the UK, six in the Near East.

RAMPING UP

These ambitious plans needed swift delivery of the aircraft concerned and Roosevelt was worried that the industry was not up to the job, the specialities of building aircraft compared with automobiles having already been a challenging obstacle to mass production in the first war. In March 1940 he chose Robert A. Lovett, a banker familiar with aircraft production methods, as special assistant to Secretary of War Stimson and in March 1941 made him Assistant Secretary of State for Air. Lovett examined the aviation industry and compared it with those in Europe which he had observed during several visits.

But the president had grander plans. Likening the effort of helping friends in need to a neighbour asking for the loan of a fire hose to quench the blaze when his house caught fire, Roosevelt created the National Defense

ABOVE: Concerned over the escalation of the war to the Soviet Union, air force planners in America look to the possible threat to the United States from long range maritime reconnaissance aircraft such as the Focke-Wulf Fw 200 Kondor and similar long-range aircraft which could reach the United States. BRUCE ROBERTSON

Advisory Commission with himself as chairman and on March 11, 1941, persuaded Congress to pass the Lend-Lease Act. This allowed America's allies to receive on loan weapons, food, oil and essential supplies they needed to fight fascism, Nazism and imperialism, only returning to the United States those items of equipment surviving after the war. In return America asked for, the rights to several foreign locations for use in fighting the war. Over time the main recipients were Britain ($31.4 billion), the Soviet Union ($10.9 billion), Free France ($3.2 billion) and the Republic of China ($1.6 billion)

The impact this had on the US aircraft industry was marked, although not obstructive, as the

THE GREATEST TEAM AAF IN THE WORLD!

AAF EXAMINING BOARD OR U.S. ARMY RECRUITING STATION

ABOVE: With growing awareness of the need to prepare for war, the newly renamed US Army Air Force uses the Martin B-26 Marauder medium bomber on its recruiting poster. USAF

AAF balanced essential types it needed to re-equip with the call from America's allies. Over the duration of the war, however, Britain and the Commonwealth countries received 26,000 aircraft, the USSR 11,450 and China almost 1400, with an additional 400 to other countries fighting Axis forces. Most of these were absorbed into a rapidly expanding production supply chain greatly improved by the efforts of Robert Lovett. But not everyone was pleased with Lend-Lease, General Arnold chafing at the complicated arrangements and diversion of quotas siphoned off for the allies.

But overall the increase in production was

Consolidated B-24

Aircraft such as the XB-15 and a failed project, the XB-19, demonstrated a deep interest in long-range heavy bombers capable of carrying large bomb loads. Consolidated Aircraft Company focused on the detail of this requirement and came up with a large aeroplane consisting of a deep box-shaped fuselage and twin tails with a Davis high-aspect ratio wing. This provided high lift qualities for a given weight and carried a low drag coefficient, presenting improved range compared to an aircraft with a conventional wing. It became the Consolidated Model 32 and was designed by Isaac M. Laddon, their chief engineer.

The detailed design was completed in January 1939 and tested in a wind tunnel before being presented to the Air Corps at Wright Field the following month, where some 30 modifications were made. The contract for a single prototype was signed on March 10, 1939, and the XB-24 flew on December 29, 1939. The initial B-24A was delivered to the Air Corps in 1941 and quickly overtook the B-17 in production, with an additional manufacturing plant started up in Fort Worth.

The B-24D, specification below, was powered by four 1200hp R-1830-43 engines and had a bomb load of 8800lb, more than double that of the B-24A. It too appeared in service during 1941. The B-24D had ten 0.50in machine guns and deployments to the Pacific theatre had already begun when the Japanese attacked Pearl Harbor, destroying the sole example there.

LENGTH	66.3ft
WING SPAN	110ft
HEIGHT	17.9ft
GROSS WEIGHT	60,000lb
MAXIMUM SPEED	303mph
CRUISING SPEED	200mph
CEILING	32,000ft
RANGE	2850 miles

ABOVE: The Army Air Force issued a requirement for a new medium bomber in January 1939, emphasising a 2000lb bomb load, high speed and a high operating ceiling. Martin proposed the Model 179 which far exceeded its competitor. The aircraft was in service by the end of 1941. USAF

ABOVE: Designed to a requirement issued in 1939 calling for a heavy bomber to exceed the performance of the Boeing B-17, Consolidated Aircraft came up with the Model 32 and produced the B-24 which was operational by the end of 1941. Seen here is the XB-24 (39-680) which first flew on December 29, 1939. More B-24 bombers were produced than any other American aircraft. USAF

working effectively, with the number of aircraft available to the AAF increasing from 2500 at the end of 1939 to 12,000 by the end of 1941. But arguably the most important contribution came from the increase in training aircraft, the total on hand rising from 700 to almost 7000 over the same period. Production rates were slow to begin with, the AAF receiving on average fewer than 100 aircraft a month during 1939, the monthly acceptance rising to 250 in January 1941 and more than 800 in December. Throughout 1941 these rates continued to increase, from around 1000 in January to 2500 at the end of the year.

The Air Forces wanted combat aircraft but the production quota for those was slowed by the priority requirement for new aircrew and by Lend-Lease which saw the number of B-17s delivered rising from only 22 in September 1939 to almost 200 in December 1941. Fighter aircraft on strength increased, from just under 500 to more than 1600 front-line types in those two years. However, fewer than 100 were the twin-engine Lockheed P-38, at least 300 were Bell P-39 Airacobra and the remainder were P-40 Warhawk pursuit types. In total, across the two-year period from 1939 to 1941, the

annual production of military aircraft increased from 2141 to more than 19,000 but this was as nothing compared to what would come.

To support this vast increase in production and delivery, airfields and training courses were mobilised to deliver the technicians, the students, the instructors and the support staff required to keep pace with the increased manpower. The personnel strength increased from 43,000 at the end of 1939 to almost 100,000 in 1940. By the end of 1941 there were more than 340,000 men under uniform in the Army Air Forces. The number of graduates alone had increased 800% in 1940,

reaching 8000 during the year and 27,000 in 1941. Technical courses turned out ten times as many specialists in 1940 as in the previous year, almost 15,000 increasing to 42,000 in 1941. The range of skills and courses expanded outwards as well, into specialist areas such as weather forecasting, engineering, administration, photography, communications and armament.

All this called for an expanded officer base and the reserve force served to enlarge the active duty strength to 6000 by the end of 1940. By the middle of 1941, the AAF had mobilised all the reservists willing to volunteer for the extended ➤

ABOVE: B-17B bombers at March Field, California, before the December 7, 1941, attack on Pearl Harbor. USAF

The 19th Bombardment Group under the command of Lieutenant Colonel Eugene L. Eubank had flown 21 of these bombers without a single accident from California to Oahu on May 13-14, 1941, setting a new record for mass flight over water. By the beginning of December the 18th Bombardment Wing was at Hickam Field outside Honolulu and the 14th Pursuit Wing at Wheeler Field about 15 miles away. One pursuit squadron was training at Haleiwa, a small outfield.

After the Japanese attacked Pearl Harbor on December 7, 1941, and brought America into the war, simultaneously sending several thousands of troops pouring south through the jungles of South-East Asia, the most immediate predicament for the Army Air Corps was how to deal with its facilities in the Philippines. Increased Japanese activity had been reported to the AAF by Naval intelligence sources monitoring movements in the region. US commanders were warned that Japanese aircraft were flying over British territory; the British were already sending reciprocal flights over Japanese territory in a tit-for-tat response. British intelligence sources made the Americans aware of two Japanese carriers in the mandated islands sending US naval and air forces on to high alert.

So concerned was the senior command at the AAF that they wanted to get a force of heavy bombers to the Philippines as quickly as possible and by the second week in November it was planned to send all the latest B-17E variants to the islands, leaving only 17 B-17s within the Zone of the Interior, the majority of which were very

hours of duty and civilians began to be recruited as the pre-war pool shrank. The integration of civilians into the AAF was a great opportunity for air-minded youth and unexpectedly high numbers were moved to put themselves forward.

With expanding capabilities, larger resources and greater manpower the AAF looked to its foreign commitments for areas to consolidate and in November 1939 the Hawaiian Air Force

was organised with 117 aircraft, none of them front-line types but good enough to send a signal. But commitments increased and by December 1941 the islands had one of the best defended territories with 231 aircraft of which half were modern fighters. Among them were 12 B-17D bombers which were sent in the belief that their long range would make them ideal for reaching out to attack a potential invading naval force.

ABOVE: A view of Pearl Harbor taken on October 30, 1941 looking southwest, with Ford Island naval station in the centre and the Navy Yard just beyond it across the channel. The airfield at upper left-centre is the USAAF's Hickam Field. US NAVY

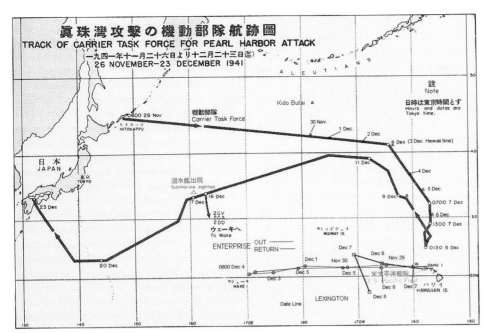

眞珠灣攻撃の機動部隊航跡圖
TRACK OF CARRIER TASK FORCE FOR PEARL HARBOR ATTACK
(一九四一年十一月二十六日より十二月二十三日迄)
26 NOVEMBER-23 DECEMBER 1941

ABOVE: The route taken by the aircraft carriers as they conveyed elements of the Japanese Navy Air Force to the vicinity of Hawaii and the US naval base at Pearl Harbor. US NAVY

ABOVE: A photograph taken by a Japanese warplane as it took part in the surprise attack, designed to eliminate the Pacific Ocean aircraft carrier force before it could respond to the invasions taking place throughout South-East Asia. US NAVY

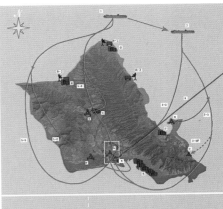

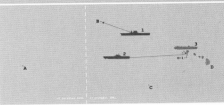

ABOVE: The Japanese attacked Pearl Harbor in two waves. The first wave was detected by Army radar at 156 miles but was misidentified as USAAF bombers arriving from the US. Top: A. Ford Island NAS B. Hickam Field C. Bellows Field D. Wheeler Field E. Kaneohe NAS F. Ewa MCAS R-1. Opana Radar Station R-2. Kawailoa RS R-3. Kaaawa RS G. Haleiwa H. Kahuku I. Wahiawa J. Kaneohe K. Honolulu O. B-17s from mainland 1. First strike group 1-1. Level bombers 1–2. Torpedo bombers 1–3. Dive bombers 2. Second strike group 2-1. Level bombers 2-1F. Fighters 2-2. Dive bombers Bottom: A. Wake Island B. Midway Islands C. Johnston Island D. Hawaii D-1. Oahu 1. USS Lexington 2. USS Enterprise 3. First Air Fleet. ANYNOBODY

up at altitude. Nevertheless, the AAF believed the British were not operating the aircraft correctly and retained their faith in what was, in 1941, the most capable bomber employed by any air force.

NEW DEPLOYMENTS

The 19th Bombardment Group took off from California in 26 B-17s on October 22 and arrived at Clarke Field, 60 miles north of Manila, on November 6. By then the AAF had 265 combat aircraft in the Philippines but the only front-line aircraft were 35 B-17s and 107 P-40 Warhawks, although 31 of those were not yet in combat units. Major General Lewis H. Brereton was there as air commander to General MacArthur, recalled to active duty by President Roosevelt and made commander of US Army Forces in the Far East (USAFFE).

Preparation for consolidation of the Philippines through the application of air power was favoured by MacArthur and his determination to build up defensive forces supported his overall strategy, which was to use the islands as a fortress from where American military and air power would counter any Japanese attempt to seize control of South-East Asia. Brereton had been asking for considerably greater resources and 1.1 million tons of equipment and supplies for the Philippines was stocked in American shipyards along the Western Seaboard awaiting shipment to the islands.

All the intelligence indicated that war with Japan was imminent and Army Air Force squadrons went on full alert as the Philippines were assessed as being a primary target for Japanese attack. With bases in China and carrier ➤

early marks. Set up specifically on the instruction of General Marshall on July 26, the AAF's Far East Air Force was considered so important that the Air Staff in Washington debated whether to send all American heavy bombers to the Philippines. As the Japanese began to show preparations for a major assault in the region, the 14th Bombardment Squadron had set out for the Philippines on September 5, flying via Midway, Wake, New Guinea and Australia.

In a prescient warning about the critical state of affairs, on November 22 officials advised that all available bombers and pursuit aircraft destined for the Philippines should be en route by December 6 – otherwise it might be too late. By this date all squadrons in the Far East were on continuous standby and to support airborne intelligence gathering, two B-24s were sent to the Philippines to carry out photographic work of a potential Japanese build-up.

Planning staffers had worked on the assumption that war with Japan would not become likely before April 1942 but the information received by the AAF was that this was too relaxed, and that there was imminent danger of an attack. While initially the build-up had been orientated toward Europe, the axis of threat shifted to the Far East and by December 7 some 913 aircraft had been deployed outside the continental United States.

With a concentration of air power in the Philippines, the Americans had high confidence in the B-17, despite misgivings by the British over its relatively poor performance in the European theatre. The first British Fortresses had entered service with No. 90 Squadron at West Raynham in May 1941 and began flying operations on daylight bombing raids on July 8. Bombing from 30,000ft on individual sorties which the Americans disliked, they were not successful, not a single bomb having been dropped on 51 sorties of which 26 had to be aborted. The RAF had difficulty with the Norden bombsight, a lot of failures with equipment and the guns had a tendency to freeze

ABOVE: A B-17B burned out at Hickam Field hours after the attack on Pearl Harbor in which 188 aircraft were destroyed and 159 damaged, some beyond repair. *USAF*

ABOVE: The USS Pennsylvania lies severely damaged with the wreckage of the USS Cassin and the USS Downes behind. In the attack, four battleships were sunk, four battleships were damaged, two other ships were sunk and nine other ships were damaged. In the attack, 2403 people were killed and 1178 wounded. *US NAVY*

forces at hand just north of the islands, the Philippines were expected to take the brunt of the Japanese steam roller pushing south, with Indo-China and Singapore to its right flank and the feared US Navy on its left flank. The attack on Honolulu was a side-blow, and the responsibility of the Japanese Navy, but not the main object of the attack, which was to neutralise Pearl Harbor.

This huge naval base was believed, by the Japanese Navy, to contain almost all the US naval air power in the region. It turned out that two American carriers were at sea and escaped the carnage but this left-hook to Pearl Harbor was meant to send America a knock-out blow while the main thrust of the Japanese forces rushed on to the Dutch East Indies (Indonesia) and Australia.

Yet the strategic direction of the territories seized made Malaya and the oil fields further south the primary strategic targets. In this

way the US State Department considered the strategic logic, the Navy to be the 'left flank' in the Pacific Ocean, and the Army Air Forces in the Philippines as the focus for the main attack. Historians write this according to the perspective of the lens they are looking through but to MacArthur and his aviators, the Philippines were the front line of defence.

MacArthur had even asked the State Department to request landing permission from the Russians for US bombers flying north to attack Japanese forces, and possibly Japan itself, by flying from Luzon, bombing Japanese ships and shuttling on to land at Vladivostok in the Soviet Union. The B-17s did not have the range to fly back to the Philippines after dropping their load. Already suffering under the Wehrmacht onslaught, the Russians were fearful of provoking the Japanese into attacking their Far East border and refused. The bombers could only operate at a radius of action which would allow them to return to Clarke Field. As it turned out, they never got the opportunity.

In the hours of destruction meted out to the Americans at Pearl Harbor on December 7, and in addition to the losses suffered by the US Navy, of 231 aircraft on the island the Army Air Force lost 64 and no more than 79 of the remainder were reported as usable. AAF casualties were greatest at Hickam Field where 163 were killed, 43 were missing and 336 were wounded. It could have been worse.

As the main Japanese attack was under way, 12 B-17s flying in from California found themselves unwitting spectators as they flew right in to the attacking formations. Stripped of guns to lighten the aircraft for the long flight, they had no means of defending themselves but the Japanese naval pilots were preoccupied with their attack runs and left the American bombers to circle round and land, mercifully with the loss of only one destroyed and three badly damaged.

Across in the Philippines on that 'infamous' day, the Far East Air Force had 33 B-17s, of which 16 were at Del Monte and 17 were at Clark Field, and 90 pursuit aircraft. Plans were

immediately laid to reinforce the Hawaiian Islands with a further 46 B-17s and the Army agreed that the Navy should command long-range reconnaissance over the islands. For the immediate future of the Philippines, a degree of uncertainty prevailed. General MacArthur heard of the attack on Oahu within an hour of it starting but in the Philippines it was night and so the Japanese were unable to attack both places simultaneously as they had desired.

The records detailing the precise sequence of events at Luzon were destroyed by the Japanese and eyewitness accounts vary greatly in how they recall the events of those hours and days. Major General Brereton insisted that he ordered an immediate strike against Japanese forces on the island of Formosa with the 18 B-17s at his disposal but MacArthur denies that such an order was ever given. The facts that can be verified are that someone did suggest such an attack but that it was vetoed until a proper reconnaissance had been made of Formosa because no intelligence information was available as to what was actually on the island, or where the Japanese were.

The Japanese too were grounded, by dense blankets of fog that swept across the area and the 100 Japanese Army bombers that were to have attacked the Philippines were unable to take off. When the Japanese finally could attack, observers were only able to catch sight of the intruders as they made the run in to Clarke Field, where the B-17s were all neatly lined up on the apron. The Warhawks took off to attack the incoming force but only three managed to engage the enemy and three waves of Japanese aircraft came across bombing and strafing, destroying all the Fortresses, which were still on the ground.

Ironically, the B-17s had been moved up to Clarke to prepare for a strike against the Japanese and would not have been there when the attack came had they got airborne. By the end of the first morning on December 9, Brereton had lost half his force.

Quite quickly, over the next two days, Clarke Field became unusable and B-17s staging through to carry out raids against the

ABOVE: Ordered by President Roosevelt, a response to the attack on Pearl Harbor was to result in the daring flight of Lieutenant Colonel Doolittle in 16 B-25 Mitchell bombers on April 18, 1942, carried on the deck of the carrier USS Hornet. US NAVY

North American Aviation B-25 Mitchell

In 1938 the Air Corps specified a medium bomber with a range of 1200 miles carrying a payload of 1200lb and capable of more than 200mph. The NA-40-1 eventually emerged from a series of design concepts, with high wing, twin vertical tails and a tricycle undercarriage. Powered by two 1350hp Wright R-2600 radial engines, it was first flown in January 1939 and shown to the Air Corps for evaluation. Initial directional instability was ironed out thanks to design changes that effectively transformed the type into a successful aeroplane.

Entering operational service in 1941 with two 1700hp R-2600-13 engines, a B-25A sank a Japanese submarine on December 24 and the improved B-25C, specification below, appeared before the end of the year. Several variants of the B-25 Mitchell, named after the famous advocate of bombers, would appear during the war with appearances in every theatre of conflict, most famous perhaps for its use as the 'Doolittle raider' of April 1942 when 15 aircraft bombed Tokyo, launched from the deck of the USS Hornet some 750 miles from the target.

The B-25 could lift a 3000lb bomb load and was armed with six 0.50in machine guns. By the end of the war, more than 11,000 Mitchells had been delivered, 9800 to the US Army Air Forces.

LENGTH	52.9ft
WING SPAN	67.6ft
HEIGHT	15.9ft
GROSS WEIGHT	34,000lb
MAXIMUM SPEED	284mph
CRUISING SPEED	233mph
CEILING	21,200ft
RANGE	1500 miles

ABOVE: Launched from the Hornet some 750 miles from mainland Japan, 15 Mitchells dropped bombs on Tokyo six hours later, one having to divert to the Soviet Union due to low fuel. US NAVY

ABOVE: Following the Doolittle Raid, eight men were captured by the Japanese including 1st Lieutenant Robert L. Hite seen here. While Hite survived, three of his fellow airmen were executed by firing squad and another died of beriberi disease and malnutrition. USAF

Japanese were forced to fall back. By the end of December 10, Brereton had just 12 B-17s operational, with 22 P-40 Warhawks and eight P-35s. The fighters were ordered not to make any more sorties because they were desperately needed for reconnaissance. Clarke Field was abandoned as a permanent base by the end of the month. Despite adequate warnings, another Japanese group had destroyed a deterrent force and just as the Japanese Navy had crippled the US Navy at Honolulu, so too had the Japanese Army destroyed the forces of retaliation in the Philippines.

As the crushing and overwhelming superiority of the Japanese forces rolled on across the Philippines, the Americans fell back and on December 24 Washington ordered MacArthur to leave and take up position in Australia where what remained of Brereton's air power could stage a resistance, with hoped-for resupply from the United States. In the weeks to come the Japanese land and sea forces swept all before them and on February 15, 1942, Singapore

fell and by early March were in possession of the Dutch East Indies. But the Americans were planning a revenge attack at the very heart of the Japanese capital and it would be carried out by Army flyers transported to an accessible reach of the Japanese mainland by a US Navy carrier.

On April 18, 1942, Lieutenant Colonel James H. Doolittle led 16 Army Air Force B-25 Mitchell medium bombers in an attack on Tokyo from the deck of the carrier USS Hornet in one of the most audacious and daring raids of the war. During a meeting of the Joint Chiefs of Staff on December 21, President Roosevelt had appealed for a way to hit back at Japan in what would amount to a signal that the Japanese could not attack US bases with impunity. While sending a message to the Japanese citizens that their country was not immune from retribution, it would, said Roosevelt, provide Americans with a "badly needed morale boost".

The Navy was recovering from Pearl Harbor and would soon engage the Japanese Navy in the Battle of the Coral Sea far to the south. Despite

that, the Navy lacked aircraft with the range to carry out such an attack on the Japanese mainland and it had fallen to the Army Air Force to deliver the first blow to an Axis power. A challenge readily taken up by General Arnold. Doolittle was a flying instructor, based in the USA during the First World War and, convinced that good pilots needed to be able to fully control an aircraft without visual cues, achieved recognition for his role in the development of instrument flying. He volunteered to lead the group he had been tasked with training on what has gone down in history as the Doolittle Raid.

While applauding the courage of the raiders, the American press called for more like it, claiming that while it had been a triumphant "sock to the Japanese jaw" it was, within the magnitude of the task now facing the country, the "too-little raid" and must be followed up with a juggernaut blow to the body of Imperial Japan. That blow would, in the reality of the Pacific war, be delivered by the Navy, until they and the Marine Corps had occupied islands within range of the Air Force's biggest bomber – the B-29. For the present. All eyes were on Europe. ✿

Chapter 6: Preparations 1941-1942

ABOVE: Adolf Hitler declared war on the United States on December 11, 1941, in this speech at the Reichstag. Senior German government officials, including Foreign Minister von Ribbentrop, advised against this – to delay engaging the Americans until Russia had been overwhelmed – but Hitler disregarded this and made the declaration as a surprise announcement. BUNDESARCHIV

The wave of Japanese invasions and occupations heading south through the Philippines and Malaysia into the Dutch East Indies to eventually push up through Burma was, claimed the Japanese, quite legal – they were merely freeing the orient of occidental occupation and imperialism achieved through past wars. And there was some twisted truth to what most saw as a perverted blend of opportunism and aggression.

The tripartite pact signed by Germany, Italy and Japan on September 27, 1940, created the Axis partnership, whereby their foreign ministries agreed to exchange the territories owned by the countries that had surrendered to Germany by that date. This included France, with the territory of Indo-China, the Netherlands, with the Dutch East Indies and Britain, which had declared war on Germany on September 3, 1939, thereby placing all its territories and possessions in conflict with Germany – and the Axis partners from the date the pact was signed.

It was the same skewed logic that Hitler used to claim that his remilitarisation of the Rhineland on March 7, 1936, had been legal because ceding territory to the victorious powers in 1919 with the Treaty of Versailles was illegal as the treaty had never been signed into law. In the literal sense this was true, because the US Senate refused to ratify it and it was, de facto, not a legal agreement but one imposed on the Germans by the British and the French alone.

While superficially seeming not to have

anything to do with the fate of the Army Air Forces these events were, in reality, enmeshed within the strategies they had evolved. This twisting and turning of history was a crucial element in the disillusionment of the American people with the idea of standing up to Hitler and using US military power to confront his Nazi government when war clouds gathered in Europe.

In the 1940s, a significant proportion of the American population was German. There was little appetite for war with Germany again and Roosevelt played a careful and frequently secret hand in manoeuvring public opinion. Just as it had in Britain, the protracted period of diplomatic parleying with Germany bought time to rearm and develop the equipment the Air Forces would need when war finally broke out. But it was with Germany, rather than Japan, that Roosevelt had been in vehement opposition publicly and through diplomatic channels.

Nevertheless, it was Adolf Hitler who declared war on the United States four days after Pearl Harbor, rather than the other way round, three days after President Roosevelt declared that "a state of war" existed between America and Japan. It was exactly what the president needed to engage the United States in the subjugation of Nazism – the enemy declaring war on the United States and in so doing propelling the country into conflict irrespective of what the President thought or did.

A REDIRECTION OF EFFORT

In staff offices across the War Department, for several months strategists had been planning the best way to defeat Hitler and what the Japanese had accomplished in the Far East provided a window to vulnerabilities in the Nazi war machine. Besieged by a US blockade for several months before the attack on Pearl Harbor, Japan was running out of vital industrial resources for both military and civilian purposes. Short on oil, steel, aluminium and rubber, Japan used all 48 million barrels of its last oil reserve to mount the massive and high-risk strategy of breaking out and lunging south to gain access through conquest to the vast resources it needed to survive. Unable to use its land-based bombers for strategic advantages it used its carrier force to neutralise American reciprocity by sea.

Strategists now planning a long-term combined bomber offensive against Germany foresaw that Hitler's war machine could be brought to a halt by starving it of the resources necessary for strategic survival, by hitting oil refineries, ball bearing factories, power production plants, coalfields and factories. It was what Hugh Trenchard, Giulio Douhet and Billy Mitchell had been saying for the past 25 years.

The pivotal turning point in Anglo-American cooperation came on December 22 when Winston Churchill arrived in America with his chiefs of staff and several officials to meet with

ABOVE: Pearl Harbor survivor Bill Johnson stares at the list of names inscribed in the memorial to the USS Arizona sunk with the loss of 1177 crewmen. On January 20, 2004, Johnson visited the memorial to pay his respects to the sailors killed that day, particularly his friend and high school buddy W. N. Royals, 64 years after the attack. While on patrol in the Pacific aboard USS Devilfish, Johnson and his shipmates survived a kamikaze attack and also managed to escape an enemy minefield. US NAVY

President Roosevelt and discuss the strategy of the war in a 'Grand Alliance'. Known as Arcadia, the conference lasted until January 14, 1942, and emphatically endorsed the president's belief that the war against Germany should be addressed as a priority over the war with Japan. General Marshall, the president's chief military adviser and confidante, spoke encouragingly of a swift and decisive blow against Germany using General Arnold's Air Forces and of an expeditionary force to liberate occupied Western Europe. He enthused over the possibility of using air power to defeat the ability of the Wehrmacht to resist ground forces but their ally was more cautious.

The British wanted to contain German expansion by involving the Army Air Forces in sustained bombing campaigns from bases in Britain and by supporting the Russians in holding off the Germans from further incursions into Soviet territory, while evicting the Italians (soon to be joined by the Germans) from North Africa during the first half of 1942. The jump across to Northwest Africa would be codenamed Gymnast and would be supported by air power. But the British also proposed a landing in Tunisia and the whole operation of clearing North Africa was modified into Super-Gymnast. Incidental to air power, US troops were to be sent to Northern Ireland to relieve British troops under operation Magnet.

To implement these plans, which were to change considerably over the next several

ABOVE: As soon as the United States was engaged in a war with Japan and Germany, a recruiting drive began to create a spirit of unity and common purpose which would have been less popular had America itself declared war on the Axis. The wounds resulting from the loss of life at Pearl Harbor ran very deep. USIA

months, on January 3 President Roosevelt sent Henry Stimson a list of requirements, calling for 60,000 aircraft in 1942 and 131,000 in 1943, for both the Army and the Navy. But while these totals remained the same the proportion of types defined within the requirement were modified by January 14. General Arnold influenced the balance between AAF type quotas, 9780 being medium, heavy and long-range bombers plus 14,350 pursuit types in 1942, with 26,190 bombers and 30,600 fighters in 1943. But the most significant growth was to be in the provision of trainers, doubling from 15,000 in 1942 to 31,000 in 1943, desperately

TOP 10 LEADING AIRCRAFT MANUFACTURERS

• North American	41,188	• Boeing	18,381
• Consolidated Vultee	30,903	• Grumman	17,428
• Douglas	30,696	• Republic	15,603
• Curtiss	26,154	• Bell	13,575
• Lockheed	18,926	• Martin	8,810

Note: Total aircraft built July 1, 1940, to August 31, 1945

ABOVE: President Franklin D. Roosevelt met with the senior British military leadership under Prime Minister Winston S. Churchill shortly after the declarations of war and gave them an overwhelming assurance that defeating Hitler and liberating occupied Europe was America's first concern. *USIA*

ABOVE: General George C. Marshall (1880-1959) was Chief of Staff under Presidents Franklin D. Roosevelt and Harry S. Truman. During the early years of the Second World War he played a vital role in balancing the over-eager expectations of Roosevelt and the reluctance of the British to engage in high-risk strategies. He was particularly helpful during the Arcadia conference beginning at the end of December 1941. *DOD*

would not achieve operational status until April 1944, that aircraft would cost $509,000.

As shown in accompanying tables, the AAF would receive a total of just over 41,000 aircraft in 1942 and 68,600 in 1943 but total production of all types for the three services amounted to 47,836 and 85,898, respectively. For the AAF, there would be just over 21,000 aircraft in the inventory at the end of 1942 and 49,018 a year later. The bill was huge, the total cost of the 1644 B-29s built by the end of the war being more than $800 million,

Curtiss P-40 Warhawk

By 1938, when the outclassed P-36 began to enter service, Curtiss engineer Donovan Berlin believed there was a way to bring it up to date and create a new fighter aircraft out of an old configuration. That rarely works but this time it did and the result was the P-40. When Berlin got permission from the Air Corps to change the 1050hp radial engine for a 1150hp inline Allison in the 10th production P-36A it transformed the aircraft. First flown on October 14, 1938, it had all the marks of a successful fighter. And it would become so. In several respects the P-40 was an interim success, developed in parallel with the Lockheed P-38 Lightning, a fast, long-range escort fighter, awaiting the arrival of the P-47 Thunderbolt and the P-51 Mustang. Nevertheless, the Army liked it and the Air Corps ordered 524 in April 1939. Deliveries began in 1940, the first of 13,738. The P-40 was the last in a long line of Curtiss aircraft and ranks third in the highest number of American fighters produced during the Second World War, eclipsed only by the P-47 and the P-51.

LENGTH	31.75ft
WING SPAN	37.5ft
HEIGHT	12.3ft
GROSS WEIGHT	7600lb
MAXIMUM SPEED	352mph
CRUISING SPEED	280mph
CEILING	32,400ft
RANGE	940 miles

needed now for the accelerated intake.

In addition to these scheduled deliveries to the AAF, the Navy was to get 10,220 aircraft in 1942 and 21,790 in 1943. To accommodate these deliveries, industry would produce just over 45,000 combat aircraft in 1942 and 100,000 in 1943, the Army Air Forces receiving 77% in 1942 and just over 78% in 1943. But the biggest financial and production burden would rest on the Army with its requirement for heavier and more costly aircraft than those built for the Navy.

Each pursuit aircraft cost from $44,000, for a P-40 Warhawk, to $51,000 for a P-51 and $88,000 for a P-47 Thunderbolt. The B-25 Mitchell, famous now from the Doolittle raid, cost just under $117,000, while a B-17 cost $187,000 and a B-24 a whopping $215,000. And, with the recognised need for a very heavy bomber, the Boeing B-29 Superfortress was on the drawings boards and although it

ABOVE: When the United States went to war the Army Air Forces were only just beginning to receive aircraft which were capable of fighting enemy types on equal terms. One of those was the Curtiss P-40 Warhawk, arguably the most famous of a line of pursuit aircraft that began with the P-1 of 1923. *USAF*

ABOVE: *To satisfy the need for large numbers of aircraft, production was key. Born May 9, 1882, to ethnic German immigrants, Henry J. Kaiser rose from humble beginnings to found the Kaiser shipyards which built Liberty boats but his contribution to the demand for increased aircraft production was an outstanding example of adaptive thinking. He died on August 24, 1967.* DAVID BAKER

about $16 billion in 2017 money values.

The war plans and scheduled production quotas at the Arcadia conference formed the basis on which the AAF began planning to move a large bombing force across to Britain. The demand on manpower was to be much greater than it had been just a few years earlier. Bombers like the B-17 and the B-24 had 10 or 11 crewmembers each, with specialised skills. Reorganisation and expansion of squadrons, groups and wings were only a few of the issues that kept the conference staffers busy responding to queries from the political leadership regarding options and possibilities, aspirations tempered by practical reality.

But the Army Air Forces were only a part of a giant war machine which was defined by Roosevelt in a radio broadcast on December 29, 1940, when he referred to America's wartime production potential as an "arsenal of democracy". As with the production demand during America's involvement in the First World War, the manufacture of domestic peacetime consumer goods was very different to the demands of fighting forces and in 1940 Roosevelt called upon the services of William Signius Knudsen and Henry Kaiser to plan American industry to supply the US war machine.

Knudsen was an immigrant from Denmark who arrived in America in 1900 and worked his way from humble beginnings to head up the Chevrolet Division of General Motors from 1924, becoming president of the company in 1937. Plucked out by Roosevelt, he became the highest ranking civilian entrant to the American armed forces when the president made him a lieutenant general to manage the war effort. Born in New York in 1882 to German immigrants, Henry Kaiser survived a very troubled childhood to become known as the 'father' of American shipbuilding, revolutionising the industry by using welding instead of riveting. Having headed up construction of the Hoover Dam project he proved his value in managing giant projects. These two men would give the Army Air Forces the aeroplanes they needed.

Yet even these giants of industry required special skilled areas of management, manufacturing and production, the field troops in the war to raise output. One such man was Charles 'Cast-Iron' Sorensen, another Dane who had made his mark on the US industrial scene. In 1941 Consolidated Aircraft was wrestling sluggish production at their San Diego plant until Sorensen was brought in to apply production skills he had put into practice at the Ford Motor Company. The B-24 was a large and complicated aircraft and the AAF wanted lots of them but the manufacturer was falling short on delivery.

ABOVE: *Aircraft manufacturing had changed dramatically in the 15 years from the mid-1920s to the end of the 1930s. Here, workers at the Keystone facility assemble an LB-5 bomber, an aeroplane that had a maximum speed of 107 mph and a bomb load of 2000lb.* USAF

ABOVE: By 1932 aircraft were fabricated with metal skin, as seen here on this radial engine Beech C-43 Traveler with upper wing staggered aft of the lower wing. But the assembly line still bears the hallmarks of the old factory method where each aircraft was assembled individually. Procured as a small aeroplane for liaison duties in the 1930s, it was eagerly sought by the AAF as an excellent communications aeroplane after war broke out – but the production methods remained the same. USAF

ABOVE: By the mid-1930s, the Curtiss A-18 Shrike attack aircraft was evaluated by the AAF but it never did receive orders. Already, there was a change to more production-line standards with specialised technicians performing dedicated tasks. CURTISS

ABOVE: Big manufacturers such as Consolidated Aircraft had outdated facilities which compromised their potential for really big-scale output. Here a production line of B-24D aircraft shows how individual airframe assemblies were put together in-situ. CONSOLIDATED

The B-24 had 488,193 separate parts making up 30,000 components and each aircraft required 140,000 man-hours to produce. Consolidated's factory had 54 separate work stations which required an average six hours for each unit to clear before it was ready to move on to the next station. It was cumbersome, laborious and time wasting. Sorensen got architects to draw up imaginary cross sections of a plant big enough to allow elements of the aircraft to be stood vertical, under an overhead crane.

What emerged would be the single biggest factory in the world, more than a mile long. Sorensen called in Albert Khan, a brilliant and accomplished engineer, to design such a plant, which eventually would turn out 100 B-24s a month and give the Army Air Forces more of this type than any other bomber – over 19,000. But there were still two defining aspects which were not addressed simply by adding capacity: what was the level of quality found desirable versus what was merely acceptable;

and was it better to move to more advanced aircraft or keep producing existing designs?

These issues would refuse to go away for the duration of the war and would only be satisfactorily resolved when the Air Force became independent in 1947. A related earlier, mass production for the automotive industry was very different to that geared up for aviation, and neither were their recognisable similarities between the industry in the First World War and the requirements of the 1940s. Materials were different and that had a great effect on the skill base needed. Women had been recruited in large numbers for war work the first time round and those numbers would swell to 48% of women aged 20 or 21 in the labour force. But overall, at the beginning of 1940 women made up only 20% of the work force, rising to 33% by mid-1942.

In January 1942 Mary Anderson, the director of the Women's Bureau, reported 2.8 million women engaged on war work. Women, it was found, were so good at riveting because, it was said, they made good seamstresses and had a better eye for specific detail. In fact, Consolidated Aircraft disclosed a preference for women, since they were each average 1000 holes a day compared with a man's average of 650.

The pop culture of 'Rosie the Riveter' was subscribed to enthusiastically by women who saw themselves just as capable as men in every conceivable industrial job bar those requiring supreme physical strength. By the end of 1943, 475,000 women were employed in aircraft manufacturing. In 1944 at least 50% of women were employed on war work in some capacity while 37% were in permanent employment. For the first time in US history, there were more married women than unmarried women in employment.

But when the war ended women went back to a more domesticated life and according to oral histories many could not wait to get back and start rebuilding homes for servicemen returning from the war. Unlike the situation in Britain, labour laws in the US gave men the same employment status they had in their respective jobs when the left to join up. Instead of retaining women on lower wages they preferred to take back the men

ABOVE: *Despite the need to maximise output, labour relations were key in maintaining a stable work force. Unions were highly influential and strikes were not uncommon. It was not unusual for the workers to be assembled to witness a particularly important rollout or first flight to enhance morale.* CONSOLIDATED

and found ways to make the women redundant.

Yet aircraft production goals, which consistently failed to deliver ambitious quotas laid down by the leadership, failed to answer the question over quality. Ford's new plant at Willow Run, Michigan, tasked with new production quotas of 600 B-24s a month could only manage 400 but by 1944 production requirements were winding down and it never did reach capacity. The aircraft produced were largely those which were in place, or entering service, at the outbreak of war in December 1941 and the AAF steered away from continuously providing the very latest in design and capability.

The B-17 and B-24 soldiered on throughout the duration, with more than 31,000 produced during the war, the Douglas A-20 stayed in production throughout 1944, more than 7000 being built before the improved A-26 replaced it. Not until 1944 did the AAF buy the last of 10,000 P-39s and continued to accept new P-38s until 10,000 had rolled out the factory. Even the venerable old P-40 stayed in production, with more than 13,000 rolling out before production of this pursuit aircraft ended in 1944.

So it was that the expansive plans worked out at the Arcadia conference challenged industry and laid the foundations for a production effort unlike anything seen before. At peak in 1943, the amount of floor space dedicated to airframes, engine and propellers grew 13-fold to reach a total of 175 million square feet. The battle to build the aircraft had been won. But how to win the war?

STRATEGIES FOR WAR

Over the weeks and months after Arcadia the Americans began to favour a different direction for the war effort and were taking a position that an invasion of occupied Europe would be the overriding priority, with such an attempt and perhaps even being mounted in 1942. But when the Americans were persuaded that this was premature, choosing a cautious attitude versus over-confidence, that was replaced with a focused effort to liberate North Africa first. The Germans were moving quickly down through the Caucasus and there was a danger that the allies would lose Egypt and the vital route to India and Australasia. But the major effort would initially fall upon the USAAF and RAF Bomber Command in attempting to erode the German war machine.

The movement of US forces across to the United Kingdom went under the codename Bolero, with the 8th Air Force specifically created to take the air war to the European Axis partners. Its roots were embedded in the plan to land in Northwest Africa (Gymnast). The advance echelon of what was designated US Army Bomber Command arrived in England on February 20, a party of six led by Major General Ira C. Eaker and the first air headquarters for the European Theatre of Operations (ETO) was established on February 22. Three days later they proceeded to the headquarters of RAF Bomber Command at High Wycombe to confer with their ally.

Earlier that month, on February 14, the Royal Air Force received a direction from the Air Ministry for Bomber Command directing it to prosecute an escalating "area bombing" campaign against German industry and the cities containing large numbers of industrial workers stipulating that this task must have "priority over all other commitments." The Combined Bomber Offensive would not be formally instituted until 1943 and cease before D-Day but from the outset there was a certainty on both the British and American sides that a close degree of cooperation would be needed to extract the most effective fighting force out of what were already two rapidly expanding forces.

For their part, when the Americans came to Britain they were reliant to a great extent on the experiences of the RAF in considering how to mount an air campaign against Germany. And that was recognised. AAF personnel coming to the UK were given instruction booklets on how to show respect and recognition for

ABOVE: *Ford's Willow Run, Michigan production facility significantly improved output using techniques borrowed from the shipping industry. Here, late model B-2J Liberators with nose turret await delivery. USAF*

ABOVE: Women workers at the Vega Aircraft Corporation employed on assembling electrical wire bundles. Manufacturers liked to show women employed on war work, supporting government initiatives to replace men with female technicians. USAF

be sent over for independent meteorological surveys highlighted the determination by the Americans to operate in parallel with the British but independently. The AAF would, in essence, be self-contained, supplied in everything they required by convoy ship and transport aircraft from the United States, so as not to be a burden on the limited resources in the host country but to give the American airmen a sense of continuity, a reassurance that they would get the same food and the same comforts they were used to back home.

In due course the 18th Weather Squadron was sent from Bolling Field and set up camp in at High Wycombe during August 1942 to begin, as Eaker put it, the "study of this beastly weather!" The unit became enmeshed with its British equivalent and the 'British' English names and pronunciations quickly became one more blended integration of American life increasingly embedded in UK life.

But there were practical challenges too. Bringing aircraft across to the UK from America required a route accessible to the shortest-range types transferred. The route required adequate communications systems and it was decided that ferry routes would take the North Atlantic route with the last leg from Iceland to Prestwick, Scotland, under British air traffic control. Initially, the British airfields utilised RAF equipment and had appropriate communications sets fitted in them before they left the United States, since none of those were available in America. From August 1942 the Americans were almost totally reliant on the British to supply the communications equipment fitted to American aircraft, for reasons of commonality with the RAF. For this, and in other areas, fresh training manuals were handed to US aircrew.

America had been a long time preparing for war and most of it fell to the AAF to organise and control the outbound leg from the United States. The logistical supply of men and resources to feed and fuel people and aircraft called for an extensive set of transport routes,

their hosts, who had already been fighting a war for more than two years, and that they had effectively stopped the Nazi juggernaut in its tracks at the English Channel in 1940.

The booklets carried extensive sections on how not to infuriate the locals, who were heavily rationed, with what would appear to be conspicuous consumption of food specially flown over from America. There was advice on how to integrate with British people and guidance on customs and the different use of language. As they bedded in, the Americans found common cause with their British allies and in the countryside around the proliferating bases they were welcomed by most people and quite quickly became the beneficiaries of food parcels to supplement tables short-changed through rationing. At Christmas time 1942 there began an annual custom of American airmen organising parties local for children, on camp and in local pubs, setting up games and play to relieve the boredom of handed-down clothing and blackouts.

But in the serious business of war the RAF was itself on a long and protracted learning curve. Beginning with vulnerable and relatively obsolete aircraft, the RAF had carried the war to Germany from the outset and while the British public may have thought of the period from September 1939 to June 1940 as a 'phoney war', the personnel of Bomber Command certainly did not. But top secret surveys of that performance made worrying reading as very little damage was being done to the enemy for considerable effort in men and machines, many bombs falling far from their targets and many aircraft being lost, until Bomber Command switched to night raids where the losses were somewhat reduced.

An area where the Americans lagged behind was with intelligence pertaining to operations planning and the assignment of targets. The AAF acknowledged on arrival that this was their weakest link and this became all too apparent to Eaker and his staff. As they

worked through the way the British did things they declared they could do no better than "to model their establishment". But the longer term solution required more intelligence people from America and Eaker put in an immediate request for 50 carefully selected servicemen from the US who could be schooled by the British at a special facility at High Wycombe.

Another aspect where the Americans came to rely heavily on the British was with weather forecasting but there were concerns that they could become too reliant on their hosts. The request to Washington for a section to

ABOVE: Assembling B-25 Mitchell medium bombers at North American Aviation's Kansas City facility where separate elements of the aircraft's structure (left) are fed in to the fixed standings for each completed aircraft. NAA

communication links and depots to marshal what was rapidly developing into a global effort.

Before America joined the war, in 1941 the Air Corps Ferrying Command had been set up to assist the British in delivering American-built aircraft, bought for cash from US manufacturers. A civilian Canadian agency had started the process by ferrying aircraft across the North Atlantic from Newfoundland to Scotland, a distance of 2100 miles. This route, from Gander Lake, Newfoundland, to Prestwick, Scotland, was one route which was now adopted as the main route taken by American aircraft when they started arriving in Britain during 1942.

Other routes accessed by the Ferrying Command were set up between Bolling Field and Ayr, Scotland, via Bermuda and the Azores. A southern route took advantage of an existing Pan American contract route from Miami down to Natal and across to a range of locations in West Africa. From there they would continue on to Cairo or across to Basra. To test the feasibility of this southern route, on August 31, 1941, Lieutenant Colonel Caleb V. Hayes, with Major Curtis E. LeMay as co-pilot, flew from Florida to West Africa via Brazil and on to Cairo, then to Basra on the Perian Gulf, returning the same way for a total distance of 26,000 miles.

To the north, two main bases in Greenland and one at Reykjavik in Iceland served as a defence line across toward the Arctic Circle and from there down to Scotland. This route, and on to Scotland, was used widely, just out of reach of German aircraft operating from Norway, which was itself heavily obstructed by the air defences of Great Britain. It was in operations from the equatorial belt of Central America and West Africa to the Arctic wastes of northern Canada, Greenland and Iceland that the Air Corps became familiar with how to operate aircraft in the most extreme of weather conditions.

A GENERAL PLAN

Because of the intention to make the RAF and the AAF Bomber Command independent of each other yet totally integrated in bombing strategy and execution, it had been decided in December 1941 at the Arcadia conference that the Americans would occupy bases in East Anglia and build their operational base in that region of the UK.

For their part, RAF Bomber Command would operate from Lincolnshire and in Yorkshire, north of the Wash which effectively separated the British and the American deployments. Much closer to north-west France, RAF Fighter Command had their defensive perimeter set up around London, the Home Counties and the south-east of England. From Kent in the south to Durham and Northumberland in the north, England was a militarised base from which the liberation of occupied Europe would be planned and set in motion.

When the Americans planned the theoretical bombing campaign in August 1941 as part of the AWPD activity, they calculated that they would have access to RAF airfields and bases and in December they were told they could have airfield accommodation for 2300 bombers by June 1943. The RAF earmarked a total of 15 airfields, eight in England, two in Scotland and five in Northern Ireland. The final, initial, selection narrowed that down to eight fields then under construction for No. 8 Group RAF Bomber Command, all

ABOVE: Boeing was used to large volume production and readily adapted to the advanced manufacturing plans where specific factories were built around the new concepts of mass production, techniques which would serve the industry well. These B-17G bombers are nearing final assembly. BOEING

ABOVE: Douglas A-30 attack bombers, a version of the popular Boston adapted for ground-attack, are moved off the assembly line at Long Beach, California.

in the Huntingdon area of East Anglia close to Cambridge and these were available when the aircraft began arriving in June 1942.

The final disposition of the American bomber zone was agreed in May 1942 at a conference between General Arnold and Air Chief Marshal Charles Portal, expanding eastwards from Huntingdonshire but unlike the RAF they insisted on their pursuit units being deployed within the bomber zone with clear determination to use them as bomber escorts whenever possible. Aircraft with sufficient range to accomplish this were needed. This requirement would result in refined designs

which by 1944 were capable of escorting heavy bomber groups all the way to Berlin and back, a capability that stunned the Luftwaffe.

Coordinating the size of airfields with the makeup of American air units required some adjustment. The RAF assigned about 16 aircraft to a squadron, three squadrons to a wing and six or seven wings to a group. The Americans organised eight to 25 aircraft per squadron, three or four squadrons to a group and two more groups to a combat wing.

The overall resource allocation made by the US War Department was based on the general strategy worked out at Arcadia but as we have ➤

ABOVE: Elizabeth L. Remba Gardner of Rockford, Illinois, a member of the Women's Airforce Service Pilots (WASP) team, takes a look around before taking off from the Harlingen Army Airfield, Texas, to deliver another B-26 Marauder fresh from a repair facility. US ARMY

ABOVE: With the need to move very large numbers of troops and airmen from the United States to the UK, ocean-going liners were pressed into service, ships like the RMS Queen Mary, seen here off New York with a record 15,740 men on board bound for England. USAF

Women Airforce Service Pilots

Shortly after the Germans invaded Poland in September 1939 and long before America entered the war, leading women pilots, well known figures on their own merit, lobbied the American government to be allowed to ferry completed aircraft from the assembly plants to the dispersal airfields where they could be delivered on to combat squadrons or operational units. Among them were Jacqueline 'Jackie' Cochran and woman test pilot Nancy Harkness Love. Despite lobbying by Eleanor Roosevelt, General Arnold turned down the initial request so some of them, Cochran included, went to England to join the Air Transport Auxiliary flying aircraft around between manufacturers and airfields. General Arnold changed his mind after Pearl Harbor and the Women's Auxiliary Flying Squadron (WAFS) was officially established in September 1942. This, and the Women's Flying Training Detachment were combined in July 1943 in the Women Airforce Service Pilots (WASP) organisation. It grew to include 1074 pilots, the first women to fly American military aircraft, flying over 60 million miles delivering 12,650 aircraft of 78 types. Thirty-eight women lost their lives in flying accidents. The records of the WASP flyers were sealed for 35 years and for several decades after the war, very few knew of their existence until a group was organised in 1975 under Colonel Bruce Arnold, the son of 'Hap' Arnold, who publicised their achievement and gained political recognition. Their example helped women gain their rightful place in the most responsible seat in any aircraft and eventually to fly as combat pilots with the US Air Force.

seen the details on that changed during 1942. The Americans were pressing for a cross-channel invasion in the spring of 1943, an operation code-named Roundup. The legal basis on which occupancy of US airfields was agreed retained ownership with the RAF. This was applied to airfields already in existence and those which the British agreed to build without cost to the Americans, who were regarded as tenants bringing their own equipment and removing it at the end of the war. All US airfields and bases would be known RAF airfields and carry that affiliation on gatehouses and manuals.

The organisational structure under which VIII Bomber Command would operate organised combat wings into three or four bombardment wings each of which would be responsible to VIII BC headquarters. But the problem of logistical supply was arguably the most important. The massive bombing campaigns being planned called for unprecedented use of raw materials, fuels, lubricants, parts, spares and munitions. As one of the most heavily industrialised countries, Britain was in a good position to produce the required goods and services, greatly assisting with the supply and delivery of these essentials.

But repair and refurbishment facilities were also essential and a series of main depots for handling the aircraft coming through. General Arnold assessed a requirement for 1000 US aircraft operating from the UK by August 15, 1942, and 3500 by April 1943. His staff toured the UK looking for appropriate facilities and were able to negotiate the use of Langford Lodge where Lockheed had already set up an assembly plant for P-38 Lightning fighters. A second depot was set up at Warton, 25 miles north of Liverpool, with a third at Burtonwood, between Manchester and Liverpool, which was destined to become the largest American overseas depot anywhere outside the United States.

Throughout the middle of 1942 the mass movement of American personnel began to

cross the Atlantic, the first shipment arriving on May 11 after a two-week voyage. A major problem for organisers was the lack of available transport ships, until the Queen Elizabeth was made available in July. The first staging contingent sailed on May 29 and arrived in the UK on June 12 with 7500 tons of equipment and supplies. With naval operations gearing up in the Pacific Ocean, the Japanese fleet steaming toward Midway Island on June 1 brought a sudden switch of priority and some aircraft and equipment were held in case they were needed there and dispatched to airfields on the west coast. A temporary expedient, the flow resumed after the battle of Midway a week later.

By the end of July the strategic priorities were beginning to be fleshed out with some degree of consistency. Some 1.15 million American fighting men were to be in the UK by March 1943 of which 232,000 were to be with the AAF. There had been a clear expectation on the part of President Roosevelt that a cross-channel landing should be attempted in 1943 but concerns expressed by the British staff had persuaded the Americans otherwise, despite General Marshall seeming to have little appreciation of the magnitude of the problem. Much of the persuasive argument for delay had been presented by Louis Mountbatten who play a significant role in the discussions.

The general agreement by this date was that the invasion of Europe would be replaced by Torch, a landing on the north-west coast of Africa so that Allied forces could sweep east to trap the German desert army commanded by General Erwin Rommel, pushed west by General Montgomery charging along the coast from Egypt. The immediate priority became preparations for the 12th Air Force to undertake Torch and while preparations for the strategic offensive against Germany slowed due to training difficulties in England, there was a realisation that operations may not be as easy to effect as many at 8th Air Force had expected. ✪

Chapter 7: Crushing the Axis 1941-1943

ABOVE: *The Martin B-26 Marauder was used early in the war against Japan and would become a familiar sight in all theatres by 1943. The heavy armament was particularly useful in the North African campaign, where frequent attacks against ground targets were called for.* USAF

While the brunt of the war in the Pacific would be borne by the US Navy, the AAF had a vital role to play in reaching out beyond the range of carrier-based strike aircraft and attacking Japanese positions. The Battle of Midway in early June 1942 was a great victory for the Americans, where four US carriers sank four Japanese carriers, losing only one of their own in the process. Rather than face the three remaining US carriers, four Japanese battleships turned for home. This, and the Battle of the Coral Sea a month earlier, sealed the fate of Japanese naval air power and marked a turning point in the use of battleships. The aircraft carrier would now become the capital ship of the world's navies. But it had been naval air power that turned the tide.

The AAF had been involved in the Japanese attack on New Guinea shortly after the Doolittle raid in April and B-17s sent to search for the Japanese ships detected a screening force and dropped some bombs but without effect. But the threats to Midway in early June were countered in part by the use of Major General Clarence L. Tinker's 7th Air Force, the redesignated Hawaiian Air Force since February 5, which was under the authority of Admiral Chester W. Nimitz, Commander in Chief, Pacific. Tinker wanted to attack Wake Island which was a likely staging post for the Japanese but the B-17Es did not have the range so Nimitz sent the 17 aircraft and

four B-26 Marauder medium-bombers, hurriedly fitted with torpedoes, to Midway where they were brought under the command of a Navy air officer.

Led by Major General Walter C. Sweeney, the B-17s attacked troop transports but without causing damage. The following morning four Marauders attacked with their torpedoes, inflicting some damage on the warships for the loss of two aircraft. On learning about the approaching carriers, the B-17s were directed toward these more vital targets, dropping 300 bombs during 55 sorties without sinking a single vessel. While Mitchell had sunk captured German battleships at moorings and on a test in a bid to prove the fallibility of naval vessels, ships manoeuvring at sea were in little danger from bombers flying at high altitude.

But the Air Force was not done yet and Tinker was determined to hit Wake Island, this time planning on the longer range, long nose, B-24 (designated LB-30), four of which were fitted with extra fuel tanks. Precise navigation and the careful management of the engines ensured minimum use of fuel but it was a dangerous flight, undertaken on the night of June 6 flying west beneath an overcast sky which prevented celestial navigation. None of the aircraft could find the atoll and mistakenly attacked a US submarine but without damaging it. The following day in a predawn attack on

Wake Island, General Tinker was killed.

In conjunction with the attack on Midway, the Japanese attacked Dutch Harbour in the Aleutian Islands and landed troops on Kiska and Attu Islands. The garrisons in the Alaska

Martin B-26 Marauder

Amid a flurry of new aircraft requirements issued in January 1939 was one for a new high-speed bomber capable of carrying a 2000lb bomb load carrying a crew of five, and four 0.30in guns for defensive purposes. Several manufacturers put up proposals but the Martin submission was far ahead of the next best design. Continuing a tradition started with the MB-1 of 1918, the B-26 Marauder was strong, robust and delivered a high performance which made it an ideal medium bomber for tactical support operations, as well as some strategic roles. Submitted to the AAC in July 1939, the design was 14% ahead of its nearest rival on points which prompted the Army to take the unprecedented step of ordering it into production straight off the drawing board, placing a contract for the first 201 in September. The Model 179 had been the brainchild of Peyton M. Magruder and had the highest wing loading of any aircraft operated by the AAC to that date at 58sq ft. Mounted at the mid-fuselage position, the relatively small wing supported two 1850hp Pratt & Whitney R-2800 Double Wasp engines but the B-26B, specified below, in service from 1942, adopted more powerful 2,000hp R-2800-41 engines. Defensive armament included four 0.50in and two 0.30in guns. For the first year of war most B-26 operations were in the Pacific theatre but the type was gainfully employed in the Middle East with the 9th AF during 1942 and 1943 and played a significant role in the D-Day landings in Normandy. More than 5000 were produced during the war and the type survived on into the postwar era for a variety of specialised roles.

LENGTH	58.25ft
WING SPAN	65ft
HEIGHT	19.9ft
GROSS WEIGHT	34,000lb
MAXIMUM SPEED	317mph
CRUISING SPEED	260mph
CEILING	23,500ft
RANGE	1150 miles

ABOVE: A B-26 in the process of being shot down. Note the package of 0.50in machine guns mounted to the side of the fuselage. All early B-26 operations were in the Pacific, three Bombardment Groups receiving this type for Middle East operations in November 1942. The first Marauders arrived in the UK in February 1943. *US ARMY*

region had been alerted to expect attack and a flight of 10 B-26s of the 77th Bombardment Group moved up to Cold Bay at the start of a consolidation to deter Japanese incursions. Extensive combat operations were mounted by the 11th Air Force but the Japanese secured their objective and achieved success where they had failed at Midway. Not before 1943 would the Americans regain the islands.

With Japanese gains throughout the region, there was increasing concern that Australia might fall and this was where the Americans decided to consolidate a defensive position and to prevent it succumbing to Japanese attack. One half of all the troops and a third of all the cargo sent overseas went to Australia, along with three fighter groups and 50 heavy bombers. MacArthur had arrived in Australia on March 17 and became commander of the South-West Pacific Area with authority over Australian as well as US troops.

But the Japanese sustained their attacks on Port Moresby, New Guinea, and this time by land. From the tiny settlement of Buna of the north side of the island they began a drive south through the jungles and over the mountains of Papua. By September they were within 30 miles of their goal. In response, Major General George C. Kenney, commander of the Allied Air Forces in the area, organised the American units in Australia and New Guinea into the 5th

ABOVE: The LB-30A, one of 75 Consolidated B-24 Liberators requisitioned from having previously been delivered to the RAF after the attack on Pearl Harbor, and deployed in the Panama Canal Zone, India and the Aleutians. It had the longer nose but no fire-proofing of fuel tanks. This example is from the Commemorative Air Force Collection. *CAFC*

ABOVE: The bomb-aimer's position on the nose of the B-24 was spacious compared with the B-17 and with British aircraft such as the Lancaster and the Stirling. NMUSAF

ABOVE: The box-shaped fuselage provided plenty of room for guns mounted either side with ample space for the gunners to move around and for storing ammunition and reloading the breech with new belts. NMUSAF

ABOVE: The spacious cockpit of the B-24 incorporated the classic yoke steering column which became a common design in American aircraft. The glazed area around the cockpit afforded good visibility but the view laterally and aft as somewhat limited compared to the B-17. NMUSAF

Air Force with headquarters in Brisbane and an advance HQ in New Guinea under Brigadier General Ennis C. Whitehead, who became Kenney's number one combat commander.

The remnants of the 19th Bombardment Group had only four of 39 B-17s in a serviceable condition, due to sustained attack and enemy action, and the P-39s operating out of Port Moresby were unable to reach the ceiling of Japanese bombers which were inflicting heavy damage on the city. Instead of trying to attack the Japanese in the air, Kenney organised attacks on the airfields at occupied Buna and Lae in attempts to drive the enemy off and several runways were knocked out of action by the B-17s and B-25s using conventional bombing techniques.

But Kenney introduced new weapons and new tactics to achieve his objective. In September, A-20 attack aircraft made low-level strikes with fragmentation bombs attached to parachutes and fitted with instantaneous fuses. In addition to the standard four 30-calibre machine guns in the nose, the A-20s had an additional four 50-calibre machine guns, a modification invented and supervised by Major Paul 'Pappy' Gunn,

who had joined the AAF during the Philippine campaign and had already made a reputation for himself as an armourer and general wizard.

By mid-September the 5th AF had gained complete control of the air over New Guinea, an achievement helped by the Japanese preoccupation with problems in taking the Solomon Islands. Pressing home his advantage, Kenney used air transport to lift 4500 fresh troops from Australia to New Guinea to help push the Japanese back along the trail to Buna. Immediately after, he switched to flying two regiments over the mountains to jungle airstrips within a few miles of Buna. Defending their ground tenaciously, the Japanese held on until January 2, 1943, where the 5th AF held complete control of the air. Continuous air support kept up delivery of 2450 tons of supplies between November 13 and January 23, where sustained Japanese attacks on shipping prevented supplies getting in by sea.

A NEW LEARNING CURVE

The first US air unit to engage the enemy in European skies was the 15th Bombardment

Squadron commanded by Major J. L. Griffith who had arrived in the UK in May 1942. They immediately began training up on RAF Bostons, the British name for the Douglas DB-7, employed by the Americans as the A-20 in an attack role. So, instead of starting operations with the development of a strategic campaign, the USAAF began with an attack by six Boston medium bombers in a low-level tactical strike against four airfields in the Netherlands.

It was July 4, the day the second B-17 arrived in the UK and the day that American airmen got to know just how close the enemy was, just a brief flight away across the relatively shallow North Sea. The six Boston bombers were joined by six RAF aircraft of the same type from No. 2 Group, 226 Squadron, based at Swanton Morley in the daylight attack which saw two of the American aircraft brought down by intense flak and enemy fighters.

During the mission an aircraft flown by Captain Charles C. Kegelman had its right propeller shot away by flak while ground fire damaged his starboard wing, setting that engine ablaze. Swinging the aircraft around, barely under control, he struck the ground and bounced back into the air. As Kegelman was getting ready to make his way back from the target he saw gunners in a machine-gun tower train their weapons on his aircraft. Turning to fly directly at the tower he blazed away with all guns as he conducted a head-on attack. The machine-gunners ceased firing.

American aviators had been flying alongside the British but not on an official AAF mission. Kegelman had been the first member of the 8th AF to drop bombs on enemy soil when he flew a mission on June 29 with 12 Bostons against Hazebrouck marshalling yard. That day also marked the first pilot fatality of the 8th when Lieutenant Alfred W. Giacomini of the 31st Fighter Group crashed a Spitfire while landing at Atcham, an airfield five miles from Shrewsbury.

The 8th AF flew its first official mission on August 17 when Colonel Frank A. Armstrong Jr. led 12 B-17s of the 97th Bombardment Group from Polebrook, Northamptonshire. The airfield had been officially turned over to the USAAF on June 28 and its four operational squadrons were to be divided between there and nearby Grafton Underwood.

Their mission was to attack the Rouen-

ABOVE: With the features and bearing of a Hollywood movie star cast in the role of a Second World War Army Air Force general, George Churchill Kenney (1889-1977) lived that life in reality, commanding air units in the Pacific theatre. Rising rapidly through the ranks, Lieutenant General Kenney commanded the 5th AF in the Southwest Pacific Area under General Douglas MacArthur. USAF

Sotteville marshalling yards in France where some 2000 freight cars had been observed in reconnaissance photographs. Armstrong was accompanied in Butcher Shop (41-2558) by Major Paul W. Tibbets, who would pilot the B-29 that dropped the first atomic bomb on Hiroshima. General Eaker flew in Yankee Doodle (41-9023) piloted by Lieutenant John P. Dowswell. For this historic flight the 12 aircraft were drawn from three squadrons (340th, 342nd and 414th) and carried a total of 36,900lb of bombs dropped from 23,000ft. The accuracy was good for a first effort and all aircraft returned from a flak-filled sky and the occasional visit by a fighter. Sergeant Kent West became the first 8th AF gunner to shoot down an enemy fighter, thus achieving his own place in history, the entire complement of 111 men welcomed back by General Spaatz.

In the hours following, General Eaker had some observations about the apparently blasé attitude of the crews and about better ways to form a defensive formation and the need for critical timing with fighter escorts, which on this occasion had been RAF Spitfires which arrived a little late. But he did note that the German fighters approached the formation "gingerly"! That would quickly change once the Luftwaffe got to know the limitations of these heavily armed bombers.

But it was a start and one which would lead to a feeling of unity between the RAF and the USAAF. On this day, Air Marshal Tedder sent a message congratulating the crews, asserting that "Yankee Doodle certainly went to town and can stick yet another well-deserved feather in his cap."

For a while the 8th AF would have to await

events in North Africa before unleashing a full strategic battle campaign against occupied Europe. Just as the USAAF was beginning to scale up its presence in the UK, the demands of Torch drew some elements away to help the Mediterranean war.

THE DESERT WAR

When Rommel's Afrika Corps drove across Egypt and pushed the British Army all the way back to El Alamein in June 1942, a detachment of B-24s were diverted on their way from Khartoum to China. This highly secret mission to China was part of a larger plan code named Halpro which involved making direct attacks on Tokyo from bases in China. But the greater danger emerging through a concerted push across Burma by Japanese ground forces made it doubtful that such missions could be supported logistically, especially if India fell.

Flying from Egypt on June 12, 12 aircraft from this redirected detachment under the command of Colonel Harry A. Halverson bombed the oil refineries at Ploesti with little result, dispersing to land back in Iraq at pre-planned locations. Nevertheless, it was the first bombing mission against a strategic target by the USAAF. Halverson would gain fame during the Berlin airlift for tossing candy out the window to children on the approach path. Ploesti would be visited again just over a year later, this time with disastrous results. But the situation in North Africa grew worse and after a direct appeal from Winston Churchill the Americans agreed to deploy nine AAF groups.

It had taken some doing to convince the

ABOVE: The threat to Australia seemed very real when the small coastal town of Darwin was bombed by a force of 242 aircraft operating off four carriers on February 19, 1942, potentially the latest in a series of toppled dominoes that carried the Japanese invasion forces south. In the foreground is HMAS Deloraine. VIA DAVID BAKER

Americans that the war against Axis forces in Europe could be won by first solving the problem from the Mediterranean and North Africa; in fact they felt it was a way to possibly lose the war altogether. But the extent to which the Germans had rushed aid and assistance to a flagging Italian army in 1941 upped the game and made it clear that by attacking south-east through Rumania and on to the Levant, and by linking up with Axis forces in North Africa, the Wehrmacht could close the door through the Suez Canal and move large forces up in the war against Russia and down into the Persian Gulf. There was much to play for and air power would be crucial in evicting Axis forces from North Africa.

General Brereton arrived in Egypt on June 28 to take command and by mid-August the 98th (heavy) and 12th (medium) Bombardment Groups and the 57th Fighter Group had arrived to support Lieutenant General Montgomery's epic struggle against Rommel. The medium bombers and the fighters went into action during September supporting the RAF Desert Air Force.

Formerly the commander of Far East AF in the Philippines, Brereton set up the US Army Middle East Air Force (USAMEAF), having been reassigned from commanding the 10th Air Force, activated on February 12, 1942, to support the China-Burma-India theatre and prevent the Japanese getting to India via Burma and thus severing the links connecting India with the allies in the Mediterranean and Europe. Now, the Middle East theatre was a vital front-line in the defeat of the Axis powers and the RAF Desert Force carried out a remorseless series of attacks on enemy shipping trying to consolidate Rommel's forces.

It has been estimated that the Afrika Corps was halted at El Alamein, and prevented from pushing the British all the way into the

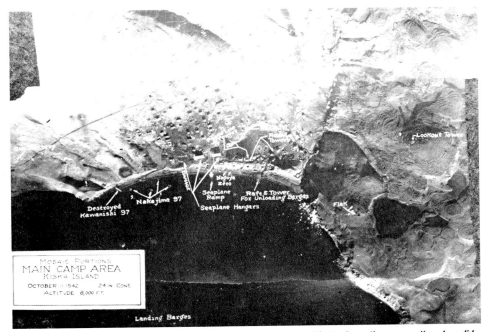

ABOVE: *Following the occupation of the Aleutian Islands by the Japanese, US attacks on the area continued, as did photo-reconnaissance flights, evidenced by this one showing the location of Japanese shipping in coastal areas during October 1942.* USAF

Suez Canal, because the RAF had sufficiently eroded the logistical flow to North Africa to make that crucial difference. Rommel had to stop at that most famous of all battle sites. Greatly impressed by what the RAF was achieving, Brereton flung the MEAF into a focused attack on enemy positions and, in turn, made all the difference that mattered in coordinating air strikes with the British.

In one of the most furious and concentrated attacks on Axis forces, the British and the

Americans mobilised air power both from Egypt and the Middle East as well as from the beleaguered little island of Malta. But just when the Eastern Mediterranean was shaping up for a major clash of forces, further drawdown came from the requirements of Torch – the landing of troops on the coast of north-west coast of North Africa in Morocco and Algeria. That operation was in need of massive air power and thus was formed the 12th AF, activated on August 20, which ran headlong

ABOVE: *Three B-17Es from Hendricks Field, the home of the Army Air Force Basic training School at Sebring, Florida, where air crews were trained on this type of aircraft before being moved across to the UK during the intensive flow of men and materiel to the European Theatre of Operations. Note the red meatball still placed in the middle of the star insignia.* USAF

into the demands coming from 9th AF, the renamed MEAF, activated on November 12.

Formed at Bolling Field, the 12th was to rapidly grow into the largest single air force assembled and it received two bombardment groups and three fighter groups from the 9th AF, initially deploying through England in September 1942 and then on to Algeria on November 9 with the Torch landings. Beginning on November 8, the landings were made possible by a massive invasion force consisting of 350 warships, 500 transports and 500 aircraft departing the UK from ports on its west and south-west ports for a 1600 mile voyage to effect beach landings on a 750 mile front extending from Safi in Morocco to Blida in Algiers.

Meanwhile, 2000 miles to the east, a major air offensive took place to prevent Rommel's Afrika Corps from receiving much needed supplies to take El Alamein and drive the British into Suez. During August, while 100,000 tonnes of Axis supplies got through to North Africa, 80,000 tons were destroyed, 32,000 tons by Allied air power. But it had been a hard month, with the Royal Navy losing its carrier HMS Eagle. Sustained attacks on ports, supply dumps and shipping brought a slow shift in the balance of available power in favour of the Allies and the Axis supply chain began to dry up. In combined air assaults on Benghazi, B-24s carried an immense load of bombs, on one occasion blowing up an 8000 ton ammunition ship which put the harbour out of action for several weeks.

LIBERATION

In one of the greatest land battles of the Second World War, on October 23, 1942, the British 8th Army began its march west, through a series of intense and bloody battles, pushing Rommel slowly back along the North African coast toward Tunisia, the destination of the Allied soldiers from Torch who were slowly moving east. Air power was crucial in this pivotal period, when the Allies first began to work intensively at cooperating on air operations. In the battle of El Alamein the Luftwaffe had about 480 serviceable aircraft to the combined Anglo-American air power of 530. But they were without adequate supplies. For the Afrika Corps it was a struggle combining retreat with attrition.

For operational reasons, in February 1943 the Anglo-American air commands in north-west Africa merged into what was henceforth known as Northwest African Air Forces (NAAF) headed by General Spaatz. Its strength was divided between the Northwest African Strategic Air Force under General Doolittle, and the Northwest African Tactical Air Force Command led by Sir Arthur Coningham, who had commanded the Desert Air Force across North Africa. The NAAF, 9th AF and the RAF forces in the Middle East on Malta were coordinated through a small supervisory headquarters known as Mediterranean Air Command (MAC), under Air Chief Marshall Sir Arthur W. Tedder.

The push to drive the Axis out of North Africa was remorseless and air power played the decisive role in clearing the offensive capability of the enemy troops for the Anglo-American forces to win the ground battles. Ceaseless and heavy bombing of the region between Bizerte and Tunis prepared ground, clearing enemy forces and allowing more than 12 forward airfields to be hurriedly prepared for the final push north

Bell P-39 Airacobra

Rarely has an aircraft been designed around a gun, this being the exception. Intrigued by the American Armament Corporation's 37mm T-9 cannon, Bob Woods and Harland M. Poyer adopted this for a loosely-defined specification from the Army Air Corps in 1936 calling for a faster way of intercepting bombers already outpacing existing pursuit aircraft. Through a series of different designs they came up with the concept of a high-calibre cannon mounted through the centreline of the fuselage, forward of the cockpit which was itself forward of the engine! The Army liked it and issued a contract on October 7, 1937, for a single prototype. Because of the configuration the aircraft had an unusual tricycle undercarriage but the single 1150hp Allison V-1710-E4 would give trouble and it was this that resulted in cancellation of all but 80 of an order for 675 which the RAF had placed through the Direct Purchase Commission in 1940. About 250 of that production order were sent to Russia as aid but the Americans repossessed a further 200 after the attack on Pearl Harbor. The principle order from the Air Forces carried deployment through the duration of the war, 9588 being produced. Defensive armament included one 37mm cannon, two 0.30in and four 0.50in machine guns and the P-39 could also carry a single 500lb bomb. A further development, of which 3300 were built, the P-63 Kingcobra was exported to Russia as war aid, very few reaching USAAF units.

LENGTH	30.2ft
WING SPAN	34ft
HEIGHT	11.9ft
GROSS WEIGHT	8200lb
MAXIMUM SPEED	368mph
CRUISING SPEED	213mph
CEILING	32,100ft
RANGE	800 miles

ABOVE: *A pleasing view of a Bell P-39 Airacobra of the 40th Pursuit Squadron, 31st Pursuit Group, displaying the unusual tricycle undercarriage and rear-mounted engine.*
BELL AIRCRAFT

ABOVE: *The P-39Q was among the final production variants and incorporated several unique features including small recessed fairings for two 0.50in guns instead of the four wing-mounted 0.30in guns. It also featured the large three-bladed Aeroproducts propeller.* USAF

ABOVE: *A close-up view of the weapons bay in the Bell P-39 with 37mm cannon shells and the yellow glycol coolant tank.* KOGO

toward the African coast on the peninsula that pointed across the Mediterranean Sea to Sicily, so close to Italy and mainland Europe. As the 8th Army pushed north, the Allied air offensive isolated the bridgehead to prevent the enemy forces escaping and to prevent them from being resupplied or evacuated.

In one raid during March the B-17s of the 301st Group destroyed some 30 acres of dock areas at Palermo and by April General Spaatz had turned his attention to Sicily, bombing and strafing ports, harbours and shipping. Known as Operation Flax, which officially began on April 5, it was a determined effort to cut the supply lines

from Sicily to the Axis forces in Tunisia. Early in the morning of the opening day, P-38s from the 1st Fighter Group swept the Sicilian Strait while 18 B-25s from the 321st Bombardment Group escorted by 32 P-38s from the 82nd Fighter Group carried out an interdiction mission in the vicinity of Cap Bon. Quite quickly they encountered a formation of German aircraft including 31 Ju 52 troop transports, about 17 fighters and a Ju 87 Stuka dive bomber, shooting down about 14 Ju 52s and three of the fighters.

In a day of enduring raids and determined attacks, B-25s from the 310th Bombardment Group and 18 P-38s from the 82nd Fighter Group attacked airfields in Sicily near Borizzo, dropping fragmentation bombs on 80-90 aircraft clearly visible and without camouflage. In another operation on April 5, the 301st Group attacked Milo airfield and destroyed 21 aircraft on the ground, damaging several, for a total of 30 transport aircraft and several fighters. Over the next week the attacks were ceaseless and intense, with Allied aircraft hitting airfields, ports and harbours, attacking shipping, boats and aircraft.

In the now famous April 18 'Palm Sunday Massacre', the 9th AF sent out all its squadrons, some 47 P-40s along with 12 RAF Spitfires from No. 92 Squadron. The Spitfires flew top-cover at 15,000ft and the P-40s stayed at 4000ft, encountering a large formation of 65 Ju 52s at only 1000ft flying north east on a return flight accompanied by about 10

ABOVE: P-39s of the 72nd Tactical Reconnaissance Group operating in the Panama Canal Zone during 1942. USAF

escort fighters. In the general melee, about 24 transports and 10 fighters were shot down, with 35 seriously damaged but managing to crash land on the Sicilian coast.

Technically, the offensive operation ended on April 27 and did considerable damage to enemy logistics supply lines, starving the Tunisian forces of fuel and ammunition. In a last desperate bid to escape from Tunisia, several single-seat German fighters crammed additional personnel in their single-seat cockpits and transport aircraft were overloaded, several crashing through excess weight. The level of desperation reached a peak during late April 1943, before the last transport flights arrived from the mainland on May 4, when 177 tons of supplies were flown in.

The final ground offensive had begun on April 22, supported by around 2000 sorties a day in a continuous assault on Axis forces which endured until the final surrender on May 13 when 275,000 German soldiers were taken prisoner. It was the biggest single loss of able manpower to the German army, almost three times the number that had surrendered at Stalingrad three months earlier.

The Casablanca conference held by the Allies in January 1943 had determined that the North Africa campaign would be followed by the invasion of Sicily, from where the invasion

ABOVE: Bell's Niagara, New York, assembly facility turning out P-39s. BELL AIRCRAFT

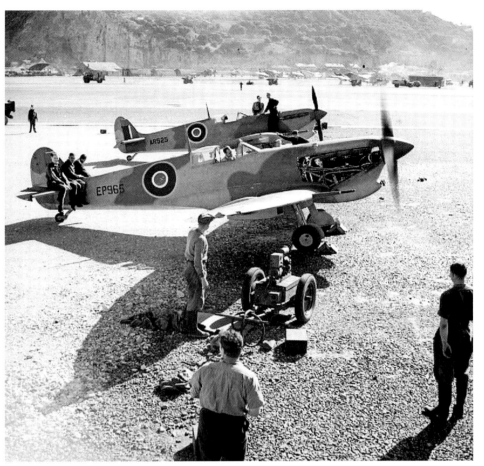

Douglas A-20 Havoc

Conceived in early 1937 by a design team consisting of Donald Douglas, Jack Northrop and Ed Heinemann, what was known in service with the Americans as the A-20 Havoc, was initially presented as a bomber. Carrying a pair of 450hp Pratt & Whitney R-985 Wasp Junior radial engines set on a conventional wing, the aircraft was quickly seen as under-powered and potentially vulnerable to more modern designs quickly tested in the Spanish Civil War and a major redesign followed. However, France quickly placed an order for the type, followed by the British with whom it was known as the Boston. Admired by pilots for its manoeuvrability and by air forces for its ruggedness, reliability and speed, the type quickly found favour. It was used by the RAF in the night fighter and night bomber role from December 1940, where it was named Havoc, and in the light bomber role from October 1941, where it was named Boston.

In parallel with these applications, the Americans bought it as the A-20 for the attack role. Power was provided by a pair of 1600hp Wright R2600-7 radial engines and armament consisted of up to eight 0.50in machine guns, with a bomb capacity of 2600lb. Unspectacular in outright performance, the A-20 was another of those wartime types that kept working to requirement, finding an operational niche with units in North Africa, Europe and the Middle East. Almost 7500 were built by the end of production.

LENGTH	48ft
WING SPAN	61.3ft
HEIGHT	17.8ft
GROSS WEIGHT	27,200lb
MAXIMUM SPEED	339mph
CRUISING SPEED	272mph
CEILING	25,800ft
RANGE	1090 miles

ABOVE: Some of the 116 tropicalised Supermarine Spitfires Mk. Vcs delivered to Gibraltar for equipping allied units. Built at Castle Bromwich, the aircraft in the foreground (EP965) was delivered to the 308th Fighter Squadron of the 31st Fighter Group. USAF

ABOVE: The Douglas Boston (to the RAF), or Havoc (USAAF), depending on which air force it was flying with, the A-20 maintained a consistent performance during the Second Word War and was one of the most widely exploited aircraft of its class. USAF

ABOVE: A group of A-20J over France, with the new modified nose section. The type was discarded by 1945 but most of this variant went as trainers, redesignated TA-20. US ARMY

ABOVE: A bomber crew of the 301st Bomb Group with their A-20 Havoc after being awarded medals on July 11, 1942. Left to right: Sergeant Bennie Cunningham, of Tupelo, Mississippi; Sergeant Robert Golay, of Fredonia, Kansas; Lieut. Randall Dorton, of Long Beach, California; and Major Charles C. Kegelman, of El Reno, Oklahoma. US BUREAU OF STANDARDS

of mainland Italy would achieve the first Allied landing on mainland Europe. The ability to support operations from the air played a critical role in deciding the best way to proceed. Some staff officers had proposed an invasion of Corsica followed by a jump across to southern France, a great distance from the supply lines and under constant threat from attacks by aircraft based in Italy. But in taking Sicily and then Italy, the entire Mediterranean would be denied to the enemy and any opposition by air would move north toward the Italian Alps.

In the preparation of Sicily for invasion, the NAAF pummelled the Italian fortress island of Pantelleria, midway between Africa and Sicily,

so as to deny it to the enemy but also to use it as an Allied fighter base. In over 5000 sorties the combined air forces dropped 6000 tons of bombs and under this rain of ordnance the island surrendered on June 11 just as naval assault forces were approaching. This was perhaps the first time air power alone had forced an island fortress to surrender without any ground forces involved.

In the bombing campaign against Sicily, almost all the 31 airfields on the island were destroyed, along with about 1000 enemy aircraft. On the day of the landings, July 9, in Operation Huskie the NAAF flew 1002 sorties to protect the beach forces and flew several thousand

more over the following days. Strategic targets had been hit many times over the preceding weeks with industrial targets hit throughout Italy and Sicily, including manufacturing facilities in southern Italy and the ports of Naples, Messina, Palermo and Cagliari. By July 20 only two airfields in Sicily remained fully operational, in all some 42,000 sorties had been flown since mid-May, destroying 323 German and 105 Italian aircraft with a loss to the NAAF of 252.

Daylight opposition over Sicily had all but ceased by July 14 with Allied aircraft ranging as far as southern France, attacking bases there from where German fighter or fighter-bombers could attack the Allied forces on Sicily, now preparing to jump across the Italian mainland. Since the Allied landings under Torch, German troops had occupied all of Vichy France, following the willing surrender of French forces in Algeria. For several weeks not a single enemy aircraft was seen in the skies over Sicily and raids which were mounted against railway systems in Italy also helped neutralise the movement of German and Italian troops in areas where they suspected an Allied landing might take place. This also inhibited the movement of troops to places which would need reinforcements.

As the German and Italian forces evacuated Sicily they took to the sea and even Allied air attacks that sank 23 ships could not stem the flow of men and materiel that moved off the island. But not all had gone as planned. Half the British glider-borne assault forces had been lost when the gliders were released too early. Unable to make it to Sicily, they came down in the water, albeit with little loss of life. The end of the Italian resistance was very near however. On July 25 Mussolini was forced to resign and would suffer an ignominious end by being mutilated and strung up on a meat hook by a population deeply disturbed and suffering direct attack from Allied forces.

On September 3, the interim government sued for peace and from that day, when elements of the British 8th Army landed on the toe of Italy, the Germans were an occupying force fighting a rear-guard action all the way back up the country to the Alps. Six days later the American Fifth Army landed at Salerno, to take the great port of Naples and cut off the German troops. The Germans had gone, having blown up all the bridges behind them.

At an Allied conference in Cairo during December 1943, it was decided to tone down the fight in Italy and begin the movement of troops back to the UK for the planned invasion of north-west Europe, some time in 1944. Back came Generals Eisenhower, Spaatz and Doolittle with Sir Arthur Tedder and their staffs. Now the NAAF would be merged with MAC into the Mediterranean Allied Air Forces (MAAF), a truly Allied theatre air headquarters, with control of all Allied air forces everywhere in that region.

General Eaker flew in from England to take command of that and of its US component, the Army Air Forces/Mediterranean Theatre of Operations (AAF/MTO). To give the theatre the same punch as the strategic bombing force in the UK, the XII Bomber Command had been transformed in November into the 15th Air Force, a strategic bombing force like the 8th AF, and placed under the command of Major General Nathan F. Twining, who had previously been in charge of the 13th AF in the Solomon Islands. ✪

Chapter 8: Combined Offensive 1942-1943

The initial air attacks on mainland Europe, begun with a mission to Rouen by the 8th AF in August 1942, preceded an experimental daylight bombing campaign which would lead directly to the Combined Bomber Offensive in June the following year. Despite the enormous volume of materiel flown over from America, there were abysmal shortfalls in required inventories, at depots, distribution airfields and on bases struggling to become fully operational. Whereas all previous US operations and those for the next year, would be largely in support of ground campaigns – in the Mediterranean and North Africa – the deployment of a strategic bombing force was something that had never been done before, and certainly not several thousand miles from home.

To get a working structure, General Eaker had organised VIII Bomber Command into three wings but by mid-August 1942 only the 97th Bombardment Group had become operational, while others were in training and en route from America.

The ambitious plan for Operation Bolero drawn up late July anticipated that by the end of December 1943, the 8th would have 137 groups, including 74 bombardment, 31 fighter, 12 observation, 15 transport, 4 photographic and 1 mapping. For this, the British had allocated 127 airfields. The early invasion of North Africa had thrown all that into disarray and by the beginning of August further delays were anticipated as a consequence of a decision to adjust the Bolero shipments in favour of the Pacific war.

Until the spring of 1943, the diversion of resources to these other theatres kept combat strength for the 8th between two and six groups of bombers and only half its aircraft were operational due to a lack of spares and proper maintenance equipment. In that period, on only rare occasions could it mount a 100-aircraft raid and bad weather coupled with faulty equipment forced many aircraft that did participate on raids to turn back before delivering their bomb loads. Coupled to which was an increasing demand for attacks on U-boat pens and submarine bases to counter an intensification in attacks on convoys crossing the Atlantic.

The first air raid by the 8th AF on a target in Germany was the attack on U-boat pens at Wilhelmshaven on January 27, 1943, when 53 B-17s made it out of 91 aircraft that set off. The B-24s were unable to find the target, due to weather conditions and poor navigation. But the raid did damage to the construction works,

ABOVE: Brigadier General Ira Eaker (1896-1987) was a foot soldier in the First World War until transferring to flying duties in 1918 and starting a brilliant career with military aviation, promoted to command VIII Bomber Command, the 8th AF, in 1942. US ARMY

ABOVE: A B-17 of the 351st Bombardment Group flying over Polebrook, Northamptonshire, a point of arrival in England for aircraft ferried in from the US via Scotland. USAAF

ABOVE: Deanie Parish, as a WASP, adjusting her parachute on the flight line at Tyndall Air Force Base, Florida, before climbing aboard the P-47 she will deliver to the next stop on its journey to front line service. USAF

power plant and the general docks, while two other aircraft attacked the submarines base at Emden. As an example of how frustrating it was becoming, on the next raid on February 2, 61 B-17s and 22 B-24s from all six bombardment groups, set off to bomb Hamm marshalling yards but all returned after finding poor weather over the North Sea. The next raid, on February 14, was abandoned too, when the 74 bombers encountered heavy weather.

Long missions proved particularly hazardous for the B-17s which at this point had no nose turrets to defend against head-on attacks, other than a hand-held machine gun. Some protection was obtained by packing 18 bombers into a tight formation known as a combat box and stacking two or three boxes vertically in a combat wing. The learning curve was steep and if the Luftwaffe was initially confused about how to approach these aircraft, the Americans too were unsure about the best way to send them on long-range missions deep into enemy-held territory.

1000 BOMBER RAIDS

Many of those who agreed to send US air forces to England nurtured a vision of organisation and command reminiscent of the situation when aircraft had been sent to Europe in 1917; a fully autonomous component of an allied effort where they were responsible for a particular set of objectives and would adhere to those. The intention had been to wield strategic air power against a robust enemy deeply entrenched behind the Atlantic wall.

But it had not turned out that way. The fact that the Royal Air Force was now a fully-fledged instrument of air power and had been fighting the Axis for three years would ensure that the optimum way for the Americans to make a contribution was to fully converge in an integrated command structure. It had worked very well in the Middle East and the Mediterranean and that transformation was now sought for the strategic

Republic P-47D

An evolution of the P-35 and the P-43 Lancer, the Republic P-47 Thunderbolt was the last radial engine fighter purchased by the AAF in large numbers and established the manufacturer as a builder of strong, robust and survivable aircraft types which would see it produce a line of fighters and fighter-bombers for the jet-age. Designed by de Seversky and Alexander Kartvelli, the P-35 had set the template for the P-43, a single-seat pursuit aircraft which was used in the early stages of the war and eventually adapted for the photographic reconnaissance role. The P-47 was designed around the 2000hp Pratt & Whitney R-2800 radial engine and from the outset there was little effort made to reduce weight.

First flown on May 6, 1941, the XP-47B had a deep fuselage incorporating a supercharger intake duct beneath the engine, an elliptical wing planform and a telescoping landing gear affording ground clearance for the large, four-bladed propeller. It had an armament of eight 0.50in guns, four in each wing, and a sliding cockpit with a razorback fuselage which did little to assist with the pilot's rear view. Deliveries of the P-47B began in 1942 and the type became operational with the 8th AF in April 1943, escorting B-17s for the first time. With water-injection for high altitude, the more powerful P-47D-25, specified below, was powered by the 2300hp R-2800-59 and block numbers from that lot incorporated a bubble canopy with a cut down fuselage, greatly improving all-round visibility.

The Thunderbolt distinguished itself with the final versions operating exclusively in the Pacific. A total of 15,683 P-47s were built and of those about two-thirds reached operational commands with 3499 lost in combat, a low loss rate of 0.7% on the 1.35 million combat hours flown.

LENGTH	36.3ft
WING SPAN	40.75ft
HEIGHT	14.1ft
GROSS WEIGHT	19,400lb
MAXIMUM SPEED	428mph
CRUISING SPEED	350mph
CEILING	32,000ft
RANGE	530 miles

war against German industry.

The area bombing directive of February 14, 1942, had widened the remit of RAF Bomber Command and given it expanded scope to destroy large industrial areas, objectives which would have been unrealistic a year earlier. But now, new and highly capable aircraft were achieving operational status, the first raid by the new Avro Lancaster being conducted on March 3, 1942, a mine-laying operation carried out by No. 44 Squadron, followed by a night-bombing raid seven days later when two Lancasters took part in a raid on Essen.

Later in 1942 the Handley Page Halifax began to dispel a dismal reputation which had attracted harsh criticism from Air Chief Marshal Arthur Harris, head of Bomber Command. Improvements and modifications since its introduction in 1940

ABOVE: General Henry H. Arnold (1886-1950) was the architect and strategist behind Operation Bolero, the mass movement of men and materiel from the United States to the UK in preparation for the liberation of occupied Europe, the bombing offensive and the defeat of Nazi Germany. USAF

allowed the aircraft, with some limitations on flexibility, to play a worthy part in 1000-bomber raids that would become an objective for Harris. But the RAF was not new to four-engine bombers, the Short Stirling having been in operational service with the RAF Bomber Command since August 1940. Stirlings had bombed Berlin in April 1941 and for two years made a major contribution. By mid-1943 they were becoming obsolete and would end their days primarily as glider-tugs.

To the Americans, the deliberate bombing of towns and cities had been a problematic area. Both moral and military objections had been raised frequently since the late 1930s and there was a strident body of opinion, as there was with British policy, that it was an immoral act, a war crime perpetrated against innocent civilians, opposed by a view which declared that munitions workers were as much in the front-line as were front-line troops on the battlefield. The debate would rumble on and has never gone away.

Yet in 1942, support for an expanded bombing campaign was increasingly becoming a driving component of British policy, pushed along by key milestones, one of which was the area bombing directive. But that had itself been endorsed on the back of a series of calculations carried out by Lord Cherwell, Professor Frederick Lindeman, and Churchill's chief science adviser, in which he attempted to demonstrate with mathematical precision how the war could be significantly shortened by not only area bombing but through the deliberate targeting of cities. The results would play a seminal role in convincing the Americans to go along with this policy.

On March 30, 1942, Lindemann sent a memorandum to Churchill which was considered during a discussion about the most effective way to utilise national resources and whether the large amounts of money now beginning to flow to Bomber Command would be better spent on the Army or the Navy. The paper has to be considered within the context of its delivery, when Bomber Command was tempering its activities awaiting the arrival of the Lancaster and better versions of the Halifax.

Lindemann used analysis of German air raids on British cities to determine that the RAF should be able to count on the average British bomber being capable of surviving 14 sorties before being shot down. Because the average lift weight of those aircraft coming into service was three tons per bomber, each aircraft could deliver 40 tons of bombs during its operational life. Based on bomb damage assessment in Britain, that would make 4000-8000 people homeless per aircraft. Lindemann estimated that 22 million Germans lived in 58 towns of more than 100,000 inhabitants and, given the productive output of 10,000 bombers a year, if half that total dropped

Block numbers

The B-17F was the first Boeing aircraft to carry the new USAAF block number system, introduced in 1941. Due to the enormous expansion of production quotas and the minor changes which were applied to successive variants, a number was applied as a suffix to the main aircraft variant letter without changing the model number.

For instance, the B-17F indicated the 17th bomber type contracted by the AAC or the AAF, with 'F' being the fifth proposed type variant. Block numbers were multiples of five, beginning with 5. A suffix -5 would indicate the initial "block" variation of the B-17F type and the next minor variation in production would be B-17F-10, and so on.

The block number was unique to each manufacturer and each aircraft type, Boeing-built B-17F aircraft for instance getting up to B-17F-30, the 605 built by Douglas getting to -80 and the 500 built by Vega reaching -50. Block numbers could only be interpreted when applied to a particular designated type, B-24, B-25, B-26, etc).

During the 1941/42 production expansion programme, two suffix letters were added to the block number, or to the type variant letter if there was no block number, to denote that the aircraft type was manufactured by a different company. A comprehensive list of manufacturing plants was prepared, each one of which had an identifying code of two letters. Some large companies had several manufacturing plants and therefore a separate code for each. For instance, Boeing had two plants (Renton, Washington, carrying code BN, and Seattle, Washington, coded BO). North American Aviation had two (NA and NC), while the majority had only one. In all, there were 130 separate aircraft manufacturing plants, each with their own two-letter code.

ABOVE: The B-17E seen flying over the English countryside, by 1943 a staging ground for attacks on Nazi Germany and an arsenal of weapons for the strategic bombing campaign. USAF

ABOVE: This B-17F (Idiot's Delight) displays the moulded plexiglass nose assembly and the paddle-blade propellers introduced on this type, plus modifications to the cowling to allow the wide blades to be feathered. USAF

ABOVE: *Some B-17E aircraft were modified for radar tracking of surface ships, as indicated by the nose antenna on this aircraft of the 98th Bombardment Squadron, 11th Bombardment Group, at New Caledonia, north-east of Australia, in January 1943.* USAF

their loads during the span of their estimated life, about 7 million people would be made homeless.

Lindemann had been a long-time friend and confidante of Churchill but the prime minister did not have unimpeachable faith in his judgements. But Bomber Command had done their own assessment and Chief of the Air Staff Sir Charles Portal argued that the force Lindemann had described could destroy 43 German town and cities with more than 100,000 inhabitants and win the war in six months. The definition of 'winning' appears to have been the stumbling block and was based entirely on conclusions that morale would collapse. It was argued that the population would panic and bring down the Nazi regime and in any case be incapable delivering the munitions essential to carrying on with the war.

Another factor was the German invasion of Russia, the end of which was nowhere in sight – initial German optimism over a rapid defeat of the USSR having been premature. It was postulated that the combined effect of a strategic bombing campaign and the attrition of German forces east of Poland would impose an unsupportable strain on the German nation and the regime would collapse. The argument had merit and the conclusion was logical but the debate had no end and continued on until Harris offered a way which he thought would prove them correct, one which would influence US thinking on the subject.

ABOVE: *Nurse Katye Swope of the 802nd Medical Evacuation Air Transport Squadron attending wounded servicemen air lifted out of Sicily in July 1942.* US ARMY

ABOVE: Nurses from the School of Evacuation, Bowman Field, Kentucky, learn how to attend wounded using the mock-up of the Douglas DC-4 fuselage. *USAF*

ABOVE: American Lend-Lease equipment being handed over to the Russians in Iran is supervised by USAAF officers. Between 1941 and 1945 America gave Russia aid equivalent in value to $153 billion in today's money. *USAF*

ABOVE: Professor F. A. Lindemann (left) with Prime Minister Winston Churchill and Dr. D. A. Crow (right) with Vice Admiral Tom Phillips watching secret radar and electronic anti-aircraft tests at Holt, Norfolk. Professor Lindemann was to make assertive claims about the ability of bombers to bring Germany to its knees. *RAF*

Harris offered Churchill and Portal a way to test the concept, to achieve a real test of the proposed policy by carrying out a raid by 1000 bombers against a single target. Bomber Command had authority over little more than 400 aircraft and trained crews, however, and sought to include operational conversion units and training groups with a combination of instructors, with some aircraft loaned from RAF Coastal Command and others from Flying Training Command. Harris wanted to prove the concept, even though it was as yet not within the ability of Bomber Command to mount independently with the resources it alone could command. It would point the way toward realisation of Lindemann's claim and the area bombing directive.

Notwithstanding opposition from Coastal and Training Commands, and delays brought about through reluctance to release their aircraft for this high profile, high-risk, plan, the force gradually came together on paper which generated further problems as nobody had assembled this number of aircraft together in the skies over England for a single operation against one target. The numerical size of the force alone was two and a half times greater than anything the RAF had mounted on a single night before and there was a degree of bravura about demonstrating to the Americans "how it should be done".

After several delays for operational and meteorological reasons, the raid was mounted with 1047 bombers taking off, mainly from airfields in Lincolnshire and Yorkshire. With concern about flying operationally with so many trainee crews the operation was mounted on the night of May 30/31, 1942, against the industrial city of Cologne, third on the list of Harris's target cities. It was great success, followed up two nights later by a second raid, to Essen, which was not on his original list. The 1000 bomber raids were difficult to accomplish until the numerical inventory of Bomber Command allowed other Commands to retain their aircraft and crews but frequently raids of 700 to 800 bombers would deliver their bomb loads over a single town or city in less than 20 minutes.

COMBINED OFFENSIVES

All this had a measurable and impressive effect on the Americans and the 8th AF command structure, opening the possibility of a combined bomber offensive which would multiply the effect by allowing the 8th to follow its own independent raids in conjunction and in close cooperation with the RAF. But the AAF was still struggling with operational readiness. By the end of 1942 only 79 missions had been flown and none exceeded 79 aircraft.

But the question of escort fighters had galled the Americans. Generally considered the best interceptor and bomber escort, because of its range, the P-38 Lightning was no dog-fighter and the senior AAF leaders considered the Spitfire the best all-round fighter of the war, admirable for interception, bomber defence and dog-fighting. But its poor range would render it unsuitable for those tasks with raids deep into Germany.

Neither had it been possible to maintain the strength of P-38s assigned to England, escort fighters being desperately needed for Operation Torch and in addition to supplying the 12th AF with aircraft, the 8th had to move 1072 aircraft, including 412 P-38s and 239 P-39s using long-range drop tanks to North Africa, also losing 2109 officers and 2817 enlisted men. But the North African campaign and the ensuing push up through Sicily had demonstrated the worth

ABOVE: *Curtiss P-40 Warhawk pursuit aircraft being assembled somewhere in Iran in a deal worked out with President Roosevelt and the Shah. USAF*

ABOVE: *Marshal of the RAF Sir Charles Portal (1893-1971), Chief of the Air Staff from 1940 to 1946, played a crucial role in working with the Americans to create a Combined Bomber Offensive in 1943, whereby separate RAF and USAAF operations would combine to a common purpose. RAF*

of the P-38 and fighters were being sought to consolidate escort capabilities for the 8th AF in the UK. But not until December 24 did the first P-47s arrive in England.

It was said to be able to protect bombers up to 200 miles inland of the enemy coast but the drop tanks that would have made that possible failed to arrive. With an internal fuel capacity of 305 gallons the P-47 had a maximum escort radius of 175 miles and further doubts were raised due to its low acceleration getting from the speed of the bomber formations to the engagement speed with enemy fighters, when they appeared. It was an acceleration problem solved in part with a paddle propeller and water-boost injection.

The commander of VIII Fighter Command, Brigadier General Hunter, believed that the P-47 would be most effective flying high top-cover,

pouncing on enemy fighters as necessary, and that the strength of the fighter escort should not be determined by the number of bombers they had to protect but by the number of enemy fighters likely to be engaged, the range at which they could operate and the relative performance of US and enemy fighters. But the numbers of escort groups considered minimal were never achieved, the set goal of 20 available by August 1943 fell short by 17 on that date, the date when the first major raids began under a new integrated planning structure which had its origins at the beginning of the year.

In January 1943 when Roosevelt and Churchill met in Casablanca, the value of high altitude bombing was discussed at length but the RAF was suspicious of American claims that they could carry out effective operations in daylight. The RAF had learned through bitter experience

the danger of daylight skies over enemy territory, full of fighters from the Jagdwaffe hunting for slow-flying bombers. And the Air Force staffers too were cautious about the effect they could have on the enemy. As late as October 1942 they had been unable to make any impact on the U-boat bases on the Atlantic coast when their 2000lb bombs, the largest they had, could not penetrate the concrete-shielded pens.

But the Americans, wedded to the idea of precision bombing with their successful Norden bombsight, were intent on continuing with the daylight campaign and General Eaker, flown out for the conference, rose to the challenge concerning the lack of American success when claiming that a "round the clock" campaign would "soften the Hun for land invasion and the

ABOVE: *The RAF had been carrying the burden of bombing German cities while attention would now focus on daylight destruction of industrial targets by the US Army Air Force. In operation since March 1942, the Lancaster was capable of carrying a wide range of bombs, from incendiaries (left) to high explosives. The 'Airborne Cigar' antennas are for jamming German radio telephone channels. RAF*

ABOVE: Developed as a fighter but pressed into service as a fighter-bomber, the Lockheed P-38 became the mainstay of British and American forces in several theatres. LOCKHEED

ABOVE: The cockpit of the Lockheed P-38 with excellent all-round visibility and a compact and functional layout. NMUSAF

kill". He persuaded Churchill to support the idea, which now became formalised: the RAF would continue with expansion of its night raids and the Americans would sustain daylight raids. Eaker got his independent mode of operation while coordinating with the British to bring maximum damage to the German war machine. But there would be no centrally directed Anglo-American campaign.

General Marshall sided with Eaker, suspicious of British attempts to siphon off US units to the night raids if a combined command was headed by the British, which, given the runaway success the RAF was now having, seemed like a natural progression. Moreover, Marshall had supreme confidence in General Arnold and his Army

Air Forces. Nevertheless, Generals Marshall, Arnold and Eaker agreed that much could be learned from the British, especially the mode of operation, demonstrated by an increasingly impressive Bomber Command who were now, single-handedly, carrying the fight to the heart of German industry and its workforce.

Now the way was clear for what both sides agreed would constitute a Combined Bomber Offensive (CBO) for the "progressive destruction and dislocation of the German military, industrial and economic system, and the undermining of the morale of the German people to a point where their capacity for armed resistance is fatally weakened". It would be prosecuted by daylight precision raids on factories and pin-point targeting of specific marshalling yards, powerplants, production facilities and ports and harbours, with the night raids assigned to burning out the cities.

The directive also called for the integration of target assignment to maximise the effect. This would at times call for the sustained air assault on a town or city by both day and night, maintaining a continuous bombardment which would prevent workers resting, emergency services from operating, or medical attention being administered to casualties. Several such examples were selected for raids which could focus continuous bombardment over the course of two days and three nights. But there were other threats to the CBO achieving its objectives, most notable the significant increase in fighter defences.

Decisions regarding specific targets were made by an Anglo-American planning committee. General Arnold relied on the Committee of Operations Analysis, composed of analysts who would use the American industrial model to assess the relative effect strategic bombing might have on particular targets. The RAF used their

P-38 Lightning

There were probably four classic fighters of the Second World War of which the P-38 was one. The type was in production when the war began and when it ended, with more than 10,000 built for every theatre involving American air fighting units. Yet it was not until the penultimate year of the war that production peaked, at 4186 in 1944 alone. Yet this aircraft was the first American fighter to destroy a German aircraft in flight, the first to make a return flight to Berlin on bomber escort, the one that shot down Admiral Yamamoto's aircraft, and the mount for the high scoring American air aces, Major Richard R. Bong and Major Thomas B. McGuire, Jr. Responding to a request for a twin-engine, high-altitude interceptor, Lockheed's legendary Kelly Johnson designed an unorthodox aircraft with twin tail booms, tricycle undercarriage and a centre-wing nacelle incorporating the cockpit and gun bay. Powered by two 1150hp Allison V-1710C engines, one installed in each boom, model 22-64-01 was presented to the Air Corps in April 1937, won the competition and received a contract for 13 YP-38 prototypes, the first of which was flown on September 17, 1940, at Burbank, California.

Major contracts followed, expanding as war loomed, and the Anglo-French Purchasing Commission placed an order for 667 in April 1941. After the fall of France the entire production lot was taken over by the RAF but after initial flight tests at Boscombe Down were unfavourable they were rejected and after Pearl Harbor the AAF took them over instead. Standard armament was one 20mm cannon and four 0.50in cannon. During the war great improvements were made and the type received the more powerful 1475hp V-1710 engines for the P-38L, specified below, capable of carrying a 3200lb bomb load. The type also operated as a night fighter designated P-38M.

LENGTH	37.9ft
WING SPAN	52ft
HEIGHT	9.9ft
GROSS WEIGHT	21,600lb
MAXIMUM SPEED	414mph
CRUISING SPEED	290mph
CEILING	44,000ft
RANGE	450 miles

ABOVE: P-38s on their way to England during a stopover in Iceland to refuel and for a short break on the long flight from America. USAF

intelligence information on the observed damage to German targets to extrapolate effects on new targets. Together, the two would converge at the planning committee and decide particular targets.

COORDINATION

To focus attacks on German aircraft factories the Pointblank Directive of June 14, 1943, authorised the coordinated USAAF and RAF attacks on selected targets designed to stem the flow of new fighters rolling off the production line. Prime targets included the Messerschmitt works at Regensburg and the ball-bearing factories at Schweinfurt. Recognising the increasing depth of defences surrounding these targets, AAF planners determined that massed firepower from the 0.50in guns of the B-17s and B-24s erected the best form of defence for the bombers. The basic formation of the time was a combat wing which was proving cumbersome to control in the air.

Essentially consisting of three groups of 18 aircraft, each with three squadrons, the formation was set out so that it presented a frontal area of 7000ft, with a height of 1000ft and a depth of 1800ft, thus presenting a solid wall of fire to a headlong attack. But manoeuvring this formation was difficult with aircraft at the farthest place from the pivot point running full throttle in a desperate effort to maintain station while those near to the pivot point were wallowing around at near stall speed. Later, as fighter protection improved, this structure would be replaced with a group of 36 aircraft before it would be replaced in 1945 with a formation of 27.

But defending against the enemy fighters was getting very difficult, even as the AAF was still on a steep learning curve. And P-47s sent out on escort duty still had to turn around at the western border with Germany, leaving the bombers to struggle on alone. Over time, the advantage of RAF Bomber Command's night raids was gradually being eroded with the advances in radar fitted to enemy night fighters hunting them down, a technology which would soon be turned against

the day raiders as well.

New and highly capable fighters were appearing in the skies over Germany, including the new Bf 109G which became operational in mid-1942 and equipping home defence units from February 1943. Known as the 'Gustav' the type had essentially the airframe of the Bf 109F but with a powerful DB 605A engine with higher compression ratio, a top speed of more than 380mph and a service ceiling of 38,500ft which gave them clear access to the incoming bomber formations.

From June 1942 the dreaded 'Butcher Bird', the Focke-Wulf Fw 190 with a top speed of around 400mph and a ceiling of 37,400ft was also joining Jagdwaffe units employed on the defence of Germany. In May 1943 the Germans began

equipping these aircraft with 30mm cannon, allowing their pilots to attack beyond the range of the B-17's guns.

Working to begin raids under the Pointblank initiative, the strength of VIII Bomber Command began to significantly improve throughout 1943. In January heavy bomber strength in tactical units considered operational was 84, growing to 112 in March and 200 in May. During May the 8th received five new bombardment groups and one resumed combat operations. In addition to the heavy groups, the 8th got the temporary addition of one medium bomber group with their B-26 Marauders.

On May 13 the availability of combat crews doubled overnight, going from 100 to 215 and to a level of strength where units had been working

ABOVE: Converted from the B-17, the YB-40 was operated as a flying gunship to protect US bombers formations but it was too slow to keep up and was a failed concept. USAF

U. S. ARMY
OFFICIAL POSTER

"The leader of the first element set his Zero afire at the top of the loop ... rolled out with a Zero on his tail ... his wing man shot it down ... Altogether these 4 P-38's met 11 Zeros on this mission, shot down 7 sure and 2 probables. They returned to base without a single bullet hole in them."

Army Air Forces report

Give us MORE P-38's

ABOVE: With most eyes on the bombing of Germany, Americans were reminded of the contribution made by the war effort to avenging Pearl Harbor with the remorseless march of naval and air forces toward the mainland of Japan. NARA

to maintain establishment in an environment of siphoned-off units to other theatres and inconsistent quantities of reserves. In July the 8th would declare 378 American bombers in England.

To demonstrate the new enhanced capability, on May 14 the 8th put on its biggest show to date when it launched a combined attack, the RAF sending forces to Berlin and other locations with the AAF allocating 217 B-17s, B-24s and 12 B-26s to Kiel, Courtrai, Antwerp and Ijmuiden, together with 118 P-47s. Of the total, 198 bombers and all the fighters effectively carried out their missions together with Spitfires of the RAF. Eleven bombers were lost, at 5.5% a little higher than the average suffered by the 8th to this date.

On June 22 the 8th AF made the first large-scale penetration of the Ruhr by daylight in a concentrated bombardment of the synthetic

rubber works at Hüls, a tactical experience but also one which provided valuable experience with heavy air fighting. One of the most important of its kind in Germany, the plant had been built under the four-year plan of IG Farbenindustrie and had expanded production by the beginning of the year to 3000 tons. It was the second largest Buna plant in Germany, accounting for nearly one-third of the country's production capacity, producing several valuable chemical by-products in addition to tyres. Since 1941 it had been bombed by the RAF in one fairly heavy and three light raids.

On this raid the 183 aircraft sent out included 11 YB-40 types, essentially B-17s refitted as bomber escorts of which 20 had been converted from B-17F types with a chin turret of the type fitted later to the B-17G and equipped with heavy machine guns of up to 40mm calibre. First used

on a raid to St Nazaire on May 29, 1943, it was too heavy and was unable to keep up with the bombers it was supposed to protect.

The raid itself was a great success, dropping more than 422 tons of bombs of which 88.6 tons exploded in the area of the plant itself. Not expecting a daylight raid, workers flocked outside to watch the aircraft flying high over the plant unaware of the bombs raining down. Some 186 were killed and more than 1000 injured while bombs cracked two of the air raid shelters, killing 90 people inside.

The effect of the raid was so severe that the plant was shut down for a month while repairs were carried out and production was not back up to pre-raid levels for a further six months. Total loss in that one Buna plant amounted to 12,000 tons, sufficient on its own to reduce Germany's total reserve stocks to approximately six weeks' supply.

During that day an additional 39 B-17s had turned to attack Antwerp while a force of 12 Mitchells from RAF No. 2 Group escorted by Spitfires carried out diversionary raids on Rotterdam and succeeded in engaging the fighters in that area so that they were unable to refuel in time to get to the heavy bomber attacks, all in an effort to confuse the German controllers. Split by the two attacks, there was a deceptive strategy under way which nevertheless could not prevent a lively air battle in which 16 main force and four secondary force bombers were shot down, a loss of almost 10%.

Weather conditions for the remainder of June prevented any significant raids but a series of important raids began to broaden the range of operations for the AAF, focusing on a determined effort at degrading the ability of the Germans to continue production of a wide range of material goods. Great improvements to the weather allowed the 8th to carry out some of the most intense and productive raids of the year, unleashing heavy and persistent attacks. With the RAF conducting nightly air raids setting new records in tonnage dropped, US heavy bombers operated on six consecutive days from July 24, penetrating deeper into Germany, dropping more bombs and expanding the range of targets.

On July 24, the AAF began raiding key targets in Norway, striking at unfinished plants for the production of magnesium, aluminium and nitrates as well as U-boat facilities at Bergen and Trondheim. The flight to Trondheim was the longest air raid attempted by American aircraft to date, involving a round trip of 1900 miles flown by the 4th Bombardment Wing. Work was severely disrupted and stalled production for more than three months while the unfinished aluminium and magnesium production plants were considered unrepairable and abandoned.

The raid had instituted a new method of assembling aircraft formations during bad weather, involving a takeoff on instruments with special beacons for group formation. The simultaneous bombing of a plant at Heroya denied the enemy 12,000 tons of primary aluminium, about 30% of all the losses from direct attack after midsummer 1943. This and further raids during July demonstrated the rapidly expanding capabilities of the AAF in the UK and in the increasing number of aircraft crews becoming available.

On July 26 more than 300 B-17s were dispatched to Germany, of which 199 succeeded ➤

ABOVE: *A soldier and a civilian look out at the Fieseler works in Kassel at fires started by USAAF bombers.* BUNDESARCHIV

ABOVE: *Robert A. Lovett, Assistant Secretary of State for Air, became a pivotal player in the fight to find a fighter that could escort bombers all the way to Berlin and back.* USAF

in bombing their targets, 92 attacking the rubber plant at Hannover, 54 the submarine pens at Hamburg and 53 out bombing targets of opportunity, the combined effect of which was to confuse the German fighter controllers and give

them a very busy day. Additional diversionary attacks were made by the medium bombers of the VIII Air Support Command and by RAF Bostons and Hawker Typhoons strafing nearby airfields.

At the Hannover targets, almost 209 tons of high explosives and incendiaries were dropped but again the raiders were unescorted except for three YB-40s which themselves suffered badly from flak and attacking fighters, with 24 bombers shot down including 13 to enemy attack and seven to anti-aircraft fire. For this, the plant lost 24% of production output for a month including the loss of 2000 aircraft tyres and 6000 vehicle tyres. But recovery was rapid and not before March 1945 was this plant finally knocked out of action altogether.

In spite of these successes, losses were building up and the Luftwaffe was receiving equipment which improved the ability of its controllers to vector defending fighters on to the incoming bombers. In one raid on July 28, 302 bombers were dispatched in two forces, but poor weather prevented more than 95 reaching their targets, the Fieseler works at Kassel and the AGO Flugzeugwerke at Oschersleben, 90 miles from Berlin where the factory was producing Fw 190 fighters. Although covered by cloud, a small gap opened almost right over the target allowing the bombers to drop their 67.9 tons of bombs on the aircraft factory. That small token drop amid

bad weather cost the factory a month's loss of production.

Despite being escorted by 123 fighters, the Oschersleben raid cost 15 of the 37 bombers that set out, a shocking 40% of the strike force, and the Kassel raiders lost 12% of their number. Yet by now the P-47s were pushing farther into Germany than ever before and, had they not been able to do so, the losses may have been greater. Equipped for the first time with jettisonable belly tanks, 105 P-47s met the returning bombers 260 miles from the English coast and escorted them back home. When they appeared 30 miles further into German airspace than ever before they caught 60 German fighters by surprise. The P-47s shot down nine of them, and only one Thunderbolt failed to return.

The presence of a long range escort was still some way off but the pressure for them was getting intense. In June the Assistant Secretary of War for Air, Robert Lovett, reviewed the American effort and sent his findings to General Arnold, impressing on him the urgency of getting escort fighters to accompany the bombers into Germany, recommending P-38s and P-51s for the job. Arnold issued specific orders demanding that a long range fighter be provided by the end of the year because "I want a fighter escort for all of our bombers from UK into Germany", to support intensive deep penetration missions he said would begin in January 1944. ✪

Chapter 9: Maximum effort 1943-1944

When General Arnold issued his demand for a long-range fighter escort it started a race against time. Attrition rates were climbing and the strategic offensive could not be sustained with the losses now being experienced. But he insisted that a solution be found "within months". Yet even that was too long as the losses began to grow even faster and reached a peak in mid-1943. Nevertheless, attention was focused on getting long range tanks on the P-38s and the P-47s, while in reality the solution would come from a very different place.

On August 15 the 65th Group used 200 gallon belly tanks supporting bombers attacking targets in France and Germany with support extending as far as Kleve. Penetrating about 275 miles into Germany, the fighters were able to see off 50-60 enemy fighters attempting to get through to the bombers, eight German fighters being shot down with the loss of only

two bombers in a force of 290. On the eve of August 17 there were four fighter groups in VIII Fighter Command, a day on which the American bombing effort reached a climax.

Also on August 17 an attacking force of 188 aircraft flying deep into Germany attacked the ball-bearing factory at Schweinfurt, where half of Germany's output was based, and 127 bombers struck the Messerschmitt aircraft assembly plant at Regensburg, where about half of Germany's fighter production was centred. The Regensburg plant was about 100 miles further on and the aircraft would transit south to land in Algeria. The plan was for the Schweinfurt raid to follow behind the Regensburg aircraft and that way avoid excessive fighter forces, since they would be occupied with the preceding formations up ahead. It was not to work out that way.

No sooner had the Regensburg bombers reached the continent and said farewell to their

escort fighters than the Jagdwaffe set upon them in a furious engagement that went on for 90 minutes, controllers vectoring fighter units from as far away as the Baltic. Special German spotter aircraft, keeping well out of the way of the bombers, maintained a running commentary on where the various fighter units, coming up from the ground, could locate their own targets. The fighters employed a wide variety of tactics, some of them never seen before.

Slicing down in groups of two or three and in packs of up to 25, using a javelin formation they attacked the bombers' nose positions in groups of seven to 15 aircraft at a time. They struck in steep bunting dives right through the formations of vertically stacked bombers, aiming for the mid-upper turrets of individual aircraft. They also used rockets with fuses set to detonate close to but not on the bombers so that they would damage various parts

ABOVE: *Delivered to Polebrook in May 1943, B-17E 41-2578 was commanded by General Ira Eaker on a mission over Germany on August 17, 1942. General Eaker continued to play a significant role in building up the AAF in the UK throughout 1943 and 1944. USAF*

ABOVE: *The 3rd Bombardment Division raids the Focke-Wulf works Marienburg on October 9, 1943, with 96 B-17s dropping 217 tons of bombs.* USAAF

of the same aircraft. Some even dropped parachute bombs on the vulnerable B-17s.

Opposition to the raids was the most intense yet encountered during the war. In the initial engagement, 24 bombers of the 127 that made it to the target were knocked down, most before reaching their target, while the remaining aircraft dropped 299 tons of bombs on the factories. But the second component of this night's operation was fouled by bad weather which delayed the despatch of the 230 Schweinfurt bombers, of which only 188 would make it to the target, by more than three and one-half hours. The Regensburg bombers had had to leave within one hour of the planned time to make landfall in North Africa before dusk.

Of the 188 B-17s from the 1st Bombardment Wing, 36 were shot down, an unsustainable loss of 19% added to the 19% losses sustained by

the 4th BW on the Regensburg raid. But the damage incurred at the ball-bearing factories ensured that production dropped from 169 tons to 69 tons in August and 50 tons in September with an increase only restoring some level of normality by November. But the raid did stimulate a move to obtain finished stock from 'neutral' Sweden and Switzerland.

Such was the importance of the Schweinfurt ball-bearing factories that the 8th executed a return attack on October 14. A total of 291 B-17s were dispatched from the 3rd and 1st Bombardment Divisions while a force of 29 B-24s from the 2nd Division were expected to fly a longer route to the south; because the B-17s were flying a route beyond their normal range an additional fuel tank was placed in the bomb bay. However, the B-24s found it impossible to form up correctly and ended up flying a

diversionary approach toward Emden. As soon as the main force reached Aachen, 240 miles from the British coast, the 196 escorting P-47s had to turn back and the Jagdwaffe attacked.

The tactic was for enemy fighters with 20mm cannon to fly right through the formations, guns blazing as they went, followed by twin-engine Bf 110s launching rocket attacks from about 1000 yards and from the rear. Meanwhile, the single-engine fighters had landed, refuelled and rejoined the fray from all directions. The fighters would focus on a single

ABOVE: *Mechanics of the 99th Fighter Squadron (Tuskegee Airmen) 332nd Fighter Group, 15th USAAF, with a 75 gallon drop tank. Installed empty and then filled, one pint from the top of the tank was removed before flight to eliminate possible water contamination.* USAF

ENGINE PERFORMANCE INCREASES 1941-1945

Engine horsepower	Original horsepower	1945 rated
Packard V-1650	*1300*	*1700*
Allison V-1710	*1000*	*1700*
Wright R-1820	*750*	*1350*
Pratt & Whitney R-1830	*950*	*1350*
Wright R-1600	*1500*	*1800*
Pratt & Whitney R-2800	*1800*	*2100*
Wright R-3350	*1800*	*2500*

ABOVE: B-17s of the 388th Bombardment Group fly over smoke screens, an attempt to hide industrial facilities in Bremen. *USAAF*

ABOVE: B-17s take the war to Schweinfurt on August 17, 1943, hitting the ball-bearing works in a raid that cost the 1st Bombardment Wing 36 aircraft and 355 aircrew. *USAAF*

ABOVE: With radar fitted to lead aircraft, the USAAF bombers were able to drop their loads through dense cloud and avoid wasting bombs on open country. *USAAF*

formation, breaking it up and picking off the lame ducks one by one. The 1st Bombardment Division was all but wiped out this way.

Despite the mauling, 229 bombers were effective over the target dropping 395 tons of bombs and 88 tons of incendiaries. The appalling losses amounted to 60 aircraft, a quarter of all the aircraft that reached their target which, when including major damage to 17 and repairable damage to 121, left only 31 B-17s out of 229 that set out fit for immediate assignment. These losses and the dire need for fighter escorts all the way out and back halted heavy air raids in daylight deep into German territory for a while. Only modest progress had been made toward providing adequate fighter escort, the P-38s becoming operational on October 15 with two 75 gallon drop tanks extending their radius to 520 miles, and with two 108 gallon tanks by February 1944 they could reach out 585 miles from base.

But it was less exotic problems that AAF air crew had to wrestle with. During the second

half of 1943 there was a tendency for the mid-upper turrets to cause a fire that could consume half the upper fuselage before being extinguished. This was caused, it transpired, by the ring-shaped rotating turret mounting chafing electrical wire and oxygen hoses. Yet the issue of the expanding inventory of enemy fighters available to address the increasingly intensive AAF raids became a serious threat to sustained operations during the second half of 1943.

With an end to the Mediterranean air war the shift of Luftwaffe forces from that theatre to north-west and central Europe dramatically increased the number of fighters available to attack the bombers. Allied intelligence was slow to accept the revitalisation in German aircraft production, a response to the sustained bombing campaign, the vast majority of which was being carried out by RAF Bomber Command in particular. Counter-intuitively, under armaments minister Albert Speer the German war effort was reaching extraordinary proportions.

As the air war intensified, for two years German aircraft production quotas had shifted. In 1942 bomber output was 28% of all aircraft production, falling to less than 19% a year later, while fighter production since 1941 had gone from 34% in 1941 to 44% in 1942 and 57% in 1943. Worse still, total German aircraft production increased from 12,400 aircraft in 1941 to 15,400 in 1942 and 24,800 in 1943. In 1944 Germany would produce 30,781 fighters, 76% of all aircraft built that year.

In terms of intensity, in July 1943 the Luftwaffe had only 30% of its day fighters on the western front while in October that had almost doubled to 56%. And all the while, the losses on the German side were escalating, thanks to the expanding scale of the air war over Europe due to the expansion of AAF and RAF capabilities for taking the fight to the enemy. In the first half of 1943 the Germans lost 5188 fighters, increasing to 7386 in the second half of the year. However, largely unknown to the Allies at the time, the intensity of the Combined Bomber Offensive had weakened the theoretical potential of the German armaments industry and delayed production by three months.

ASSET STRIPPING

These raids had been the real test for the strategic initiative with Combined Bomber Offensive but the first serious losses, which also caused a halt to planned raids, were suffered during a raid mounted by the 9th AF against the Ploesti oilfields in Rumania. That had taken place on August 1 against this most important production plant delivering 60% of Germany's crude oil and a third of its liquid fuel. Ploesti had been attacked by Russian aircraft in 1941 and again in 1942, with little effect. Too far away to be attacked from bases in England, it would fall to the 9th AF flying B-24s from North Africa to carry out a low level raid dropping a planned 311 tons of high explosive plus 430 boxes of incendiaries, some 170 more than was considered necessary to destroy the plant.

Assigned to carry out the mission, 177 aircraft in two groups from IX Bomber

➤

ABOVE: Exceptionally heavy losses to the 8th AF in raids on Germany led to the introduction of the B-17G in late 1943 with a chin turret below the nose equipped with twin 0.50in guns, almost 9000 of this variant being built. USAAF

FACTORY CAPACITY (THOUSANDS OF SQUARE FT)

Date	Airframes	Gliders	Engines	Propellers	Total
1940 Jan	9606		3018	492	13,116
1941 Jan	17,973		6463	1050	25,456
1943 Jan	77,536	2486	31,829	5240	117,091
1943 Dec	110,423	3558	54,189	6835	175,005
1944 Dec	102,951	1664	54,888	7888	167,391

Command and three on loan from the 8th AF in England carried out intensive low-level training activities near Benghazi in preparation for their audacious attack. The complexity of the raid was confounded by operational and technical delays carried out at altitudes of less than 500ft. When the 93rd Bombardment Group went in it dropped to 100-300ft and headed straight for the refineries, just missing tall chimneys and high buildings. The bombs it dropped caused explosions which the 98th and 44th had to fly through following similar routes. Instead of turning back they flew directly on into the flak, exploding bombs, flames and dense choking smoke concealing balloon cables and more tall chimneys.

Although the targets were hit hard, even the official report on the raid claims the B-24s went down "like tenpins", and as the groups departed the scene they were set upon by marauding fighters all the way out. Unable to follow pre-arranged flight patterns, the remaining B-24s scattered to find their own individual paths back toward North Africa, making for Malta, Sicily or Cyprus. Some went to Turkey, mostly those in the greatest distress. Of the 177 that hit the target, only 88 made it back to various airfields. Total losses were 54 in enemy skies and three which crashed at sea, a total of 32% of the force which set out and the loss of 532 airmen.

Yet the Ploesti raid has become one of the most remembered, for the sheer grit and determination displayed by the airmen who set out on one of the most dangerous missions of the entire war. Highly accurate bombing and a high success level of exploded bombs resulted in serious damage which took out 42% of the plant's refining capacity and 40% of

ABOVE: The crushed front of a B-17G after returning from a raid on Cologne, the chin turret only just remaining attached to the fuselage. USAAF

ABOVE: *B-17F 41-24408 returns from a collision with a Bf 109 over France, the tail section only just intact.* USAAF

ABOVE: *Salvaging useable parts from a distressed B-17 at the 390th Bombardment Group located at Framlingham, Suffolk, between July 1943 and August 1945. A lot of recycled parts were saved in this way.* USAAF

ABOVE: *Women Airforce Service Pilots (WASPs) provide the photographer with a posed walk past a line of B-17s which will be delivered to service units by this group of elite American women pilots.* USAAF

the cracking capacity for at least four months. Surprisingly in retrospect, no further raids were made against Ploesti until late spring of 1944 and yet it was always considered one of the most important strategic targets of the war. Other targets considered to be of greater tactical or strategic value preoccupied the Mediterranean air forces for some time and the bombers never returned with such force.

One impediment to an increase in strategic missions from England was in the inability of the supply chain to deliver adequate resources for the AAF in Britain. The claims from other air forces in other theatres, not to mention the demands of an increase in momentum in the Pacific war against Japan, had sapped the slowly growing logistical deliveries from the US. As a general guide, at the beginning of 1943 it had been hoped to build up an AAF personnel strength of 500,000 men, of whom half would be dedicated to the strategic bombing offensive and 46% to the tactical air forces but as of May the strength stood at less than 75,000 compared with a planned 485,000. Set in August, the goal was for 115 groups and 6800 aircraft but the revised estimate at the end of November envisaged 98 groups in the European Theatre of Operations by July 1, 1944 and, incredibly, that number was actually achieved.

All these aircraft needed fuel and the actual amount on hand in the UK was around one million gallons for the first five months of 1944. With the D-Day landings anticipated for mid-year, it was agreed that instead of tankers delivering oil to English west coast ports they would dock in London, within easier reach of East Anglian bases. This would alleviate pressure on the road tankers and supply lines from having to deliver it right across the middle of the country. The British built pipelines from the Thames up to the AAF bases, eliminating the need for road transport from the west of the country. Storage facilities were greatly expanded increasing capacity at each base from 72,000 gallons to 144,000 gallons, even 216,000 gallons at some airfields.

But fuel was only one problem, as there was also a shortage of trucks and vehicles to haul the increasingly heavy bomb loads around and carry out general transport of essential goods. British firms were pressed into service to supply clothing, blankets and containers, while the Ministry of Aircraft Production began to gradually take over the entire replacement requirements for tyres and tubes needed by the AAF.

The need for jettisonable fuel tanks was

ABOVE: Approaching the area at a height of 500ft, the August 1, 1943, raid by the 9th AF on the Ploesti oil refiners in Rumania remains one of the more outstanding examples of audacious bravery in the history of the American Air Forces. *USAAF*

ABOVE: Dropping down to little more than 200ft, the B-24D heavy bombers skim chimney tops, fly through blast waves and broiling smoke from bombs already dropped by aircraft up ahead, as they strike strategic targets at Ploesti. *USAAF*

repair also reached new levels. Where it had been necessary to repair about 500 a month during late 1943, by April 1944 the total reached 1600. The flow of aircraft into the European Theatre of Operations grew at a pace which was only just within the capabilities of the administrative and operational management structure of the Army Air Forces, as displayed in an accompanying table.

THE FINAL PUSH

Development of the truly long-range escort fighter came through the further development of the North American Aviation P-51 Mustang, which owed its origin to a British requirement for a fighter with a performance which simply did not exist in America at the time. First flown in October 1940, initial models were powered by a 1100hp Allison engine and while the aircraft proved satisfactory and with a surprisingly good performance, largely due to its unique laminar-flow wing and the provision of smooth nose entry by placing the radiator inlet well back in the ventral position to provide the smallest frontal cross-section to minimise drag. Developed by the NACA, the wing had its maximum thickness well back from the leading edge and provided almost as much camber above as below, reducing turbulent flow, reducing drag, increasing speed and extending range.

The first Mustangs reached the UK in October 1941 and caught the attention of Ronald W. Harker, then a test pilot with Rolls-Royce, who concluded that the aircraft had disappointing performance at high altitude. Harker told his employees that the aircraft would perform much better if it was fitted with the Merlin 61, with two-stage, two-speed supercharger but there was opposition within the Ministry of Aircraft Production. Harker had also been responsible for suggesting that the unimpressive Avro Manchester bomber would be improved if its two Rolls-Royce Vulture engines were replaced with four Merlin engines, transforming a lacklustre aircraft into the Lancaster bomber.

The RAF began an experimental programme with modified airframes carrying the Merlin 65 and known as the Mustang X when trials began on October 13, 1942. Harker knew that the type had a very efficient design and had a very low drag coefficient but simply lacked the right engine to

growing with the expanded demand for escort fighters and here the British too began to supplement deliveries from the USA, saving time and shipping space. By the end of 1943 alone factories in the UK had turned out 7500 paper tanks of 108 gallon capacity with some 18,000 on hand at AAF stations across the UK. Paper tanks were effective and cheap, being compressed pulped paper which were quite adequate for a single mission.

Quite methodically, during the second half of 1943 and the first half of 1944 British manufacturing began to take on an increasing responsibility for supply and replenishing the fighting airmen of the Army Air Forces. But all this material needed to be delivered and sustained production began to stress the country's rail networks, the burden increasing from 750,000

ton-miles per month at the beginning of 1943 to a monthly average of 1.7 million ton miles each month at the end. Also by the end of the year, an express truck service was mounted between the rail heads and the base depots and from there on to the advance depots and support airfields.

Air transport too was a growing demand, some 3.3 million lb of cargo and mail and 13,400 air passengers being moved around in the last five months of the year, with 8000 aircraft moved from ports to airfields during 1943, rising to 16,000 in the first half of 1944. The entire country was on a war-footing far greater than anything it had seen during the Battle of Britain in the summer months of 1941 or the blitz that followed on into early 1941.

The growing burden of aircraft assembly on arrival at ports and of general maintenance and

USAAF AIRCRAFT BUILD-UP PRIOR TO D-DAY

1943	Total aircraft	Combat aircraft
June	1841	1671
July	2069	1895
August	2452	2275
September	2827	2619
October	3310	3061
November	4152	3835
December	4618	4242
1944		
January	5685	5133
February	6917	6045
March	8562	7171
April	9645	7875
May	10,737	8351

ABOVE: A group of Tuskegee Airmen, Afro-American volunteers, a group which flew and fought in the 332nd Fighter Group and 477th Bombardment Group. USAAF

Tuskegee Airmen

The bid to get African-Americans into the Air Forces really began when Eleanor Roosevelt, wife of the President, took a flight piloted by a representative of this ethnic group, Alfred Anderson, in March 1941, thus opening the door to a group which had previously been barred from joining as flight crew. The 99th Pursuit Squadron was formed at Chanute Field in Rantout, Illinois, on September 11, 1941, and was declared combat ready in April 1943.

The first assignment was to North Africa where they flew during the invasion of Sicily. With increasing numbers of pilots becoming qualified, the 332nd Fighter Group was formed in February 1944 and had been sent overseas with three fighter squadrons. Based in Italy, they carried a crimson colour on the tails of their P-47 and P-51 aircraft but they also flew P-39 and P-40 types. Primarily employed defending bombers flying up into the south-eastern regions of Europe, they also flew strafing and combat missions into France.

The 332nd received a Distinguished Unit Citation for outstanding performance on March 24, 1945, when they escorted B-17s to a tank factory in Berlin, fought back heavy attack from enemy fighters and strafed transportation facilities while flying back to their base at Montecorvino, Italy. The 477th Bombardment Group was beginning to form up when the war ended and the 332nd was returned to the USA in November 1945 and disbanded.

get the best out of it. Flight tests demonstrated a top speed of 432mph, far superior to the Spitfires of the period and significantly better in overall performance than either the P-47 or the P-38. The American Packard Motor Co had a license to build the Merlin as the V-1650 with a single supercharger for the Curtiss P-40F.

In America, an experimental XP-51B was fitted with the V-1650 and first flew on November 30, 1942, exhibiting distinctly superior performance to earlier P-51s in every way. A slight modification to the radiator and its air scoop, to eliminate a problem with the different metals reacting with the glycol coolant, improved the aerodynamic performance even more, the air flow of the aft radiator flap providing a secondary boost through a more efficient air flow. An obvious winner, the aircraft immediately went into volume production and began equipping the AAF in the UK from September 19, 1943.

Responding to complaints from pilots that the rear view was compromised by the type's razorback fuselage decking, the P-51D appeared with a bubble canopy and a cut down top fuselage for a first flight on November 17, 1943. This variant, which rapidly became standard for the AAF had a maximum speed of 437mph, nearly 50mph faster than the P-51A, and a maximum range of 2300 miles with drop tanks. Eventually, 7956 P-51Ds would be built, more than half the total number of 14,819 built for the AAF before production ended.

The first P-51 mission into enemy skies occurred on December 5, 1943, when 36 aircraft of the 354th Fighter Group, along with 266 P-47s and 34 P-38s, escorted 548 B-17s and B-24s to strategic targets in the vicinity of Paris. The P-51s escorted the bombers from the French coast to Poix, southwest of Amiens, where they were relieved by P-47s. The success of the aircraft over the next several weeks prompted a change in allocation and on January 24, 1944, the British and American commanders agreed that most P-51 units would be placed with the AAF, and that the 8th would be equipped almost exclusively with this type, the P-38s and P-47s going to the 9th AF.

By March, P-51s were accompanying the bombers all the way to Berlin and back, to the considerable astonishment of the Luftwaffe's senior leadership, following a winter in which operations had been considerably hampered by poor weather. This led to a concerted effort to develop an adequate form of radar bombing, which would allow the AAF to bomb through cloud. The RAF had already made considerable progress with radar and late in 1942 General Eaker had developed a pathfinder unit which could lead the bombers to their target using H2S, the airborne ground scanning radar which became a core part of RAF Bomber Command's operations. Aircraft of the 482nd BG had used this since September 27, 1943.

In the drab winter months of January and February, General Spaatz regretted the decision by the Combined Chiefs to mount an invasion of mainland Europe around mid-year, before his air forces had demonstrated an ability to end the war by air power alone. While the RAF had been operating at effective strength for some time, the 8th and 9th AFs were only just getting toward the levels anticipated by the Combined Bomber Offensive. Nevertheless, the decision to mount Operation Overlord without waiting

ABOVE: Tuskegee Airmen attend to P-51B-15-NA 44-15569 assigned to the 100th Fighter Squadron, 332nd Fighter Group. USAAF

ABOVE: Sergeant Harold Rogers of the 401st Bombardment Group, activated in England during 1943, with his mascot 'Mister', equipped with his own oxygen mask! USAAF

ABOVE: The Glenn Miller Band gave 800 performances in England, raising morale and gathering dedicated supporters of his inimitable music and its unforgettable renditions of classic jazz pieces. Miller died on December 15, 1944, while flying across the English Channel. *USAAF*

ABOVE: Key to the precise bombing of daylight targets from high altitude, the Norden bombsight was developed before the war yet played a crucial role in allowing bomb aimers to get more of their bombs on target. *USAAF*

further for success with the CBO, would take away some of the strategic targets to which the RAF and AAF had been dedicated.

Bomber Command had been remorseless in burning down the German cities at a level and at a pace unimagined even at the height of blitz on Britain three years earlier, with firestorm raids now a contrived part of imposed destruction, while the Americans were systematically proceeding to destroy industry and the ability of Germany to provide electricity for power, coal for heating homes and food for its people. And through it all, while fighting a determined, resolute and highly experienced cadre of Luftwaffe fighter pilots determined to bring down the bombers at all costs.

Soon, the priority would begin to shift, away from the strategic to the tactical support of the Overlord plan, where the heavy bombers would be used increasingly to prepare for the invasion of Europe. Before that, a new plan, under

Norden Bombsight

One of the most important technological devices to come out of the war was the piece of equipment that did as much to put bombs accurately on target as the aircraft that carried men and machines on their assigned missions. It originated in the creative imagination of a Dutch engineer, Carl Norden, who worked for the Sperry Gyroscope firm from 1911 and then for the US Navy. Focused on a wide range of stabilisation systems, he sought ways to improve the standard Course Setting Bombsight (CSBS) which had been designed by Harry Wimperis for the Royal Naval Air Service in Britain, the standard bomb-dropping aid in the First World War. Norden was tasked by the Navy to come up with a superior design and developed the Mark XI. This required the bomb aimer to calculate the amount of time it would take for the aircraft to reach the target and enter that into a countdown clock. When the target lined up with a set of iron sights the timer was started as the bombardier rotated a telescope round a vertical mount to start a mechanical link to a second sighting scope which moved twice as fast, providing a correct aiming angle when the timer ran out, a second set of sights showing the time to the drop.

Successive phases of development over several years produced a fully synchronous system, which Norden had first believed was impossible to design, and the technology was considered so secret that it incorporated a thermite grenade which could be set off should the aircraft crash in enemy territory, melting all the components. Bomb aimers were sworn to defend its secrets with their lives and Navy aircraft which adopted it had flotation devices removed so that, should the pilots have to ditch, the aircraft would immediately sink and take the Norden's secrets to the seabed.

With this device, 32% of bombs dropped were placed within 1000ft of their planned targets from an average altitude of 21,000ft, a value about the same as that achieved through radar bombing.

the RAF had mounted its first 1000-bomber raid and now the 8th AF had matched that. To the airmen it was a coming of age and from this date the inertia built up through increased momentum, was only going to grow.

Between February 20 and 25 the 8th AF mounted 3300 bomber sorties while the 15th AF flew 500 against a dozen or more factories and assembly plants. Losses were an average 6%, better than in previous months, and the damage caused set back German aircraft production by two months. On March 4, the 8th AF went after Berlin, serving notice that the Allied bombers could attack any target in Germany at will. Two days later, and again two days after that, American B-17s struck Berlin a second and third time but there were heavy loses, with 69 out of 672 that reached the target falling on March 6 and 37 out of 539 heavy bombers falling on March 8.

With fighters now pressing their escort duties throughout the flight path, bomber patterns were more consistent, the attention of the enemy aircraft diverted to the increasing numbers of P-51s tangling with the Bf 109s and the Fw 190s. But this was taking a toll on Allied fighters too, with 11 lost out of 801 on March 6 and 18 of 891 on March 8. The job of escorting the bombers was deliberated upon and approval given for the American fighters to leap ahead of the massed formations and engage the enemy before they could fall on the lumbering bombers, trailing along at little more than half their speed.

When they understood what was happening, many German fighter leaders were disgusted. During the Battle of Britain, they had been prevented from using the same tactic by the direct orders of Hermann Göring, head of the Luftwaffe, who demanded that their Messerschmitt Bf 109Es stayed close around the bombers. Now the tables were turned, the Germans were on the defensive and knew that this tactic would work in favour of the bombers.

Moreover, it was eating into the Luftwaffe's reserves and this American use of aggressive air power and defensive screening was knocking down far more enemy fighters than ever before. During February and March the Jagdwaffe lost around 800 day fighters where once they would have hunted with impunity.

This was a tipping point for the Luftwaffe and in the run-up to the D-Day landings (Operation Overlord), it served the dual purpose of protecting the bomber formations while eroding the ability of the fighter forces to protect the beaches during the Normandy landings. And it was this next war front that began to swing the operational applications of the entire Army Air Forces toward the single objective of liberating occupied Europe and marching on Germany itself. In any measure of the importance of the Allied bombing campaign, especially the Combined Bomber Offensive, the collapse of the Luftwaffe's ability to take and hold possession of the sky was probably the single most important part of preparing the ground for invasion.

In October 1943 the 9th Air Force, a new air force and not the one which had been created for the Mediterranean war, had been set up in England with the task of supporting Overlord. Composed of medium bombers, fighter-bombers, troop carriers and support aircraft it was the largest single tactical air force in the world, a record which stands unchallenged today and one which is unlikely ever to be broken. ✪

Chapter 10: Supreme Endeavours 1944-1947

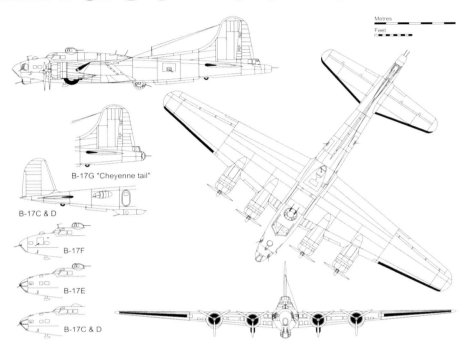

Metres

Feet

B-17G "Cheyenne tail"

B-17C & D

B-17F

B-17E

B-17C & D

ABOVE: During its protracted career with the USAAF, the Flying Fortress underwent considerable improvement, visually defined largely by its evolved nose area, resulting in the B-17G with chin turret. VIA DAVID BAKER

The Supreme Allied Commander, General Dwight D. Eisenhower, set up his headquarters in England alongside Gen. Spaatz's new United States Strategic Air Forces (USSTAF) which had been established out of the 8th AF on February 23, 1944, especially to re-configure the general administrative command and control of Allied forces com-

ing up to D-Day, June 6, 1944. The strategic planning staff remained intact and held authority over the 9th AF and the British 2nd Tactical Air Force, which were the operational arms of the Allied Expeditionary Air Forces (AEAF). To some degree the operations of the 12th and 15th Air Forces were also embraced by USSTAF and VIII Bomber Command was inactivated, on paper.

North American Aviation P-51

Flown for the first time on October 25, 1940, in response to a British requirement for a fighter it could purchase for RAF fighter units, the NA-73 model was powered by a 1100hp Allison V-1710-F3R engine. Production began quickly, designated P-51 because under the terms of the purchase agreement two examples had to be supplied to the Army for evaluation. The first of those took to the air on May 20, 1941, but the USAAC was slow to realise its potential, only rushing to order 310 after Pearl Harbor. Britain had already proposed installation of the Rolls-Royce Merlin for which a lip intake for the up-draught carburettor was necessary. The modified variant, with a US-built Merlin, the Packard V-1650, was the P-51B which carried four 20mm cannon in the wings. Further development through the P-51C led to more powerful engines and the P-51D had a bubble canopy and lowered fuselage upper deck aft to the tail, which considerably improved pilot visibility. It was powered by the 1490hp V-1650-7 engine. By January 1944 the aircraft was operating well into German skies, the range of 1300 miles being achieved by increasing internal fuel capacity from 184 gallons to 269 gallons, extended to 2080 miles with the adoption of two 110 gallon drop tanks. With a performance outstripping any other US fighter of its day, the P-51 was capable of staying with the heavy bombers to any target anywhere in occupied Europe. Equipped with six 0.50in guns, the P-51 was ordered in large blocks due to its essential and unique role in being able to conduct close escort – the USAAF never compromised on range for its escort fighter. Moreover, the aircraft's ability to match almost anything the Luftwaffe could put in the air brought it success for its pilots, many increasing their personal scores on the P-51D, of which more than 15,000 would be built, and flown by many operators after the war.

LENGTH	32.25ft
WING SPAN	37ft
HEIGHT	12.2ft
GROSS WEIGHT	11,600lb
MAXIMUM SPEED	437mph
CRUISING SPEED	362mph
CEILING	41,900ft
RANGE	950 miles

ABOVE: The North American Aviation P-51D which would play a significant role in the defence of daylight bomber formations, was a vital factor in the dramatic survival rates among bombers on accompanied missions from early 1944, that and the fighter's ability to engage with the Jagdwaffe and degrade the attacks. NAA

ABOVE: Analysts of the 7th Reconnaissance Group at Chalgrove pore over photographs from a British automated film processing machine which could turn out 900 prints an hour. USAAF

AIR FORCE PERSONNEL STRENGTH 1907-1949

Year	Strength
1940	51,165
1941	152,125
1942	764,415
1943	2,197,114
1944	2,372,292
1945	2,282,259
1946	455,515
1947	305,827
1948	387,730
1949	419,347

Throughout 1943 there had been concerted analysis of the need to resupply the invasion beachheads and to replenish troops on shore and increase their numbers at a rate exceeding the ability of the enemy to move ground forces into the area. It had been decided that, had the rail transportation system been left intact the invasion would fail within days and the test of whether tactical air power could be used to such effect was more than an academic exercise.

RIGHT: C-47A Skytrains deliver gliders and paratroops to the Normandy area on June 6, 1944. USAAF

But another, equally vital necessity, was to drive the Luftwaffe out of Western Europe and across to the East and for that Pointblank had been a decided success, with the 8th AF attacking production factories and assembly plants.

Originally scheduled for June 5 but delayed a day to secure a window in the weather, the long awaited invasion of the Normandy beaches began in the early hours of June 6 supported by what was the largest aerial armada ever assembled in support of a single objective. For weeks the operational readiness of squadrons had been a top priority, the response of the enemy uncertain, resistance to the landings largely unknown and the outcome in doubt for several days after the first waves of soldiers had walked ashore and the initial parachute drops had been made.

More than 4,000 aircraft with the 8th AF had been made ready for action this day, with an equal number plus 1,300 troop-carrying aircraft at the disposal of General Brereton's 9th AF. In all, more than 10,000 aircraft, of which 2200 American, British and Canadian bombers attacked targets along the coast and further inland.

Huge losses were suffered by the French civilians as villages and towns were flattened to prevent German reinforcements reaching the advancing allied forces, roads and coastal areas strafed and bombed to destroy all infrastructure of use to a defending force. But France had suffered greatly already and throughout the five years of German occupation and attacks by British and American air forces, some 68,000 French civilian had been killed by bombing alone – more than had been killed in the British Isles during the same period. In addition, more than 100,000 were injured and 432,000 houses completely destroyed in air raids.

Most astonishing of all was the almost total lack of enemy air activity to counter the invasion, only three Fw 190 fighters being chased off and only 22 Luftwaffe aircraft attacking the shipping after nightfall. Moreover, VIII Fighter Command had been unable to make contact with enemy aircraft in the air during an early morning offensive sweep. But there had been plenty of target

Douglas C-47

Arguably one of the most famous aircraft in the world, the Douglas C-47 Skytrain was a development of the DC-3, which had its origin as the Douglas Sleeper Transport (DST), first flown on December 17, 1935. This all-metal twin-engine transport had evolved from the DC-1, which had made its first flight on July 1, 1933, at the behest of Trans-World Airlines executive Jack Frye. Then the vice-president in charge of TWA operations, Frye had wanted a competitor to United Air Lines' Boeing 247, which the manufacturer insisted on delivering only when it had fulfilled the order backlog from that airline. Fry requested bids for a substitute which could be delivered quicker. Donald Douglas came up with the DC-1 and when other bids fell short he got the contract. This led to the DC-2, a stretched version, which flew for the first time on May 11, 1934, and was also used by TWA.

The DC-3 was produced to a requirement from American Airlines for a sleeper service to replace its Curtiss Condor biplanes and to compete with TWA's DC-2 fleet. Douglas fitted the basic DC-2 with more powerful engines, launching a type of which more than 16,000 would be built in a wide range of variants and for a large number of customers. But the Army first purchased a variant of the DC-2 in 1936 and found it 50mph faster than any existing transport aircraft it operated. This type went under a series of designations including C-32, C-33, C-34 and C-39, depending on the engine and other fitments. When war broke out several aircraft operating with airlines were sequestered.

By 1940 the Army specified several changes, including a strengthened floor, large cargo door on the port side, a hoist and more powerful engines. Operating weight grew from 25,000lb to 29,300lb and some to 35,000lb and initial versions were powered by the 1,200 hp Pratt & Whitney R-1830-92. From the time it entered service with the USAAC in 1941, the C-47 Skytrain was the aerial packhorse which had exactly the right performance, size and operating capabilities the Army was looking for, extending its reach to every theatre of war.

LENGTH	63.75ft
WING SPAN	95.5ft
HEIGHT	17ft
GROSS WEIGHT	31,000lb
MAXIMUM SPEED	224mph
CRUISING SPEED	160mph
CEILING	26,400ft
RANGE	1600 miles

ABOVE: The ruins of Cologne, the familiar twin spires of the cathedral standing amid the rubble and the devastation, its bridges all but completely destroyed. USAAF

ABOVE: The crew of the B-29 (42-24598) "Waddy's Wagon", 497th Bomb Group, pose to duplicate the caricatures on their aircraft, lost on January 9, 1945. USAAF

opportunity, had the Jagdwaffe been in a position to take advantage of the day. A massive pre-dawn raid by 1361 B-17s and B-24s dropped 2,944 tons of bombs on the coastal batteries and shore defences, most having to be dropped through the heavy overcast skies using radar, the last bombs being dropped ten minutes before the first waves went ashore. Most fuses were set to detonate on contact, reducing the number of craters to impede the anticipated advance of allied soldiers.

Throughout the first day several hundred medium bombers attacked peripheral areas to seal off defensive units of the German Army, hitting roads and transport links outside the area immediately accessed by the allied troops coming ashore, and carrying our harrying attacks on roads and camps. The major pre-invasion raids quickly changed to tactical air action on the day itself, 528 heavy bombers being dispatched to hit chokepoints in Thury, Harcourt, St.-Lô,

and Caen. Heavy cloud prevented all but three groups returning home. Nevertheless, 566 B-24s destroyed all of Caen except for a single bridge, which seriously delayed the 21st Panzer Division.

In addition to these operations by the USAAF, on the night of June 5/6 the RAF flew 1211 sorties, with 1012 aircraft attacking ten artillery batteries covering the invasion beaches, flattening wide areas of the immediate inland zones. A major contribution from the RAF involving 483 bombers on the night of June 8/9 saw the first use of the 12,000 lb Tallboy bomb against the Saumer railway tunnel, which effectively sealed off a major access route for the German Army, bringing down 10,000 tons of earth in the process.

In all, 11,950 aircraft of the USAAF and the RAF were directly involved in the Normandy landings, 7722 dispatched by the 8th and 9th AFs alone. Losses came to 71 aircraft, brought down by flak and anti-aircraft fire. What was needed over the next days and weeks was a support through tactical air strikes by the combined air forces and a resumption, specifically by RAF Bomber Command, of the strategic assault on German towns and cities while the 8th AF got back to targeting the industrial heartland of the Reich. In the period June 6 to July 31 the RAF and the 89th and 9th AFs dropped 35,500 tons of bombs involving 15,000 sorties on freight yards alone, while 16,000 sorties and 24,500 tons of bombs were directed exclusively against bridge targets. An average of more than 1000 tons a day. Even by mid-July, these raids had successfully reduced the volume of German freight traffic by 57%.

In August and September the Allied forces pushed 400 miles eastward and the pace became a matter of logistical supply, new supply routes

for gasoline and maintaining the requirement for munitions, plus the day-to-day supplies required for the ground troops, limited the rate of progress as the front line advanced up toward Paris. By mid-September, however, the US 3rd Army could advance only at the pace of the supply chain and was regulated by that factor alone. German forces were being overwhelmed at an increasing rate but dangerously short on gasoline, the Allied forces were brought to a halt along the Moselle River and the Siegfried defences.

On April 30, 1945, Hitler committed suicide and on May 8 the war was over. In the first week of May the 8th AF flew 4147.1 tons of emergency food, dropped to the starving populations of distressed and famine-stricken Netherlands and surrounding areas. With the war technically still going on, the Germans acquiesced to this humanitarian assistance, and together with the RAF, US air forces dropped in total 11,000 tons of food rations.

As a final mark of gratitude for the work they had done to keep the bombers armed and flying and the aircrew equipped and fed, around 30,000 ground personnel were taken on sightseeing tours by air of the targets they had sent the aircraft to bomb. Yet even as the aftermath of war in Europe was drawing together the forces of a new confrontation, continuing to suck in ever greater munitions and logistical requirements from America, the USAAF was gearing up for a major air assault on mainland Japan.

On March 12, 1944, the Joint Chiefs of Staff had ordered Ad. Chester W. Nimitz, chief of naval operations in the Pacific, to seize the Marianas islands for the use of Boeing B-29 Superfortress bombers by June 15, so that this mighty aircraft could make its operational debut against targets on mainland Japan from bases hewn out of these atolls. Consisting of Saipan, Tinian and Guam, the Marianas were about 1500 miles from Tokyo and would operate as an effective base from which to operate, easily resupplied by sea.

On August 6, 1945, a single B-29 piloted by Col. Paul W. Tibbets, Jr., dropped one bomb on the city of Hiroshima – an atomic device which had been developed with the help of British and German scientists, the latter having fled Nazi Germany before the war. It destroyed 4.7 square miles of the city and was followed three days later by a second bomb, on Nagasaki. On August 10 the Japanese decided that they could not go on and formally declared acceptance of the surrender terms offered, the formal ceremony coming in Tokyo Bay aboard the USS *Missouri* on September 2.

But signs on the international stage presented a forbidding glimpse of a dark age of communism, threatening to devour the remaining free countries of Europe not yet in the grip of Soviet oppression. Seeking to undo the shame of Brest Litovsk, when the Bolshevik government had sued for peace in March 1918, giving up Finland, most of its Baltic territories and the Ukraine, Stalin was holding fast to territory on which its troops came to a halt in May 1945. The eastern sector of a divided Germany, as well as Poland, Czechoslovakia, Ukraine, Hungary, Bulgaria and Romania, were now under direct influence from Moscow. As Winston Churchill was to say in a speech in Fulton Missouri on March 5, 1946, "From Stettin in the Baltic to Trieste in the Adriatic, an iron curtain has descended across the continent." ✪

COMBAT AEROPLANES ON HAND BY MAJOR TYPE

Year	Total	Heavy bombers	Medium/light bombers	Fighters
1939	1269	39	738	492
1940	1356	92	639	625
1941	4002	288	1544	2170
1942	11,139	2079	3757	5303
1943	26,734	8118	6741	11,875
1944	40,157	13,790	9169	17,198
1945 (Aug)	39,192	13,930	8463	16,799

ABOVE: Named Bockscar, the B-29 that dropped the second atom bomb on Nagasaki on August 9, 1945, is seen here at its base in the Marianas but is today preserved at the National Museum of the US Air Force.

Chapter 11: Cold War challenges 1947-1960

ABOVE: A pile of aluminium scrap in 1946. Decommissioned B-29s were taken apart on Tinian in the Marianas, a scene typical of several hundred air bases around the world where aircraft were broken up where they were rather than shipped back. USAF

Immediately after the war, the headlong rush to disarm took place with an almost embarrassing haste. In September 1945 the Army Air Forces had 2,282,000 men on the payroll and 68,400 aircraft in the inventory. It was the largest assembly of air power in the world and had a greater strike potential than all the Axis air forces combined. Only the Royal Air Force in the UK came anywhere near the awesome power of the US Army Air Forces.

Within the last 18 months of the war, the United States had acquired technology for gas turbine engines which were already being designed into the first generation of US jet fighters, while a new class of bomber capable of delivering weapons on targets half a world away, without landing or making use of mid-air refuelling, was about to go into production. Air-to-air missiles were being talked about and some were on the drawings boards of companies specialised in the new sciences, while new generations of advanced early-warning radar were being introduced.

The story of how the air forces became an independent arm of the military really began with the campaigning zeal of General Arnold for separation of the air forces from the army, a move which had already begun with a memorandum subsequently dubbed as the 'declaration of independence'. Dated July 21, 1943, it was a defining document from General George C. Marshall reasserting the four sectional responsibilities of US land-based air power: strategic aviation to destroy the enemy nation; tactical air power to destroy its military on the battlefield; defence of the US mainland; and logistical support of these objectives.

In a seminal report dated November 1945, General Arnold envisaged a defence force of "three autonomous services, each of which has an equal and direct share of the total responsibility". The success of the strategic bombing campaign against Germany and Japan was a demonstration of the coming of age for an independent US Air Force. The tools to wage strategic war against aggressor nations had been supplemented by the advent of atomic weapons, of which the United States would retain a monopoly until Russia achieved technological parity in 1949.

With amazing prescience, Arnold argued that soon "aircraft, piloted or pilotless, will move at speeds far beyond the velocity of sound," prophesying that guided missiles would travel between continents, asserting that "until such time as guided missiles are so developed (and) there is no further need for manned aircraft, research in the field of 'conventional' aircraft of improved design must continue".

It was this emphasis on the future design of combat aircraft that drove Arnold to extricate the designs of the Whittle jet engine from the UK and to launch a major development programme in the US based on gas turbine propulsion, first from Britain and then from captured German engines and associated technical research results.

On September 7, 1947, Chief Justice Fred M. Vinson, administered the oath of office to the first Secretary of Defense, James V. Forrestal, setting into being the National Military Establishment – the Department of Defense. The following day W. Stuart Symington was sworn in as Secretary of the Air Force, followed by General Carl Spaatz as the first Chief of Staff, United States Air Force, on September 26.

Succeeding Arnold, Spaatz foresaw an air force based around the Marshall proposal and set up Strategic Air Command (SAC), Tactical Air Command (TAC), and Air Defense Command (ADC), reflecting the combat commands which had been established during the Second World War. The headquarters for Continental Air Command, set up initially as a planning group for demobilisation on December 1, 1948, became HQ for Strategic Air Command, which had first call on men and materiel. It would also serve as a coordinating agency for tactical aviation, air defence and training of the Air National Guard.

AIR FORCE PERSONNEL STRENGTH 1950-1957	
Year	Strength
1950	411,277
1951	788,381
1952	973,474
1953	977,593
1954	947,918
1955	959,946
1956	909,958
1957	919,835

Lockheed P-80

The invitation to build what would become America's first all-jet combat aircraft in full operational service came on May 17, 1943, when Lockheed was asked to capitalise on in-house work it had already being conducting on jet concepts and complete an XP-80 prototype within 180 days. A design team led by Clarence 'Kelly' Johnson beat that by two days and the first flight took place on January 8, 1944, powered by a 3000lb thrust H-1 engine, replaced on successive aircraft by the 3750lb thrust General Electric J33. Contracts for 5000 aircraft were placed with Lockheed and North American Aviation but 3000 were cancelled on VJ Day, deliveries commencing in December. Long before that, on October 20, 1944, four YP-80As were sent to Italy but none saw combat and a spate of crashes began. The aircraft was very different to prop-types, with difficult slow speed handling and the sluggish acceleration of all first-generation jets made conversion fraught with hazards. Top scoring air ace Major Richard Bong lost his life in a P-80A and after further crashes the aircraft was grounded. This ban was lifted by November but there were still difficulties, 61 examples being involved in accidents by September 1946.

The type's service life had begun in December 1945 when three YP-80As were delivered to the 31st Fighter Squadron, 412th Fighter Group, followed by production aircraft replacing that Group's P-51 Mustangs. Almost immediately the AAF began a series of spectacular flights to show off the aircraft's capabilities, Colonel William Councill took just four hours, 13 minutes, 26 seconds, to fly the 2,453.8 miles between Long Beach, California, and La Guardia, New York, at an average speed of 580.93mph with a 310 gallon drop tank. More records toppled as the Army showed off its newest hot ship and entered the P-80 in the first post-war National Air Races.

In 1948, the designation system was changed, the P-80 becoming the F-80, the definitive major production variant being the F-80C, specified below. The P-80C carried six 0.50in guns, two 1000lb bombs or 10 x 5in rocket projectiles. During the Korean War the type was outclassed by Russian jet fighters but on November 7, 1950, Lieutenant Russell J. Brown became the first pilot to shoot down a MiG-15 in the first jet-on-jet combat.

A lack of adequate airfield facilities in South Korea hampered F-80 operations but the type had vindicated itself and some 1715 were built. The design would be reborn as the T-33 trainer, of which a further 6557 were built, and would form the basis for the F-94 Starfire.

LENGTH	34.5ft
WING SPAN	39.9ft
HEIGHT	11.3ft
GROSS WEIGHT	16,856lb
MAXIMUM SPEED	580mph
CRUISING SPEED	439mph
CEILING	42,750ft
RANGE	1380 miles

Tactical Air Command would be managed from new headquarters at Langley Air Force Base, Virginia, inheriting its traditions and its inventory from the legendary 9th and 12th air forces. Air Defense Command would have to get along as best it could with what was left over. And there was, potentially, a lot of excess hardware, but very little of it fit for the postwar Air Force.

The industrialisation of manufacturing, assembly and production had generated vast quantities of hardware. During 1944, almost 70,000 aircraft had been delivered to the Army Air Forces, of which 34% were fighters and almost 36% were bombers of one class or another – almost 200 delivered every day. Most of those were already outdated.

However, despite this rapid demobilisation and with dramatically lower funding now being made available for the Air Force, new aircraft were about to reinvigorate its mission. The Convair B-36 would soon enter service with SAC and the North American B-45 Tornado was about to reach the 47th Bombardment Group as the first jet-powered light tactical bomber.

The F-86 Sabre jet fighter had just flown for the first time and would soon establish a world speed record, and 'Chuck' Yeager had become the first man to fly through the sound barrier in level flight. Elsewhere, Republic was capitalising on its success with the wartime P-47 Thunderbolt by producing a jet successor, the F-84F Thunderjet.

For the future, Boeing was putting the swept-wing, six-jet B-47 medium bomber through its paces. With a bomb load of 20,000lb and a range of 4000 miles, it was a sign of the times that an aircraft which would, by Second World War standards, have been a heavy bomber was now relegated to the 'medium' category.

Following in its tracks, the mighty B-52 Stratofortress, an eight-engine bomber

with a load capacity ultimately extended to 70,000lb and a range of more than 7000 miles. All these futuristic types would be in service within a few years of the Second World War, and one would remain in front-line service right up to the present day.

ABOVE: The scene at Tempelhof airport, Berlin, as a conveyor belt of C-47s and other transport aircraft throw a lifeline between the West and Eastern Europe to the beleaguered citizens of Berlin. USAF

ABOVE: A USAF Douglas C-54 Skymaster, another of the multitude of unsung heroes bringing aid to Berliners during the historic airlift. USAF

BELOW: The P-80 developed as America's first operational jet fighter, F-80 under the new designation codes, introduced in 1948 was the epitome of the new generation of combat aircraft. USAF

ABOVE: A B-29 (44-69963) gets a boost into the air with a RATO (rocket assisted-takeoff) pack fitted to increase the maximum loaded weight of the bomber. *USAF*

While SAC had the first claim on men and aircraft, seeing strategic deterrence as a way to avoid future aggression and the escalating price of the new jet bombers was set against potential cost-saving measures sought through force reduction. For a few years after the war, the strategic bomber force would still have to rely on the piston engine Boeing B-29s and B-50s, each of which cost $509,564 in 1945 money. By comparison, a B-17 cost $187,742, a B-25 Mitchell cost $116,752.

Each new Convair B-36, with hemispheric capability, would cost $4.1 million, or a modest $54 million in 2017 money. This escalation cut deep with a cost-conscious Congress, because the level of expenditure necessary to help win the war against the Axis powers had been very high.

In 1944 America had been spending 37% of its GDP on defence and in 1945 the US government's federal budget had been $92.7 billion, of which $82.9 billion (89%) had been spent on the war. Everything else the government was responsible for received less than $10 billion. This is the reason why serious consideration was given to disbanding a permanent professional military force, eliminating a standing army, drastically reducing the Navy and relying solely on air power to deter any attack, which was deemed to come without warning, swiftly and with great violence.

Calls to disband the US military and save essential funds were countered by the need to robustly protect the United States using the threat of atomic annihilation and the defensive screen of tactical fighters to keep America safe.

To operate an efficient structure Spaatz instructed that of the 16 operational air forces, 11 were to be retained and five disbanded due to a lack of resources. SAC assumed direction of the 8th and 15th Air Forces, TAC the 3rd, 9th and 12th Air Forces, and ADC the 1st, 2nd, 4th, 10th, 11th and 14th Air Forces.

While this new and leaner force was being established, the wholesale reduction of what had been the wartime resources of the Army Air Force went ahead. By April 1946 the USAAF had been cut to 485,000 men and

women and within a year that number fell to 304,000. The best went first, the skilled trades departing to better paid jobs in engineering and manufacturing, the number of trained mechanics dropping from 350,000 to 30,000 while pilots, bombardiers and navigators wanted to stay in – their numbers disproportionate to the requirements of a slimmed down service.

The inventory of aircraft suffered a similar fate, some 35,000 airframes being turned over to the Reconstruction Finance Corporation, a federal organisation set up to dismantle the 'arsenal of democracy'. As production lines spilled out their existing airframes and engines, the Corporation took them straight to the breaker's yard. The total number of airframes on hand dropped from nearly 70,000 in 1944 to 24,000 by the end of 1947, of which little more than 4000 were serviceable and safe to fly. And with fewer aircraft came a reduced need of airfields, only 177 in 1947 remaining from a total of 783 in 1943. There were now fewer landing strips than there had been in 1940.

NEW THREATS
The United States Strategic Air Forces in Europe (USSTAF) had been re-designated as the United States Air Forces in Europe (USAFE) on August 7, 1945, and tasked with managing the demilitarisation of its former Axis enemies under the command of General LeMay. Within 18 months it had been reduced from a force of 17,000 aircraft to 2000 and

ABOVE: A legacy fighter from the Second World War, this F-51 Mustang finds taxying difficult in wet conditions during the Korean War. *USAF*

from 500,000 personnel to 75,000.

This proceeded successfully, despite the uneasy relationship which now existed between the Western Allies and the Soviets. Then suddenly, on June 22, 1948, the Russians cut off all road and rail access to West Berlin, managed by British, French and American sectors. At a stroke, more than two million Berliners were left facing potential starvation – since there was no way of bringing in the vital supplies they needed over land. Yet between June 26, 1948, and September 30, 1949, an Anglo-American airlift transported 2.325 million tons of food, fuel and supplies into Berlin, 77% of which had been flown in by the USAF.

BUDGETS FOR US ARMED FORCES 1950-1957

Fiscal year	Army	Navy	Air Force
1950	4.2	4.1	4.7
1951	19.4	12.5	15.9
1952	21.6	16.1	22.3
1953	13.6	12.5	20.3
1954	13.0	9.4	11.4
1955	7.1	9.4	11.4
1956	7.1	9.6	15.7
1957	7.8	10.4	17.7

Note: Figures are in millions of US dollars

ABOVE: Providing close air support, the Air Force lends the Army a hand as both fighting services learn to work effectively with each other on the battlefield. US ARMY

ABOVE: Despite the improvement in fuel consumption of later jet fighters, their short range frequently called for a helpful top-up, courtesy of a Boeing KB-50J. USAF

This ability to respond rapidly to crisis and to become a tool for political and diplomatic resolution transformed the way the Air Force was measured, both in worth and value. The Berlin Airlift was a humanitarian effort of extraordinary proportions – it mobilised the effective assets retained from a force of ageing transport types to overcome a new

challenge presented by an aggressive state. The new model USAF had already proven it could get the job done – not through fighting but through sheer logistical prowess.

When the pro-Soviet communist faction seized power in Czechoslovakia in 1948, General Lucius D. Clay, the US Military Governor in Germany, sent a message to Washington asserting that war between America and Russia might "come with dramatic suddenness". Those fears were reinforced on August 29, 1949, when the Soviet Union detonated its first atomic device.

Seven and a half months later, on April 14, 1950, the National Security Council presented President Harry S. Truman with NSC-68, a position paper which would become the 'Truman doctrine', which stated that containment of the global communist expansion required the development of thermonuclear weapons (the hydrogen bomb) and a national strategy of deterrence based upon the belief that the Soviet Union would not risk aggression if it became certain that the US would respond with overwhelming nuclear force.

The implications were shattering: the atomic bomb had been 1800 times the explosive yield of the biggest conventional bomb dropped during the Second World War (22,000lb) but the thermonuclear bomb would demonstrate that it could be up to 2000 times more powerful than the bomb dropped on Nagasaki.

Matters became yet more precarious with the unexpected invasion of South Korea by the North on June 25, 1950. The United Nations had been formed in October 1945 to govern a peace-loving world of independent states but one of its first acts was now to sanction the use of military action to suppress unwarranted aggression.

In a strange mix of what would become the last conventional air war and the first war of the jet age, the USAF had its first test as an

North American Aviation F-86 Sabre

The design of the USAF's most famous first-generation fighter originated in the US Navy FJ-1 Fury, a straight-wing carrier based aircraft which was modified with a swept-wing for the Air Force. This wing came directly from research work liberated from Germany at the end of the war, which showed better performance toward the transonic region. The first XP-86 flew on October 1, 1947, powered by a single 3750lb thrust Allison J35 jet engine and in the spring of 1948 it became the first aircraft to safely exceed Mach 1 in a shallow dive.

The first production order for the F-86 was placed on December 28, 1947, and the first F-86A, specified below, took to the air on May 18, 1948. The type was in volume production when the Korean War broke out in 1950 and ushered in the era of the jet fighter when it went into combat against the Russian MiG-15. With modifications to the wing resulting from this experience, the type so equipped was re-designated F-86F and subsequent variants included the F-86D carrying a nose-mounted radar and an afterburner, and the F-86H tactical fighter-bomber.

The F-86 remained in production until December 1956 after almost 10,000 had been built. Many were sold to foreign air forces. Standard armament included six 0.50in guns, three each side of the forward fuselage, with options on two 1000lb bombs or 16 x 5in rocket projectiles. The 5700lb thrust J47 engine fitted to the F-86D had an afterburner thrust of 7630lb.

LENGTH	37.5ft
WING SPAN	39.1ft
HEIGHT	14.7ft
GROSS WEIGHT	16,357lb
MAXIMUM SPEED	675mph
CRUISING SPEED	527mph
CEILING	48,300ft
RANGE	785 miles

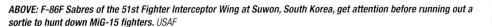

ABOVE: F-86F Sabres of the 51st Fighter Interceptor Wing at Suwon, South Korea, get attention before running out a sortie to hunt down MiG-15 fighters. USAF

ABOVE: B-26 medium bombers hit targets in Wonsan as further tactical support for the ground campaign to drive the communists from South Korea, a UN operation to evict the invader. *USAF*

1248 aircraft in the 37 months of combat.

In all, the force was built up to 20 groups which together completed 720,980 sorties plus 167,552 from the US Navy and 44,873 by other UN-sanctioned air forces including those from Britain.

The FEAF's bombers had delivered 467,000 tons of bombs and napalm on targets right across North Korea in a strategic assault reminiscent of the raids on Japan, but it also supported tactical needs from ground forces and much was learned about integrating air force units as a separate fighting entity. During the conflict, the first jet air battles had taken place, the Russian MiG-15 acquitting itself with distinction, frequently let down only by a less than effective performance from its pilots. The FEAF lost 1466 aircraft with 1729 casualties.

With the war still raging, on October 31, 1952, the prototype of an American hydrogen bomb was detonated on the island of Eleugelab leaving a crater one mile across and two miles deep. The strategic deterrent received top priority both in the government and the Air Force and the combination of the hydrogen bomb and lighter nuclear weapons fuelled a dramatic expansion in Strategic Air Command and its ability to deliver the ultimate punch.

At the outset of the Korean War in 1950, SAC had 962 tactical aircraft of which 58 were the new

independent fighting force. The war began during the tenure of President Harry S. Truman and would end, with an uneasy armistice on July 27, 1953, with President Dwight D. Eisenhower in the White House. Between those dates the size of the Far East Air Force (FEAF), established in 1944 to fight the Japanese, had grown in personnel from 33,635 to 112,188, with an average of

B-29 Superfortress

Boeing responded to a surge of interest in very long range bombers with carrying capacity of up to 20,000lb as a result of worsening relations with Germany and Japan, recognising that America might have to fight enemies at great distance from its own territory. Competing designs from Consolidated, Douglas and Lockheed set the scene for a surge in large comber designs which would underpin requirements in the early post-war years.

The B-29 was an enormous venture, both for Boeing and the Army Air Force and presented production difficulties too, not least because of its sheer size. Frequent upgrades meant that aircraft straight off the line had to be sent for installation of the latest upgrade kits before delivery. The B-29 was unique in US bomber design in that the cockpit comprised the nose of the aircraft, a 'stepless' design which lacked the separate cockpit area on top of the extreme forward fuselage.

The B-29 was powered by four 2200hp Wright R-3350 radial engine fitted with a dual supercharger for high altitude work. Armament comprised four remotely controlled barbettes each with two 0.50in guns plus tail armament of three guns. The maximum bomb load was 20,000lb. The B-29D introduced the more powerful 3500hp Pratt & Whitney R-4360 Wasp Major engines but this was re-designated the B-50 which first flew on June 25, 1947 and would be the first new type introduced with Strategic Air Command. Adaptation of the B-29 into the C-97 Stratofreighter led to the postwar Stratocruiser, a commercial airliner capable of carrying up to 100 passengers on its double-deck configuration. After the war, the Air Force employed the KB-29 as a cargo lifter and refuelling tanker, greatly expanding the capabilities of the Air Force to project its influence beyond the range of existing aircraft. Several B-29s found their way to Russia, primarily aircraft that got off course flying back from the China raids in 1944, and the type was urgently requested by the Soviets as part of the Lend-Lease arrangement. That request was denied but the Russians built a version of their own anyway, the Tupolev Tu-4. Impediments faced by the Russians stemmed from different steel gauges and the metric system of measurement which rendered straight duplication extremely difficult.

LENGTH	99ft
WING SPAN	141.25ft
HEIGHT	29.6ft
GROSS WEIGHT	71,360lb
MAXIMUM SPEED	358mph
CRUISING SPEED	230mph
CEILING	31,850ft
RANGE	4100 miles

LEFT: This B-29 is caught dropping 1000lb bombs on targets in North Korea, effectively using precision bombing learned from the war against Japanese industrial facilities. *USAF*

ABOVE: *Precursor to the Boeing B-52 Stratofortress, a B-47B gets assistance from jet assisted takeoff rockets, April 1954. In 1959 Strategic Air Command had 1540 aircraft of this type in the inventory.* USAF

ABOVE: *The XB-70 carried the hopes of many senior officers in Strategic Air Command for a supersonic answer to the vulnerability of subsonic bombers n enemy airspace.* USAF

B-36 and RB-36, a type which was now fitted with twin pods of paired turbojet engines attached to pylons beneath the outer wings outboard of the six reciprocating engines. With the ability to stay in the air for up to 50 hours with internal belly tanks, the type was admirably suited to high altitude, long range reconnaissance, a task which carried it to the borders of the USSR and beyond. But the aircraft was a hybrid mix of propeller and jet, an intermediary, complex and expensive to maintain, and slow. The rest of the SAC inventory consisted of Second World War types. But by 1960, SAC boasted 2992 tactical aircraft including an all-jet bomber force supported by KC-135 jet and KC-97 piston-engine tankers.

But the emphasis on massive retaliation to aggression also fuelled concerns about US vulnerability and the Air Force had also begun to address the secondary issue of air defence, expanding the budget for the new Air Defense Command (ADC), separate to Continental Air Command from 1951, which established a radar warning line just north of the Canadian border. Complemented by new generations of air defence fighters such as the Lockheed F-94 Starfire, the distant early warning radar line was extended from Alaska along the Arctic Circle to Greenland. As small and lightweight tactical nuclear weapons became available, derivatives were used in air-to-air missiles capable of being fired by interceptors into massed Soviet bomber formations, should they attack North America over the North Pole – the shortest route.

New aircraft began to appear and new technologies were applied to improve existing designs. A new 'century-series' of fighters began as the numbering system reached 99, the F-99 being the unmanned Bomarc air-defence missile. The first of these 'century-series' types was the world's first fighter to achieve supersonic speed in level flight, the North American F-100 Super Sabre. Operational with Tactical Air Command from September 1954, the type was joined by the first delta-wing aircraft to enter Air Force service, the Convair F-102 Delta Dagger, designed from the outset as a missile carrier for air defence using the Hughes Falcon, some capable of carrying a nuclear warhead. This was the first dual weapon system of the missile age and became operational in 1956.

But technology was helping advance the capabilities of existing aircraft too. When the F-102 encountered unexpected drag at transonic speed, the NACA's Richard Whitcomb delivered a solution in the form of the area rule. Discovered by Otto Frenzl in Germany during the war, it offered improvements by reshaping the constant diameter of the fuselage – a regular tube – into a Coke-bottle shape, avoiding the onset of strong shock waves by pinching the fuselage in at the place where the wing was attached. This made the total area of fuselage and wing at that point as equal in cross-section as the forward, more bulbous fuselage. Area rule influenced the design of both the F-102 and the F-106 Delta Dart, a more powerful redesigned derivative.

In seeking an advantage over the enemy, the Air Force wanted a supersonic bomber and achieved that in part with the General Dynamics B-58 Hustler, of which 86 were ordered. This Mach 2 bomber was introduced in 1960 but its comparatively short range and limited weapons load made it less useful that had been hoped and it was withdrawn in 1970. But the ultimate objective of a Mach 3 strategic bomber was epitomised by the XB-70 Valkyrie, a remarkably advanced aircraft capable of very high penetration into enemy airspace. It combined Mach 3 with search-and-strike capability for seeking out Soviet rail-mobile missiles and destroying them. Developed during the second half of the 1950s, it was cancelled by a cost-conscious Kennedy administration in 1961 but two XB-70s were built and flown. ✪

ABOVE: *Convair F-106 Delta Darts from the 5th Fighter Interceptor Squadron, over Mount Rushmoor. Air defence became a vital counterpoint to strategic retaliation as conventional response to an attack on the United States took over a more important role.* USAF

Chapter 12: Vietnam

ABOVE: The Republic F-105D Thunderchief with a full warload of MN117 750lb bombs over Vietnam in 1968. USAF

AIR FORCE PERSONNEL STRENGTH 1958-1969

Year	Strength
1958	871,156
1959	840,028
1960	812,213
1961	820,490
1962	883,330
1963	868,644
1964	855,802
1965	823,633
1966	886,350
1967	897,426
1968	904,759
1969	862,062

The USAF had not long re-established a new combat rationale after the Korean War when it was required to provide further support for America's allies in distant places, whether in suppressing local aggression or internal subversion. United States National Security Council document NSC-162/2, signed by President Eisenhower on October 30, 1953, ensured the American nuclear shield would protect friendly countries, which would in turn use their own armed forces to suppress disruptive acts of violence or terrorism, from internal or external sources. In this way America would not need to get directly involved.

It was expected that these countries would call upon the conventional might of the United States to help with those tasks only in dire circumstances. This was why the United States provided a willing hand to disrupt what Secretary of Defence Robert McNamara called "the domino" effect, whereby a series of communist incursions might flow across borders and politically prejudice an entire region. And so the concept of flexible response began to influence the shape and structure of the US Air Force, but there was considerable debate about whether that should be achieved internally by revolution or evolution. As it turned out it was neither but rather by a process of osmosis.

The US Air Force had been an extraordinarily willing helper on the world stage, in evacuating escapees from communist aggression, using transport aircraft and routes in and out of beleaguered states, in engaging in famine relief and providing succour to victims of natural disasters. It had been doing that since the food aid drops on Holland in the Low Countries in 1945 when millions of civilians faced starvation at the end of the war. But it was becoming apparent that not every political, or even military, crisis could

be averted with the threat of nuclear retaliation alone. The United States began a concerted effort to train up military personnel in friendly countries, including Vietnam, where the folly of a politically flexible response really became apparent.

A meeting between General Thomas S. Power and Secretary of Defence McNamara explains the way the Air Force evolved during the 1960s and the tenures of Presidents Kennedy and Johnson. General Power explained to McNamara that the Single Integrated Operational Plan, or SIOP (the general war plan involving nuclear weapons, formally instituted on July 1, 1961), required the use of massive force involving, for instance, the destruction of entire countries in the East European sector to inhibit Soviet capabilities. To McNamara, a statistician who had worked the numbers during the AAF raids on Japan, this seemed illogical and a new doctrine of 'proportional response' emerged.

The US Army Chief of Staff, General Maxwell D. Taylor, had greatly influenced President Kennedy's decision to focus on conventional warfare and match a proportional response to the level of provocation. It sought to build up military forces to whatever level was necessary to bring about the desired solution. And it was exactly that policy of reciprocal, reactive action that got the Air Force into difficulties in South-East Asia, when the political judgment of the civilian leadership in Washington was to use only proportionate force as a measured response rather than setting a goal and allowing the military to reach it by whatever means necessary.

The involvement of the USAF in Vietnam began during France's struggle to retain control of Indochina (Vietnam) when Ho Chi Minh, the leader of the communist rebels, sought to evict the French and gain control

of the whole country, eventually settling for a division into North and South similar to that settled on Korea at the armistice in 1953. After what amounted to a victory for Ho Chi Minh in 1955, the Americans continued to send military assistance to South Vietnam. USAF advisers helped to modernise the country's air force, which had been established in 1951.

This was a volte face for the USAF, imposed by American political imperatives; military supplies had been parachuted to Ho Chi Minh during the Second World War so that he could fight the Japanese occupation forces. As US aid to South Vietnam expanded between 1961 and the end of 1963, increasing quantities of military aid flowed from the North to the guerrilla forces of the Viet Cong in the South, who were encircling Saigon. The Kennedy administration sought to limit the clandestine aid provided but an increasing amount of US equipment was being flown in to support the government of South Vietnam against the terrorists.

With the code name Farm Gate, the

ABOVE: Late of the Pacific air war in World War 2, General Curtis LeMay became a controversial figure in the escalating war in Vietnam, advocating massive strategic bombing campaigns against North Vietnam, stifled by political manipulation. USAF

ABOVE: The Douglas A-1E Skyraider became a useful workhorse for slow-speed ground-attack, strafing and tactical strike in Vietnam. USAF

USAF AIRCRAFT IN VIETNAM AND THAILAND

Year	Total	F-105	F-4	B-52
1965	460	79	18	-
1966	889	126	188	-
1967	1429	129	182	10
1968	1768	108	218	28
1969	1840	70	288	39
1970	1602	65	212	44
1971	1132	12	216	44
1972	989	30	355	54
1973	675	24	218	53

Note: Figures are for June 30 each year; additional B-52s, between 30 (in 1965) and 150 (in 1972) were based on Guam in addition to 45 FB-111s in 1972.

ABOVE: A Douglas A-1E of the 34th Tactical Group based at Bien Hoa supports a patrol package low over the paddy fields of South Vietnam on June 25, 1965. USAF

aid programme quickly escalated beyond plausible denial and General Taylor sought US ground forces for South Vietnam to buttress the native army. Contrary to this view, General Curtis LeMay, now US Air Force Chief of Staff, proposed the use of massive air power against North Vietnam to wipe out the government and unite the country, which became the agreed aim of the United States.

To halt the flow of arms and munitions from the communist north down what eventually became known as the Ho Chi Minh trail, and to clear areas where Viet Cong units were preparing to ambush government forces, defoliation runs were made by USAF Fairchild C-123 aircraft spraying a chemical cocktail believed at the time to be harmless to humans.

Using Agent Orange, a British defoliant used during the Malayan Emergency of the 1950s, Operation Ranch Hand ran from 1962 to 1971 during which 20 million gallons of defoliant was sprayed across five million acres of Vietnam, Laos and Cambodia from 20,000 sorties using C-123s with the call-sign Hades. Most operations were run from the Bien Hoa Air Base and the Air Force flew 95% of these sorties.

US forces had been engaged in Vietnam since 1961 in these and various other support roles but after the destroyer USS Maddox reported it had been attacked by North Vietnamese patrol boats (a claim that has since been refuted) on August 2, 1964, Congress authorised "all necessary steps". Within days, 12 F-102s had been dispatched to Tan Son Nhut and Da Nang, joined in theatre by eight F-100s to Takhli Air Base and eight F-105s to Korat. In addition, fighters were deployed to the Philippines and SAC flew 48 KC-135 tankers from Hawaii to Guam to support the combat aircraft. When 13 out of 18 Martin B-57 bombers deployed to Bien Hoa were damaged and five destroyed in a Viet Cong attack, the Joint Chiefs ordered B-52 strikes on North Vietnam, hitting the oil storage areas around Hanoi and Haiphong.

Re-elected as president in November 1964, a year after the death of President Kennedy, Lyndon Johnson began escalating the conflict but tried to find a middle way between the policies of his predecessor, in supporting the South Vietnamese government, and escalating to all-out war. It was in that capacity of support that the US Air Force was employed to hit targets in Laos and South Vietnam. On February 7, 1965, after the Viet Cong bombed an officers' residence in Saigon killing eight and wounding 104, Johnson removed all restrictions placed on the military through Farm Gate.

In what some analysts believe was a flawed judgment, Johnson attempted to control the pressure brought to bear on the North Vietnamese by managing the rate of escalation in an air bombing campaign named Rolling Thunder that commenced on March 2, 1965, with a bombing raid on an ammunition storage dump near Xom Bang. The raids, planned as an eight-week campaign, were constrained and did not have the flexibility needed to totally suppress communist activity. Rolling Thunder would continue until November 1968, with Johnson reluctant to bomb very far north of the border for fear of discouraging the North from possible peace talks.

The first aircraft lost to surface-to-air missiles was on April 5, 1965, and on June 18 the USAF began the Arc Light B-52F bombing raids on Viet Cong targets – without very much success

ABOVE: *Fairchild UC-123B defoliation Ranch Hand operations using Agent Orange chemical spray to strip vegetation and cover for Viet Cong activity. USAF*

ABOVE: *US Secretary of Defence Robert S. McNamara pursued a flawed policy on 'war by statistics' until replaced with Clark Clifford by a disillusioned President Johnson on February 29, 1968.*

at first. Since 1964, aircrews had been trained in using the B-52 for conventional bombing and the modified B-52F variant was capable of carrying 31,500lb, usually 24 x 750lb bombs and 27 x 500lb bombs. In December 1965 it was decided to convert the B-52D in a 'big Belly' modification, each aircraft carrying 84 x 500lb bombs, or 42 x 750lb bombs internally, and 24 x 750lb

bombs under the wings distributed between two pylons. Maximum bomb load was 54,000lb.

The first bombing raid on North Vietnam took place on the night of April 11/12, 1966, and from this date the nature of the war changed appreciably, aircraft continuously coming under intense fire from air defences provided by the Soviet Union. The infamous

SA-2 Guideline SAM was the most lethal, driving new SAM-suppression measures relentlessly pursued throughout the war.

With tactical air support increasing and strikes on bridges, supply lines and covert transportation of munitions into South Vietnam continuing,

ABOVE: *With black undersurfaces to avoid detection by searchlights, a B-52 drops its bombload on Hanoi during air raids aimed at eliminating the military potential of North Vietnam. USAF*

ABOVE: McDonnell Douglas F-4D Phantom II fighter-bombers from the 435th Tactical Fighter Squadron fly formation on a Boeing KC-135A tanker aircraft over Vietnam. USAF

when the Army, the Navy and the Air Force adopted a common numbering system. Fighter types designated F-1, -2 and -3 were Navy aircraft, making the F-4 the first USAF numbered fighter under the new system.

Designed essentially as a Navy fighter, where the pilot would fly the front seat and the radar intercept officer the back seat, the Air Force flew rated pilots in both seats, although the rear cockpit had fewer instruments and an appalling view forward. Tactical Air Command first got the F-4 on loan from the Navy in January 1962 with the dedicated F-4C joining the Air Force in November 1963. Increasingly, the role

specifically under Operation Rolling Thunder from March 2, 1965, to November 2, 1968, the North Vietnamese became more open in expressing a desire for peace. On March 31, 1968, President Johnson ordered a partial halt to the bombing over North Vietnam in return for talks, extended to a complete halt from November 1. Just over four months later President Richard M. Nixon authorised B-52 raids on North Vietnamese and Viet Cong sanctuaries in Cambodia.

END GAME

The air war over North and South Vietnam was characterised by a strange blend of aircraft which owed their origins to the early post-Second World War era, while others were just entering service and some were flown there experimentally to evaluate their combat effectiveness under fire. One such type was the F-111, the product of a requirement placed by the US Navy for an

air combat fighter merged with a successor for the Air Force's F-105 Thunderchief.

The General Dynamics design was selected in November 1962 and two versions of the F-111 were developed: the F-111A for the Air Force and the F-111B for the Navy, each slightly different to accommodate the separate needs of the two services. The Navy never did deploy its variant and continued on a path which would result in the F-14 Tomcat, while the Air Force flew 4000 combat missions with the type in South-East Asia for the loss of only six aircraft. A much maligned design, it more than justified its development and would play a significant role in future USAF missions in the decades ahead.

One aircraft above all others was defined by the Vietnam War. The McDonnell F-4 Phantom II had initially been designated the F-110 immediately prior to the 1962 tri-service re-classification of aircraft types

Boeing B-52

Preceded in service by the B-47, a six-engine medium bomber conceived in late 1943 and delivered to the Air Force from mid-1951, the B-52 was a response to an April 1945 requirement for a turboprop powered bomber. Boeing responded to changes in specification and flew the first jet-powered YB-52 on April 15, 1952. It followed the design profile of the B-47 in having thin laminar flow wings with 35° of sweep supporting eight engines in paired pods attached to pylons. A production order was placed and the type entered service with SAC in June 1955, the B, C, D and E models powered by eight 10,500lb thrust Pratt & Whitney J57-P-29W turbojet engines. The B-52F and G had 14,750lb thrust J57-P-43WB engines.

A lifelong anachronism of the B-52 was its relatively small bomb bay located between fore and aft fuselage-mounted main landing wheel bogies, the aircraft stabilised by wing-mounted outriggers. The size of the bomb bay was driven by the exclusively nuclear mission for which it was designed but this did limit some payloads from being carried. Modifications for the Vietnam War allowed some B-52D variants to carry a bomb load of 54,000lb. Some 744 were produced between 1954 and 1963 and the most significant change came with the B-52H, equipped with eight 17,000lb thrust Pratt & Whitney TF33-P-33 turbofan engines, specified below. When SAC transferred the primary role of surface-to-surface nuclear strike to its expanding inventory of ballistic missiles such as Titan and Minuteman, the Hound Dog stand-off weapon gave it a life extension, followed later by its role as a conventional bomber used most effectively during the Vietnam War. Since the 1960s, the type has continued to serve as a front-line conventional bomber carrying out a wide variety of heavy-lift and specialised roles, making it the longest serving front-line aircraft, albeit only just beating the Lockheed C-130 Hercules, introduced in 1956.

LENGTH	159.25ft
WING SPAN	185ft
HEIGHT	40.7ft
GROSS WEIGHT	488,000lb
MAXIMUM SPEED	650mph
CRUISING SPEED	525mph
CEILING	50,000ft
COMBAT RADIUS	4480 miles

ABOVE: A string of bombs from a B-52 during the Arc Light raids on Vietnam dig out the earth below. USAF

ABOVE: Republic F-105 Thunderchiefs await their turn for a top-up from the KC-135. USAF

ABOVE: Much feared by aircrew over North Vietnam, Russia's mobile SA-2 Guideline SAM rocket on a ZIL-131 truck. VIA DAVID BAKER

ABOVE: Bombs get a direct hit on the Phuc Yen airfield, the first North Vietnamese air base capable of supporting jet aircraft. USAF

B. DeBellevue gaining his sixth. Of the 107 MiG 'kills' achieved by Air Force pilots, 14% were with the aircraft's gun, with the first gun kill during supersonic flight on June 2, 1972, when Major Phil Handley shot down a MiG-19 at Mach 1.2, an achievement unmatched to the present.

As the communists expanded the use of littoral states to transport munitions the air war resumed with Operation Linebacker, a code for attacks by the 7th AF and the US Navy Task Force 77 in an interdiction campaign lasting from May 9 to October 23, 1972. As the Paris peace talks appeared to stall, and as the communists continued to export the war to neighbouring states, Linebacker II began on December 18 and lasted for 11 days in an all-out mass bombing campaign assigning 207 B-52s and 2000 tactical aircraft.

After the peace deal was signed on January 27, 1973, with the intention of a cessation to hostilities, the communists continued to violate the agreement and B-52 strikes continued into April but as the war migrated to neighbouring Cambodia, the fighting continued until the fall of Saigon on April 30, 1975.

Overall, between 1965 and 1973 the Air Force flew 351,949 sorties to North Vietnam alone, of which 171,408 were with fighters and 7303 with B-52s. In addition, the Air Force flew 518,578 sorties against communist targets in South Vietnam, the B-52s logging 28,380. The total number of USAF sorties of all categories and in all parts of the war amounted to 5.226 million compared with 710,886 in Korea and 2.362 million in the Second World War.

At 6.166 million tons of munitions expended, the total dropped during the Vietnam War was far greater than the Korean War (0.454 million tons) or even the Second World War (2.150 million tons, of which 1.613 million tons had been consumed in Europe).

The intensity of the B-52 raids stands out in the statistics – the number of sorties with this type on targets in South Vietnam increasing from 4290 in 1966 to 6611 in 1967 and 15,505 in 1968. The first bombing missions into Cambodia were flown in March 1969 and these were so secret that the crews did not know the country they were bombing, only the navigational coordinates. By May 1970, 3630 sorties had dropped nearly 100,000 tons on Cambodia.

During the Second World War the USAF lost 22,948 aircraft. In the Korean War it lost 1466 and in the Vietnam War 2257. Across those three

of the rear-seater was for mission support.

Deployed to the 45th Tactical Fighter Squadron, 15th Tactical Fighter Wing, on July 10, 1965, the F-4C shot down a MiG-17 using AIM-9 Sidewinder missiles but on July 24 another F-4C became the first F-4 victim of SAM (surface-to-air-missile) fire. On April 26, 1966, an F-4C from the 45th became the first US aircraft to shoot down a North Vietnamese MiG-21 but on October 5 another F-4C was the first US aircraft shot down by an AAM (air-to-air-missile) fired from a MiG-21.

While many of the air operations involving F-4 Phantom IIs were flown by the Navy, the F-4D arrived with Falcon missiles in June 1967, but these were designed for shooting down slow-moving bombers rather than agile, fast moving targets. They were ineffective and quickly replaced by Sidewinders. With both Navy and USAF aircraft developing the fine art of fighting with missiles, evolution of types and tactics made optimal use of the Vietnam War to develop new fighting concepts and different weapons, the AIM-7E-2 Sparrow eventually becoming the AAM of choice and, responding to threats from the Soviet S-75 Dvina SAM, USAF F-4Ds were

fitted with radar homing and warning antennas.

The aged F-105G had been hauling most of the iron-bomb delivery runs up to 1968, when the USAF F-4D began to take over the ground-attack role, carrying warloads of up to 16,000lb. From November 1970 it became the primary tactical bombing system in the inventory, added to which was the F-105's anti-SAM radar 'Wild Weasel' role with EF-4C aircraft, later re-designated without the 'E', equipped with radar-seeking missiles to take out the 'eyes' of SAM sites.

By 1972 there were 353 F-4s based in Thailand, a peak year for Air Force Phantoms in theatre, and during the long protracted war a total of 445 F-4 fighter-bombers and 83 reconnaissance versions (RF-4C) were lost, a total of 528. Of that number, 442 (84%) were shot down during combat. When added to F-4s operated by the Navy and the Marine Corps, the United States lost 761 Phantoms of all variants carrying out a wide range of operational missions.

But the type had seen the first USAF 'ace' of the war, when Captain Steve Ritchie shot down his fifth aircraft on August 28, 1972, followed on September 9 by Captain Charles

ABOVE: Colonel Robin Olds of the 8th Tactical Fighter Wing, triple ace from the Second World War, Korea and Vietnam, on the occasion of his 100th and last combat mission over Vietnam, September 23, 1967. USAF

wars the loss rate per thousand sorties fell from 9.7% to 2% and 0.4%, respectively. The most common cause of loss was ground fire (64%) followed by operational losses (22%), anti-aircraft fire including surface-to-air missiles (4.9%) and to ground-attack by the enemy (4.2%). Only 67 aircraft (3%) were lost to aerial combat.

The lessons for the future of the Air Force were profound. The most immediate and urgent requirement was to re-equip after severe and brutal losses, that and the introduction of a completely new generation of combat and support aircraft as equally influential in changing doctrine as the Century-series fighter had been in the 1950s. To some observers the war had not tipped into a more dangerous confrontation solely because of Soviet-Chinese rivalry: Moscow aligned itself with Beijing over North Vietnam but declined to get directly involved. China aligned with the Khmer Rouge in Cambodia and did not want a direct confrontation with Russia. In the end

though, it was a war managed and controlled by politicians, prosecuted by military professionals, and lost due to civilian control over policy.

After the Americans withdrew from Vietnam it was considered by politicians to have been a negotiated success, though a large body of public opinion believed it to have been a failure. And the collapse of trust in big-government appeared justified by many after the Watergate scandal sent President Nixon prematurely scurrying from the White House in August 1974 to avoid impeachment. But the Air Force felt it had been betrayed in Vietnam, by media coverage that focused on the grim realities of bloody conflict rather than the reasons they were there and by a cadre of civilian decision-makers shaping the war for political purposes, turning operations on and off like a tap.

The problem faced by the Air Force in the 1970s was a product not only of civilian mismanagement but also of the redirection of effort away from the guiding principles which had been at its core for several decades – adequate force structures and adequate personnel. The Vietnam War itself had degraded numerical force inventories, which had not been maintained at necessary levels due to attrition and the extended lead-time in procurement, each unavoidable. A consequence of that effort was the total financial commitment to the war across all four armed services which prevented the Air Force from getting funds for modernisation.

As for personnel, the Kennedy and Johnson era of Department of Defense planning responded to the fixed ideas of Secretary of Defense Robert McNamara. He believed that there was no need to expand pilot training because he calculated that for every aircraft there were three pilots – utterly failing to comprehend that not all pilots were trained for all types of aircraft. But to McNamara, who ran flow charts, management control diagrams and who had come to run the military from a high executive position at

the Ford Motor Company, it was simple.

The senior generals in the Air Force disagreed, and knew that the heart of the service was the quality of its pilots. With the war over there was a desperate shortfall in the required numbers of suitably trained air crew. During the Vietnam conflict there had been urgent requests for expanded training programmes but these had not been granted. It took several years after the war to bring the numbers up to required levels. But one of the greatest predators – commercial airlines – continued to be a source of attraction for qualified pilots opting for higher pay. ✪

McDonnell Douglas F-4 Phantom II

Arguably one of the most important military aeroplanes of the post-Second World War era, the F-4 began life as a US Navy attack aircraft in which the Air Force took an interest when it emerged as a far superior fighter than anything flying at that time. With dihedral on the outer wing panels, anhedral on the horizontal tail and two J79 engines mounted side by side in a fuselage displaying area rule at the fuselage mid-point, it was faster and could carry more weapons than any other comparable aircraft of its type.

As a fighter-bomber, the F-4 gave the Air Force air superiority over enemy aircraft in Vietnam but it became vulnerable to anti-aircraft fire despite its strong and rugged design. The F-4 entered Air Force service in November 1963 and the type was instrumental in evaluating a rising emphasis on electronic and digital avionics. Cockpit-mounted mission support systems tended to drench the pilot in visual and audio cues to the detriment of his innate skills as a warfighter, to the extent that pilots began to switch them off and rely on experience and pure flying skill – a valuable lesson from Vietnam which helped transform fighter design.

The Phantom II has a standard 20mm M-61A1 rotary cannon in a fixed forward-firing position and provision for a wide variety of munitions, having a stores capacity of up to 16,000lb. The F-4E is powered by two 11,870lb thrust General Electric J79-GE-15 turbojet engines.

A total of 5195 Phantom IIs were built between 1958 and 1961 and the aircraft is still in service with many air forces around the world, the USAF retiring its last at the end of 2016. Among foreign users, the UK's Royal Navy operated the Phantom II from April 1968 to November 1978 and the RAF from September 1969 to October 1992.

LENGTH	62.9ft
WING SPAN	38.5ft
HEIGHT	16.5ft
GROSS WEIGHT	61,650lb
MAXIMUM SPEED	1500mph
CRUISING SPEED	484mph
CEILING	62,250ft
RANGE	1300 miles

ABOVE: A McDonnell F-4C Phantom II destroyed during the Tet Offensive, emblematic of a military operation that lasted 14 years and failed because of political meddling. USAF

Chapter 13: Cold War arms race

ABOVE: *An air view from a photographic B-29 of the atomic bomb detonating over Nagasaki on August 9, 1945. LANL*

ABOVE: *An underwater atomic test at Bikini Atoll on July 25, 1946, as viewed from three miles away. LANL*

In an Air Force already challenged by the pressures of independence, the race for supremacy in arms and operational capability really began in the last few months of the Second World War, when a new weapon of unusual potential was tested three times. The atomic bombs developed under the Manhattan Project resulted in the successful detonation of a fission device at the Trinity site near Los Alamos, Alamogordo, New Mexico on July 16, 1945.

Subsequently, an atomic bomb was dropped on Hiroshima on August 6 and on Nagasaki on August 9. These three devices, each successful, ushered in the atomic age and committed the US Air Force to the literal application of a proverb articulated by President Theodore Roosevelt to "speak softly but carry a big stick…" He was effectively advocating the tactical use of caution mixed with non-aggression while preserving the means to do violence if required.

The United States was to excel in an arms race that would rapidly envelop industry, government, research groups, technology and engineering. But it would be implemented not through a proverb but through the United States Air Force in an expression of power far greater than anything that could have been imagined when the Second World War began.

The origin of that race can be traced back to December 17, 1944 when the 509th Composite Group was activated at Wendover Army Air Field, Utah, under the 2nd Air Force. When it deployed to Tinian in the Mariana Islands in May 1945 it became part of the 313th Bombardment Wing of the 20th Air Force. Its sole purpose was to operate 15 B-29 bombers adapted to carry atomic weapons, supported by C-54 transports aircraft, and to drop those weapons on designated targets on the Japanese mainland. As such it was the direct forerunner of Strategic Air Command.

The 509th CG was commanded by Lieutenant Colonel Paul W. Tibbets, who commanded the B-29 (Enola Gay) that dropped the Little Boy atomic bomb on Hiroshima. Major Charles W. Sweeney commanded the aircraft (Bockscar) that carried Fat Man to Nagasaki. After these special operations the 509th was assigned a variety of conventional targets before returning to the US on November 6, 1945, where it was stationed at Roswell, New Mexico. While there, on March 21, 1946, it was one of the 10 bombardment groups assigned to Strategic Air Command, which absorbed most of the men and inventory of Continental Air Forces, which had been set up during the war to defend the continental United States (CONUS).

In and of itself, the development of the atomic bomb had not signalled any radical change in warfare or in the doctrine of tactical or strategic operations. The political gulf between East and

ABOVE: *The arms race would rapidly escalate with the development of the hydrogen bomb, several thousand times more powerful than the atom bomb, evidenced here by the 1.9 MT yield of a test weapon during Redwing Apache on July 8, 1956, a weapon type used in the Regulus cruise missile. The US would conduct 1149 detonations of nuclear devices, the Russians 969. LANL*

of the free world. There was now an expanding need for information and intelligence on the level of Soviet military developments, the state of its munitions and armament facilities and the possibility of new threats to American air power.

Since the late 1940s the Americans had been flying spy missions over Russian airspace, many operations entering the USSR over the Arctic wastes where there was little or no air defence. The first incursion was made by an RF-80A from Misawa Air Base in Japan over the Kuril Islands in the Soviet Far East on May 10, 1949, followed in March 1950 with overflights of Vladivostok which was at the time closed to foreigners. At first there was little resistance to these flights as the Soviet mind-set was orientated in a completely different direction but that would quickly change.

Trapped in the war they had just helped win, the Russians were slow to realise that it was air power that could threaten the very survival of their system and its people and that the massed hordes of Red Army troops could now be stopped by a few strategically placed atom bombs, turning their battle edge into a lifeless wasteland. The Russians were only too well aware of the potency of the high-altitude B-29 and had begun to make copies of examples that had landed in Russia during the war and not been returned. But the ability to wage strategic war from the air was not in their thinking. Nevertheless, overflights were carried out by a wide range of US aircraft which increasingly came under attack from Soviet fighters.

When it became clear that Soviet preparations for possible war went beyond the theoretical and that there was a real prospect for conflict in Europe, it became essential for the USAF to know precisely where the key tactical and strategic targets were located in the Soviet Union. Russian maps were deliberately inaccurate to confuse invading armies and early progress on photo-analysis of the precise location of key targets was made using captured German photographs liberated from Luftwaffe files. A full and comprehensive set of coordinates for key targets were a vital contribution, also useful for planning more targeted photo-reconnaissance missions with RB-45C Tornado jet bombers and RAF Canberra camera-carrying aircraft, which began in the early to mid-1950s.

West which quickly became wider in the late 1940s, however, resulted in a Cold War race for superiority in weapons and in aircraft, a race for both quantitative and qualitative advantage. It was applied not only through aircraft, rockets and missiles but also in the size and flexibility of nuclear and conventional forces.

The spark that ignited that race occurred on August 29, 1949, when Russia detonated its first fission bomb using a plutonium device similar to that of Fat Man, followed up by a second test on September 24, 1951, delivering 38.3 KT (38,300 tons of TNT equivalent). Less than a month later, on October 18, 1951, the Russian scientists dropped a 41.2 KT device from an aircraft flying at an altitude of 33,000ft which detonated at a height of 1300ft. In achieving this

the Russians were just over six years behind the Americans but events in that interim had gathered a harvest of intelligence information crucial to the beginning the arms race proper.

At the end of the war the Americans reacted to Soviet belligerence over East European states, the sealed road and rail access to the western sector of Berlin, and the presence of a large Soviet standing army close to the border with Western Europe by setting up the North Atlantic Treaty Organisation (NATO) on April 4, 1949. In one stroke this ensured the return to the UK and continental Europe of an American presence at airfields they had vacated at the end of 1945. It enhanced the role of the independent US Air Force and imposed a new requirement on this nascent service: protector

ABOVE: *A North American Aviation RB-45C is refuelled by a Boeing KB-29P of the 91st Strategic Reconnaissance Wing. Spyplanes became an essential element in gathering information about Soviet activities. USAF*

ABOVE: *A Convair GRB-36F reconnaissance version of the B-36 bomber engages in flight evaluation of a parasitic fighter concept. A Republic F-84F Thunderflash would be carried to enemy skies for release where it would perform fast, low altitude reconnaissance runs before retrieval by the mother-plane and carriage home. It was never introduced. CONVAIR*

ABOVE: Classed as a medium-bomber, the B-47 was frequently deployed to Europe and the Far East during the 1960s to 'carry the flag' in an increasingly dangerous world, reaching a peak of 1291 with Strategic Air Command in 1961. USAF

STRATEGIC FORCES

Year	SAC bombers	SAC personnel	US nukes	Soviet bombers	Soviet nukes
1950	605	85,473	299	12	5
1955	1688	195,997	2422	20	200
1960	1848	266,788	18,638	138	1605
1965	825	216,681	31,139	173	6129
1970	501	154,367	26,008	152	11,643
1975	489	140,735	27,519	152	19,055
1980	488	145,869	23,368	152	30,068

Note: Not shown here are the number of ICBMs operated by SAC, increasing from 12 in 1960 to 880 in 1965 and 1039 in 1970 and thereafter. The USSR had two ICBMs in 1960, 281 in 1965, 1472 in 1970, 1469 in 1975 and 1338 in 1980. It should be noted that the US had many more submarine-launched missiles than did the USSR and that it was superior in numbers of strategic strike systems through the 1980s.

ABOVE: A Bomarc missile battery stands guard from the bunker ramps in New Jersey, October 1960, as one added role to the Air Force's growing inventory of defence systems. USAF

Eventually, during the mid-1950s the Air Force began using the RB-57 for electronic surveillance at, and frequently across, the borders of communist countries including the USSR and China, but it was with the RB-36, the photo-reconnaissance version of the 10-engine bomber, that most very high-altitude flights were undertaken deep into hostile air space. Even as these were taking place, however, the Russians were making great strides with air defence measures including SAM batteries and anti-aircraft artillery increasingly supported by radar and heat-seeking warheads operating to ever higher altitudes approaching the ceiling of existing aircraft. What was needed was a very high-altitude dedicated photo-reconnaissance aircraft to more fully evaluate the real threat posed by the Soviet Union.

REVISING THE FUTURE

Three key decisions were made in 1954 that would accelerate a technological race with the USSR: the decision to build an aircraft capable of flying above the reach of air defence missiles; the agreement to build an

intercontinental ballistic missile operated by the Air Force; and the go-ahead for a military spy satellite capable of crossing the Soviet Union in space. Taking pictures vital for establishing that country's state of war readiness, the satellite would also provide information about its weapons output and aircraft manufacturing capability, which the US Air Force would have to match to stay ahead in this heightened arms race. Through these programmes the affiliation of the Air Force leadership connected with the intelligence gathering elements of the government to an unprecedented and increasingly complex level of association.

Intelligence gathering was vital for obtaining detailed operational planning and for the first time the Air Force sought a dedicated aircraft specifically built for speed and high-altitude flight. In 1954 Lockheed's Clarence 'Kelly' Johnson proposed the CL-282 with a slender fuselage, high aspect-ratio wings and a ceiling in excess of 70,000ft. It was not what the Air Force wanted but the Central Intelligence Agency (CIA) grabbed it and the subsonic U-2 spyplane was born under the code name Aquatone. The Air Force would

operate the U-2 and overflights would provide valuable and detailed intelligence information vital for a greater understanding of the status of Soviet programmes. But the information fuelled a further desire for a very fast reconnaissance platform, one which was capable of not only very high altitude cruise but speeds in excess of Mach 3.

From the very first overflights of Soviet airspace in 1956 the Russians were tracking each incursion, mostly with their A-100 radar, and the Air Force recognised that it was only a matter of time before one was shot down, which did happen on May 1, 1960, on its first mission right across the Soviet Union in a flight intended to take it from Peshawar, Pakistan, to Bodo in Norway.

For several years scientists had been working on ways to make an aircraft less visible to radar and that would result in Project Rainbow where the very shape of the aircraft itself would reduce the radar cross-section – as will be seen in the next chapter. In the meantime, it was thought that high speed was the solution to survivability. Radars of the day had a problem with tracking supersonic aircraft, which would cause the screen 'blip' to fan out at a rate proportional to the velocity of the target, making the returns almost invisible.

The search for the ultimate spyplane resulted in two competing designs under the CIA's Oxcart programme. Lockheed proposed a series of design options under the Archangel designation, A-11 going in direct competition with Convair's Kingfish concept. Certain elements of Kingfish were superior to those of the A-11 so Johnson modified it to blend with promising design features and renamed it A-12.

The Air Force liked the A-12 and placed the type under contract in August 1959 as an unarmed successor to the U-2. The first of 25 flew on April 26, 1962 and between 1963 and 1968 the CIA used them on covert operations. But the role of supersonic spyplane for the Air Force was not met by the A-12, rather by the two-seat SR-71, an aircraft which had its origins in the A-12 programme.

Two two-seat A-12s had been produced as part of the original production batch. Intended for launching D-21 drones, they had been unsuccessful in that role but the type was put up as an advanced interceptor designated YF-12A to fill the Air Force's SOR-220 requirement for a very high performance aircraft. Three of the 25 A-12 aircraft on order were completed with Hughes AN/ASG-18 radar which had been taken from the cancelled North American XF-108, a

ABOVE: *An early Lockheed U-2 spyplane which made numerous incursions over Russia and China between 1956 and 1960. LOCKHEED*

ABOVE: *The Lockheed A-12 which began as an unarmed supersonic successor to the subsonic U-2, this aircraft being the ninth in the development batch. LOCKHEED*

ABOVE: *The first Lockheed YF-12A, modified to the configuration of a Mach 3 missile-carrying interceptor from an initial order for an A-12 spyplane, first flown at Groom Lake on August 7, 1963. The Air Force placed great expectations on this but funds were never forthcoming, the design eventually appearing as the SR-71. USAF*

contender for the SOR-220 requirement, and with the provision for up to four AIM-47 missiles. The XF-108A would have had a top speed above Mach 3 and an operating ceiling of 80,000ft.

The F-12A never went into production but as the SR-71 it did provide the Air Force with the strategic reconnaissance system it had wanted. The story of the part played by the SR-71 in development of stealthy aircraft is told in the next chapter but the requirement for very high performance aircraft remained a key feature of US Air Force policy, stimulated by increasing intelligence gathered about the encroaching threat of Russian long-range jet bombers, such as the subsonic Tupolev Tu-16 then entering widespread service.

The search for a supersonic bomber for the US Air Force had been only partly satisfied by the Mach 2 B-58 Hustler, which had been studied as a requirement since 1949 and was formally requested in 1952. The first B-58 flew on November 11, 1956, an aircraft designed to carry an external pod beneath the fuselage containing additional fuel and a nuclear weapon. By this time it was apparent that the Hustler would not satisfy the ultimate driving requirement for a Mach 3 bomber and a new requirement issued in 1954 resulted in competing contenders from Boeing and North American Aviation. NAA won the contract for its XB-70 design which was truly revolutionary.

With a length of almost 186ft and a wingspan of 105ft, the aircraft would have a maximum take-off weight of 542,000lb, cruise at 2000mph and fly at 77,000ft. For maximum lift the aircraft would take off with fixed wings but at subsonic cruise the outer 20ft of each wing would deflect down at 25°, drooping to 65° for speeds above Mach 1.4. In this way the aircraft would ride on its own shock wave, improving lift, allowing smaller twin tail fins and compensating for the delta wing's rearward shift in its centre of lift at increased speed.

The Air Force found staunch advocates in the fraternity of leaders of strategic bombing campaigns in the Second World War but they were out-voiced by the abundance of ex-fighter pilots achieving high positions in the Air Force. The XB-70 Valkyrie was strongly opposed by President Eisenhower and the programme was scaled back in 1959 with considerable debate about the relevance of such an aircraft at a time when strategic missiles were coming into service, and considerable funds were being spent on B-52 production.

In March 1961 the Kennedy administration cut it back further and only two prototypes ever flew. The first made it into the air on September 21, 1964, the second suffering a catastrophic loss of control when struck by an F-104 flown by ace test pilot Joseph 'Joe' Walker on June 8, 1966, while flying in formation for a photo-shoot.

REDIRECTION

To many it seemed that the dream of fleets of supersonic bombers flying with impunity deep into enemy air space was becoming a nightmare of entangled politics and premature application of futuristic designs calling for untried technology. No better example of that perhaps than the Convair B-58B Super Hustler, another offering on the altar of exaggerated expectations seeking superiority in the Cold War race for ascendency over an enemy increasingly feared for its own technological prowess. In October

ABOVE: A Hughes AIM-47 Falcon, much modified from the original Falcon and here shown about to be installed in a YF-12A, four being carried by aircraft of this type. USAF

Year	Strength
AIR FORCE PERSONNEL STRENGTH 1970-1980	
1970	791,349
1971	755,300
1972	725,838
1973	691,182
1974	643,970
1975	612,751
1976	585,416
1977	570,695
1978	569,712
1979	559,455
1980	557,969

1957 the Russians launched Sputnik 1, the world's first artificial satellite, and within four years had placed the first cosmonaut in orbit.

The B-58B was designed as a 'mother-plane' for a parasite package known as FISH (First Invisible Super Hustler), a pod taken to Mach 2 by the carrier and released for free flight whereupon its three ramjet engines would ignite and climb to 95,000ft and Mach 4.2. Studies into this variant began in 1957 and were inextricably connected to the development of

the requirement which resulted in the SR-71 but dissatisfaction with the basic B-58 had led to a very wide range of potential growth versions from which FISH evolved as both a reconnaissance platform and a nuclear delivery system.

All these futuristic developments were part of an accelerated arms race driven by uncertainties in the strength and potential of America's prime ideological opponent and many projects were supported by politicians all too well aware of the threat to US superiority by Russia. And there had

been a significant amount of money to spend on advanced concepts. Between 1947 the US defence budget had increased from $54.2 million to $442 million, but under the eight years of the Eisenhower administration it would gradually reduce and stand at $344 million in 1961.

It was an era in which a multitude of highly specialised and very advanced concepts were proposed, many of them impossible to achieve due to an ignorance of the untested environment in which they were designed to operate. In those years were forged the war-fighting tools crafted by a new generation of scientists, engineers and managers, architects of a wizard-war on convention and traditional ways of managing new weapon systems.

An entirely new approach to designing and producing large and complex weapon systems had emerged from the Second World War – systems engineering – which was used and improved to give a new generation of uniformed technocrats powerful tools to fast-track highly advanced and complicated weapon systems. Systems engineering was applied to the development of the Intercontinental Ballistic Missile (ICBM) which was managed by the Air Force, the second of those seminal projects that garnered political and military approval in 1954.

ICBMs were one leg of a triad also embracing manned strategic bombers and Submarine Launched Ballistic Missiles (SLBMs), the latter managed and operated by the Navy. This triad, with the Air Force responsible for the first two, was an integral strategy against a single technical

ABOVE: In its search for a high altitude, Mach 3 bomber capable of hunting down rail-mobile ICBMs, the Air Force turned to the North American XB-70 Valkyrie, cancelled by the Kennedy administration when it began to emphasise conventional, flexible response rather than all-out retaliation to Soviet aggression. USAF

ABOVE: Carried to altitude and high speed by a much enlarged B-58B Super Hustler, the Mach 4.2 mission pod would have conducted reconnaissance and weapons deployment. LOCKHEED

ABOVE: Downscaled from the Super Hustler studies, the Kingfish concept envisaged a Mach 3.2 cruise capability utilising two J58 engines buried in the rear fuselage. It was dropped in favour of the stealthy A-12 which eventually provided the Air Force with the SR-71. *LOCKHEED*

fixed launch pads above ground but later Atlas E utilised a 'coffin' semi-buried in the ground affording some protection from attack with side-opening doors that allowed the missile to be erected vertically for launch. Atlas F was installed vertically in silos with massive concrete doors over the top, hardened protection against an overpressure of 100lb per square inch.

Fuelled by kerosene at ambient temperature and liquid oxygen kept at minus 297 degrees Fahrenheit, the missiles required several hours for preparation and could only remain fuelled for a limited period due to oxygen boil-off. This was also a problem with the Martin Titan I, built as a hedge against problems with Atlas, as it too used these propellants. Deployed with the Air Force from 1961, it gave way to the Titan II, essentially a new missile with storable liquid propellants at ambient temperature which allowed it to remain fuelled and ready for rapid launch. First deployed in 1963 it remained in service until 1986, carrying a 9 MT nuclear warhead, the largest fielded by the US.

However, even Titan II required some time to prepare for launch and the solution to potential destruction by a surprise attack was found in an

failure with a specific weapon system disabling the entire deterrent. In 1954 the ICBM was viewed as a feasible proposition and by 1960 the Air Force had the first Atlas missiles in their silos and ready for use. A clear example of the use of a strategic deterrent to unravel a diplomatic stalemate was the Cuba missile crisis of October 1962. When President John F. Kennedy threatened retaliation against Russia if it failed to remove nuclear missiles from Cuba, massively outnumbered by US nuclear weapons the Soviet Union was obliged to turn back from the brink.

The development and growth of the US Air Force ICBM programme is a book in itself but the influence it had on strategy and doctrinal policy was more profound than that achieved by any other weapon system since the advent of the truly effective strategic bomber of the Second World War. Systems engineering played a key role in fulfilling the requirement to strike Soviet targets with ballistic missiles fired from the continental United States, an idea mooted since the mid-1940s. The very real example of the V-2 missile and its impact on civilians in London and Antwerp was a constant reminder of the potential inherent in the rocket. Paradoxically, only through the development of guidance systems and stable gyroscopic navigation platforms was the desire made plausible.

Initially, the ICBM selected for design was the product of work that had already been under way at Convair since the late 1940s. However, lacking confidence in its practicality, no approval had been given for the Air Force to develop a liquid propellant missile before separate technology reviews came together in 1954 when approval was granted to build Atlas. First launched on June 11, 1957, this and the next launch were failures before the first successful flight on December 17 that year.

A series of development flights preceded operational deployment of the Atlas D series in September 1959, when six missiles went on alert with the 576th Strategic Missile Squadron, 704th Missile Wing, at Vandenberg Air Force Base, California. Initially, deployment was on

ABOVE: The Atlas Missile, the first US ICBM, stands ready for a test launch from pad 12 at Cape Canaveral in December 1957. *USAF*

ABOVE: The 'coffin' deployment of the Atlas missile with a round being elevated to vertical for launch. USAF

saw the decision to develop and launch spy cameras into space. Along a protracted timeline the Air Force eventually got the information it sought from an expanding inventory of reconnaissance satellites which obviated the need for direct overflights of enemy territory within the atmosphere. The Cold War arms race, packed with unlikely contenders, eventually reshaped the Air Force into the modern fighting service of today.

In retrospect, the Air Force had already soared to heights unimagined when it was formed in 1947 but involvement in South-East Asia during the 1960s and 1970s had brought a new reality, cancelling ideas for exotic vehicles which in retrospect seem more at home in the pages of a science fiction novel than on the runways of US Air Force bases. The 1980s would see a return to the need for stealthy access to enemy territory, not for reconnaissance but for tactical and strategic strike. ✪

BELOW: The first successful launch of a Titan ICBM on August 10, 1960. USAF

ICBM that could be launched within seconds, long before an incoming warhead could reach the silo where it was on standby. The solution was the solid propellant Minuteman missile. First fired in February 1961, it was much simpler to make, cheaper to build and less costly to operate, factors that appealed to the incoming Kennedy administration and its new Secretary of Defence Robert McNamara. The first Minuteman unit was operational in July 1963 with a peak deployment of 1000 Minuteman and 54 Titan II operational from 1974. Minuteman remains in service today.

The dawn of the missile era that began during the late 1950s represented a period of technological folly and unwarranted optimism, a hubris seeking possibilities and capabilities of aircraft and aerospace vehicles far beyond concepts mooted during the Second World War only a few years earlier. Highly secret at the time, the Air Force supported another highly advanced concept, the Aerospace Plane. A hypersonic trans-atmospheric vehicle which was expected to fly into space and reach speeds of Mach 6-12 in a hemispheric reach with nuclear weapons delivery and reconnaissance activity, it never got beyond the planning stage.

In reality, it too was far ahead of the technology of the day, and remains so even in the 21st century, although during the 1950s the Air Force did attempt to develop DynaSoar, a conflation of 'dynamic soaring' where the vehicle is launched into space and uses the atmosphere for a series of lifting trajectories. It too was cancelled, in 1963. But while the Army was attempting to get political approval for flights to the Moon and bases on the lunar surface, the Air Force was a little more pragmatic.

When the space programme came along at the end of the 1950s, it attempted to get its pilots into space through the NASA two-man Gemini programme of the mid-1960s but that too came to nothing – as did a successor programme for a Manned Orbital Laboratory to carry spy cameras and human occupants, cancelled in 1969.

Added to the decision to build a dedicated spyplane and dedicated ICBMs, 1954 also

Chapter 14: Getting Stealthy

ABOVE: Decidedly non-stealthy but essential to the expanded mission roles, a Lockheed C-5 Galaxy of the 445th Air Wing, the heavy-lifter defined as an urgent requirement through the Heavy Logistics System programme of 1964. USAF

ABOVE: The first US combat aircraft to be designed specifically for fly-by-wire control in a moderately unstable airframe for maximum manoeuvrability, the Lockheed Martin F-16 Fighting Falcon was a conduit for some of the essential flight control systems of stealth types. USAF

For reasons more associated with emerging technology than for any forethought, the early 1970s saw a burgeoning advance in aircraft capabilities. In 1970 Rockwell International, formerly North American Aviation, developed the B-1A which, like the FB-111, had variable sweep wings. The first prototype did not fly before the end of 1974 and the type was identified by President Jimmy Carter as redundant, pending the arrival of a new low-observable, or LO (stealthy), bomber eventually known as the B-2 and designed for low-level penetration.

This highly secret project was veiled from public scrutiny but Carter cancelled the highly publicised B-1. Nevertheless, the aircraft was resurrected as the B-1B by President Ronald Reagan in 1981 as an interim bomber pending the arrival of the still highly secret B-2. Paradoxically, both types are still in service.

The early 1970s also saw the development of a new range of fourth generation fighters for the Air Force, including the heavyweight McDonnell Douglas F-15 Eagle and the lightweight and highly manoeuvrable fighter, the General Dynamics (now Lockheed Martin) F-16 Fighting Falcon. By the early 1980s these new types were entering service, with the F-15 replacing the F-4 Phantom II in the fighter-bomber role. But combat aircraft were not the only new types introduced for the revitalised Air Force.

Logistical movement of men and materiel had long been a strong requirement for theatre and battlefield support and to supplement existing transport aircraft such as the Lockheed C-141 Starlifter the Air Force invested in what would for some time prove to be a troublesome programme – the C-5 Galaxy. The Starlifter entered service in 1965 as the first jet cargo-lifter, with 285 aircraft eventually being built and capable of carrying loads of up to 92,000lb. Through a series of modifications and upgrades, the C-5 was able to fly 3500 miles carrying a

load weighing 291,000lb. It entered service in December 1969 and was subject to a considerable rework into the C-5B, with more powerful engines and better serviceability.

While force modernization and stabilisation after Vietnam characterised the decade of the 1970s, by the early 1980s a new level of technology was re-shaping not only the role of the Air Force but redefining the way its combat aircraft would fly and fight. The appearance of the cruise missile in the late 1970s was an overnight game-changer and re-energised the flagging B-52 force, hanging on to a redefined role as a low-altitude, conventional attack asset.

In seeking a dedicated cruise missile platform, from a stand-off launch system kept out of harm's way, the Air Force examined

ABOVE: Generally unrecognised at the time as the first aircraft to be designed specifically with stealth quantities, the A-12 soars into the sky over Groom Lake in 1962. USAF

AIR FORCE PERSONNEL STRENGTH 1981-1990

Year	Strength
1981	570,302
1982	582,845
1983	592,055
1984	597,125
1985	601,515
1986	608,199
1987	607,035
1988	576,446
1989	570,880
1990	535,233

ABOVE: A re-designated A-12, the M-21 was a CIA programme named Tagboard carrying an unpiloted D-21 both of which incorporated early stealth applications in design and materials. USAF

modified commercial aircraft without finding a viable contender. Extensive evaluation of the B-52 confirmed that it could perform the role of cruise missile carrier, with six missiles carried on pylons under each wing inboard of the inner engine pods and eight internally. The B-1B was eventually capable of carrying 24 cruise missiles, each with a range of 620 miles.

While the B-2 was slowly evolving behind a classified veil that would not see it publicly rolled out until 1988, it was in reality the second generation LO aircraft. The search for survivability in hostile airspace had deflected several aircraft programmes since the Second World War. Russia's extensive deployment of surface-to-air missiles beginning in the 1950s had threatened the viability of the manned penetrating bomber, and directly resulted in the low-cost/low-flying cruise missile capable of saturating air defences with pilotless weapons. It had dramatically changed the role of the B-52. The losses of aircraft to ground fire and anti-aircraft defences amounted to almost 70% of all combat air losses in the Vietnam War and that had stimulated new types of aircraft dedicated to radar and SAM suppression to reduce that risk.

Because radar was the cornerstone of air defence, the real solution was to reduce the radar signature of the manned aircraft, shrinking the identifiable cross-section so that it was not detected as a flying machine at all until it was so close it was too late to respond. That, plus air-defence suppression missiles launched outside the observable range of the carrier-plane, would restore the viability of the non-stealthy packages of penetrating strike or combat aircraft.

Since the 1950s aerodynamicists and engineers had been trying to produce a low-observable aircraft through aerodynamic shaping and the use of radar-absorbent materials (RAM), coatings which absorbed radio waves, rather than reflecting them back to a receiver. The first LO aircraft specifically designed with aerodynamic-shaping to

achieve that had been the family of Mach 3 Lockheed A-12/SR-71 aircraft. Configurations like this were on the edge of controllability due to compromises in aerodynamic shape, which made them hard to detect.

In the early 1970s, advances in fly-by wire (FBW) and electronic flight control systems provided a radical new approach, one which would focus on a distinctly un-aerodynamic, multi-faceted external profile that gave the aircraft extreme inherent instability. Only through the use of advanced electronic control and FBW systems could the aircraft remain flyable. Some of the product from electronic flight control development had been introduced on the General Dynamics F-16, to good effect. Achieving a new rationale for aircraft design was seen as

a way of reintroducing the combat aircraft back into enemy skies without the exposed vulnerability driven by the advent of advanced radar detection equipment in the 1960s.

Vietnam had proven the extreme need for reduced radar signatures but added to this was the need to suppress the thermal image too. The burgeoning development of new and effective air-to-air missiles balanced detection systems between infrared and radar-homing methods and it was argued that merely making an aircraft difficult to detect on radar was of little use unless the homing signature too was drastically reduced. Eventually, this would lead to acoustic suppression techniques, opening the way for a return to deep penetration strikes, effective and survivable.

Lessons were also learned from the 1973 Yom Kippur War where the Israeli Air Force lost 109 aircraft to SAM fire in 18 days. Assessments were made that if the same kind of equipment was used by Warsaw Pact forces against NATO, as it would be, the entire package of air strike missions would be destroyed within two days. Added to which was an awareness that Soviet technology was producing a wide range of radars in various spectral bands which could punch through conventional suppression systems.

That in itself had stimulated development of radar-suppression tactics using Wild Weasel aircraft. Moderately effective in Vietnam, they would find difficulty in knocking out the primary air defence radars of the Soviet Union on the scale they were known to have been deployed. And this was the case, if only because the Wild Weasels would fall prey to the radars before they could launch their weapons. Moreover, the value of stealth was seen quite early on as being a force-survivability multiplier, because it would allow radar-suppression attacks to effectively blind the electronic 'eyes' of the enemy, opening flight paths for less stealthy aircraft to follow through and deploy their weapons.

Clearly, this was seen as one of the 'silver bullets' of the net-centric world of electronic air warfare and the organisation that would lead the development of possible ways to acquire

ABOVE: The Lockheed SR-71 was coated with a layer composed of miniscule metallic balls treated to absorb radio waves and turn them into thermal energy, an application used in the next generation of truly stealthy aircraft. USAF

ABOVE: With a very different wing to its successor, the Have Blue concept demonstrator was markedly different to the definitive F-117A but verified the underlying principles behind faceted design features to minimise radar cross-section. LOCKHEED MARTIN

ABOVE: Grey Dragon, an F-117A displaying the unique design configuration creating an inherently unstable aircraft with redundant quadruple flight control systems. USAF

Lockheed F-117A

Developed as the world's first all-stealthy attack aircraft, misrepresented as a fighter by designation, the type evolved through a programme in the mid-1970s seeking survivability during penetration of enemy air space. Based on a requirement that had arisen through combat experience in Vietnam, the type was concept-proven through the Have Blue precursor, which first flew in December 1977. A total of five prototype and 59 production aircraft were built and deployed with the Air Force between October 1983 and April 2008.

The aircraft was powered by two General Electric F404 turbojet engines, each with a thrust of 10,600lb, with inlet screens to shroud radar-bright fan blades and exhausting through horizontal slits on the top section of the aft fuselage. Configured for the Paveway laser-guided bomb, it could also carry the B61 nuclear bomb but had no defensive armament.

LENGTH	65.9ft
WING SPAN	43.3ft
HEIGHT	12.8ft
LOADED WEIGHT	52,500lb
MAXIMUM SPEED	617mph
CRUISING SPEED	Mach 0.92
CEILING	45,000ft
RANGE	1070 miles

those capabilities was the Defense Advanced Research Projects Agency (DARPA), which had been set up by President Eisenhower as ARPA in February 1958 in direct response to the launch of Sputnik 1. The organisation was tasked with creating a military technology superior to, and more advanced than, that of America's enemies.

DARPA had been instrumental in advancing the technology in a wide range of programmes, the majority being highly classified, and the organisation had worked with all government agencies, managing a relationship with industry as design and development tasks required. Stealth technologies were a focal point for

DARPA research programmes in 1974 and highly secret approaches were made to five aircraft companies for reports on two considerations: what were the thresholds at which aircraft became totally invisible and what were the possibilities for designing and manufacturing an aircraft capable of matching that requirement?

NEW BUILD

Only two companies responded satisfactorily and McDonnell Douglas and Northrop were awarded separate contracts to continue their research. Lockheed had not been active in the fighter business for some considerable time and was not invited to bid but during meetings at the Department of Defense, Lockheed's manager for science and engineering got to hear about the programme and received permission from the CIA for the company to present its work on the A-12 and on the stealthy characteristics of the D-21 drone. Lockheed had applied iron ball paint absorption to the exterior of the A/12/YF-12A and SR-71 series and this had significantly reduced the aircraft's radar cross-section (RCS).

Iron ball paint consisted of minute spheres of electrically isolated carbonyl iron balls in a double-base epoxy paint application. Each tiny sphere is coated in quartz to act as an insulator. When hit by radio waves the alternating magnetic paint causes molecular oscillations which convert the energy into heat instead of reflecting it back to the source of the beam. There are many steps and processes involved and most of those required to fabricate and to adequately prepare the material for use are either proprietary or secret.

With this technology already developed and in operation on an existing aircraft, Lockheed's Dick Scherer wanted to apply a more radical solution and requested a set of possible shapes for an aircraft composed entirely of a large number of separate, faceted surfaces so that only a very limited range of angles would be reflected back to the radar transmitting antenna. With the help of Denys Overholser, the design team came up with a computer programme that could shape the faceted surfaces into an aircraft with sufficient flying surfaces for an adequate lift/drag ratio. By May 1975 Lockheed had produced a design that was evaluated by the US Air Force Systems Command and several months later the Air Force asked Northrop and McDonnell Douglas to come up with suitable designs.

Of the two, only Northrop could do that and in November, along with Lockheed they were asked to provide full-scale mock-ups and test rigs for evaluating the separate designs and in

April 1976 Lockheed received the development contract. In a move of extreme prescience, DARPA asked Northrop to keep its stealth team intact as the Air Force had already intimated to that body that it was about to launch its Battlefield Surveillance Aircraft Experimental (BSAX) programme, which was to lead to Tacit Blue and eventually on to the B-2 programme.

Meanwhile, Lockheed proceeded with the Have Blue programme which was to serve as a precursor concept demonstration aircraft. It was completed in mid-October 1977 with several weeks of testing preceding the first flight on December 1, 1977, with Lockheed's test pilot Bill Park at the controls. The aircraft was inherently unstable because low RCS claimed priority over every other performance aspect and for that it had a quadruple redundant fly-by-wire system to allow the aircraft to remain in the air and flyable. Later, the prototype suffered a technical malfunction and Park had to eject before it crashed in the vicinity of Groom Lake.

Under the code name Senior Trend, on November 1, 1978, Lockheed was tasked by the Air Force with developing a pre-operational aircraft refined through multiple test flights with the two Have Blue aircraft and Tactical Air Command ordered five development airframes and 25 production aircraft. These were significantly modified from Have Blue and incorporated changes resulting from previous work both in the air and in the laboratory. The first YF-117A was flown for the first time from Groom Lake on June 18, 1981, and the first production aircraft was delivered in 1982 with operational capability declared in October 1983 at the 4450th Tactical Group at Nellis Air Force Base, Nevada.

Not until November 10, 1988, did the Air Force publicly acknowledge the existence of the aircraft, by which time it was well into production, the last of 59 being delivered on July 3, 1990. In addition, the aircraft was deployed with the 37th Tactical Fighter Wing, the 49th Fighter Wing

and the 412th Test Wing, the latter at Edwards Air Force Base, California. Although designated F-117A, the aircraft performed a tactical strike role and it was to demonstrate that capability with resounding successes in two major conflicts.

But even as the Air Force was announcing the existence of the F-117A, in Palmdale, California, it was getting ready to unveil its stealthy long-range bomber, the B-2, the result of a programme which had its origins as early as 1976. From the early studies for a small attack/fighter that generated the Have Blue programme came the genesis of the much larger stealth bomber. The Air Force remained quiet about its development but the press got word and speculation only grew with the announcement of the Advanced Technology Bomber (ATB) in 1979. Northrop teamed up with Boeing to produce the Senior Ice study and Lockheed with Rockwell International to come up with competing designs under Senior Peg.

Both teams went after a flying-wing design, eliminating all conventional tail surfaces in a shape following the ultimate blending of wing and body into a conformal profile where the separation between the two is a matter of structural assembly rather than external wetted area. Lockheed, already heavily involved with the F-117A, put up a design which did have a small tail. But the Northrop concept was pure wing, taking a lot from the early work in the early 1940s on the piston-powered YB-35 and the jet-powered YB-49. Both of these earlier Northrop types had competed with the Convair B-36 and when technical problems beset the flying wing designs they were cancelled in favour of the more conventional bomber.

Second time around, Northrop won the ATB contract and received the go-ahead on October 20, 1981, the date for the official designation and the name Spirit, from its seemingly invisible presence. At this date the B-2 was designed for high-altitude work but a change to low-altitude mission profiles brought a refinement in the shape of the aircraft. The Air Force received guidance from several outside sources and the overall programme was more politically debated than the F-117A had been, despite the stealth bomber being veiled in unprecedented secrecy regarding the specific manner in which it was made so. To the general public, however, it was a tantalisingly vague project.

The first public disclosure came on November 22, 1988, when the first example, AV-1 (serial number 82-1066) was rolled out of its hangar at Plant 42 in Palmdale, California, before a specially invited audience of the political, military and contractor leadership. The aircraft made its first flight on July 17, 1989, and the first operational aircraft was delivered to Whiteman Air Force Base on December 17, 1993, reaching full operational capability on January 1, 1997.

These stealth projects emerged at a time of political change in the United States, where the one-term President Jimmy Carter sought to make funding cuts and reshape the way international relations were conducted. Criticised by the campaigning team of Republican opponent Ronald Reagan, which accused him of having disarmed America, Carter chose to forego development of the swing-wing Rockwell International B-1 supersonic bomber and to rely on the eventual deployment of the stealthy B-2. The Air Force wanted 169 stealthy bombers but when President Reagan took office in January

ABOVE: The Northrop YB-49 flying wing made its first flight on October 21, 1947, and very nearly received approval for operational deployment. NORTHROP

ABOVE: Maintenance crews service a B-2A Spirit at Andersen Air Force Base, Guam, before a long duration mission, flights routinely using several refuelling tankers to extend their reach beyond its 6900 mile range. USAF

ABOVE: The B-2A incorporates radio, thermal, acoustic and visual detection suppression using cooled air for reducing the temperature of the engine exhaust gases, exiting above the aft body area and a radar absorbent coating on external surfaces with serpentine exhaust inlets to prevent radar reflections off fan blades. USAF

ABOVE: The B-2A has a bomb load capacity of 40,000lb. Here loaders lift a 2000lb BDU-56 guided bomb into the spacious bay. USAF

1981, a subsequent review reduced that to 132.

The initial requirement generated by the Air Force was not made on the basis of cost but rather on the operational needs of the service, nor was there consideration of the total price to the taxpayer. When the true level of expenditure required to develop and produce the B-2 became apparent, political objections drove down the number to 75 and when the collapse of the Soviet Union and the democratisation of East European states formerly under the grip of the USSR occurred in 1991, President George H. W. Bush reduced that to just 20 aircraft.

The combination of new technology and 'stealth' design and materials technology allowed radar signature reduction to come together in the B-2, which also suppresses the infrared signature both in engine exhaust and in the general heating of the airframe due to RAM. The introduction of stealth technology would come to dominate fighter and strike aircraft right through to the next century but it still had to prove itself in warfare. That opportunity came unexpectedly with powerful consequences for both the Air Force and for the restoration of national pride in America's military air power.

Northrop Grumman B-2A Spirit

Emerging from the same stealth development studies as the F-117A, the B-2A is the world's first all-stealth long range bomber serving both nuclear and non-nuclear roles, with tactical and strategic strike capability. Originating in the Advanced Technology Bomber programme calling for a survivable aircraft capable of loitering in enemy airspace and hunting down road and rail-mobile ICBM launchers, it has found a role as a supplement to the B-52 force.

Only 20 production aircraft were ordered but after the crash of AV-12 due to water in a pitot tube sending incorrect air data, the flight test aircraft was modified at a cost of $500 million to maintain the full inventory. Due to the high cost of the B-2, each reportedly priced at more than $2 billion, and the high cost of flying the aircraft – twice that of the B-52 and the B-1B – the aircraft has limited operational application in the conventional role. The primary purpose for which it was designed has changed although the general configuration is believed to be a model for its successor, the B-21.

The B-2 is powered by four non-afterburning General Electric F-118-GE-100 turbofan engines with exhaust products cooled by ingested air for suppressing the thermal signature. It has no defensive armament, a bomb load of 40,000lb and can carry a range of conventional munitions or up to 16 B61 or B83 nuclear weapons.

LENGTH	69ft
WING SPAN	172ft
HEIGHT	17ft
MAXIMUM LOADED WEIGHT	376,000lb
MAXIMUM SPEED	630mph
CRUISING SPEED	560mph
CEILING	50,000ft
RANGE	6900 miles

Chapter 15: Gulf War

ABOVE: *An F-15 of the 71st Fighter Squadron displaying its large area wing, a type that performed strike duties in Desert Storm as well as combat air patrols and interception missions.* USAF

US military forces were engaged in several short-lived operations, not all of them glorious, during the years immediately after the American withdrawal from Vietnam in 1975. A pivotal event in US military planning and its relationship to civilian oversight and control began when a revolution broke out in Iran on January 7, 1978, to overthrow the monarch, establish a politicised Islamic state and fuel the rise of terrorism around the world.

Less than a year later, on November 4, 1979, Iranian students fomented into action by Islamic extremists, occupied the US Embassy and seized 52 American diplomats and civilians. At the direct order of President Jimmy Carter, Operation Eagle Claw sought to rescue the hostages in a daring operation whereby a force of helicopters and transport aircraft would land in the desert (Desert One) and conduct an assault operation to free the captives.

Heavily opposed by senior military and civilian officials, President Carter insisted on mounting an attempt to liberate the hostages, taking personal control from the Pentagon and from the Situation Room at the White House. The attempt combined elements from all four armed services and failed in a cascade of misjudgements, bungled commands and unwise decisions leaving aircraft abandoned or burning on the desert floor and the political reputation of Jimmy Carter in tatters. In the post-mission analysis an unspoken agreement was reached that, once sanctioned by the civilian leadership, decisions about how to fight should be left to the professionals.

The importance of this to the administration, direction and control of the Air Force was to liberate the military authorities from management by decree, which had been a disastrous

aspect of how the Vietnam War had been run and was finally laid to rest as a result of Operation Eagle Claw, which set back American diplomacy in the world by several years.

In the meantime, on December 24, 1979, the Russians invaded Afghanistan and began a continuous conflict that would last more than nine years and cost the lives of more than 14,000 Soviet soldiers and at least 75,000 Afghans. It brought renewed fears of a Soviet advance toward the Persian Gulf which never came.

After Vietnam and the Desert One debacle, regional military command structures were set in place, with General Norman Schwarzkopf in charge of the Middle East.

Schwarzkopf changed US doctrine, from planning around a possible mass invasion by Soviet troops of Saudi Arabia to a focus

on how a regional dictator would seize a neighbouring state and how the US would respond. The preparations he made to counter such an eventuality were highly, and uncannily, prescient. And if war were to break out in the Middle East, America had a new, post-Vietnam inventory of equipment and manpower.

During the 15 years after the Vietnam War, the US Air Force introduced the F-15 Eagle and F-16 Falcon fighter and ground-attack aircraft, and the Fairchild A-10 Thunderbolt II close air support aircraft, the latter emerging from a design competition set in 1967 and defined as A-X. It arose from direct experience in Vietnam – the clear need arising for an aircraft requiring minimal ground support facilities and capable of carrying large ordnance loads. First flown in May 1972, the A-10 was equipped with a GAU-8A Avenger

GULF WAR AIR REFUELLING

Desert Shield

Aircraft	Sorties	Hours	Recr a/c	Offloads (lbs fuel)
KC-10	4117	23,262	4253	87,340.800
KC-135A	10,128	37,095	23,312	263,379,200
KC-135E	3040	14,476	5545	90,297,600
Total:	17,285	74,833	33,110	441,017,600

Desert Storm

Aircraft	Sorties	Hours	Recr a/c	Offloads (lbs fuel)
KC-10	3278	16,717	10,915	283,616,000
KC-135A	9897	34,635	27,390	353,030,000
KC-135E	3690	14,886	13,391	164,090,000
Total:	16,865	66,238	51,696	800,736,000
Grand Total:	**34,150**	**141,071**	**84,806**	**1,241,753,600**

ABOVE: General Norman Schwarzkopf led the coalition forces during Desert Shield/Desert Storm. DOD

ABOVE: The General Dynamics F-16 played a vital role in the Gulf War and has subsequently incorporated upgrades resulting from lessons learned in that operation. USAF

multi-barrel cannon and the ability to carry a 16,000lb warload. It represented a significant addition and one which would greatly outlast its projected service lifespan. All three aircraft would play pivotal roles in conflicts to come.

DESERT SHIELD

On August 2, 1990, Iraqi armed forces invaded the independent neighbouring state of Kuwait and three days later President George Bush addressed Congress to begin the process to gaining United Nations approval for a coalition of forces to evict them. That UN approval was granted and by January 1991 Operation Desert Shield had assembled a force of 10 coalition countries to drive back the invader. But how did this happen and why did the United States fight the most intensely planned and coordinated battle since the D-Day landings of June 1944?

The origins of the war lay in the regional ambitions of Iraqi President Saddam Hussein, when he attempted to create a military basis for conquest after the 1973 Arab-Israeli war by constructing a 1.25 million man army and beginning the development of nuclear, biological and chemical (NBC) weapons. With substantial modernisation of his air, land and naval forces, Saddam Hussein's aggressive foreign policy took the country to war against

Iran in 1980 in a conflict that lasted eight years and saddled Iraq with a debt of $80 billion and a reconstruction programme costing $320 billion.

Adopting a belligerent attitude toward former Allies, he demanded $30 billion in aid and threatened to invade any country that refused. Increasingly tense negotiations between Iraq and Kuwait over territorial claims led to the movement of eight Republican Guard divisions to the border, the full invasion on August 2 resulting in Iraqi forces being at the border with Saudi Arabia within 24 hours, to which country the Kuwaiti Air Force had fled. Few US military advisers had anticipated the invasion and existing plans traded space for time with rapid deployment of US forces.

An early decision by President H. W. Bush was to give the military full and independent decision over the size of force required, mobilisation and deployment plans and about the prosecution of the war. The revised deployment plan worked out by Schwarzkopf envisaged a deployment phase lasting four months, ultimately requiring command arrangements with 38 countries. But with the potential for a full-scale Iraqi invasion of Saudi Arabia, he decided to deploy combat elements first, deciding on air power

General Dynamics F-16

Responding to lessons learned in Vietnam, the F-16 was defined by a lightweight fighter requirement and served as a supplement in the Air Force to the larger and less agile F-15. Five companies competed for a contract awarded to General Dynamics in January 1975, with delivery to the Air Force beginning on January 6, 1979. With 4600 delivered to date the lightweight and highly economical fighter has found favour with many air forces around the world.

The first fighter designed to be aerodynamically unstable for minimum energy loss in high manoeuvring, the F-16 has been adapted for a wide variety of roles and an expanded series of different variants for various customers. Selected by the USAF Thunderbirds aerobatic team, the F-16C, specified below, is powered by a single 28,600lb thrust General Electric F110-GE-129 engine and can carry a maximum weapons load of 17,000lb. It is scheduled to remain in service with the USAF until 2025.

LENGTH	49.45ft
WING SPAN	32.7ft
HEIGHT	16ft
MAXIMUM TAKEOFF WEIGHT	42,300lb
MAXIMUM SPEED	1320mph
CEILING	50,000+ ft
COMBAT RADIUS	340 miles

ABOVE: Vietnam-era aircraft continued to play a vital role in the Gulf War. An F-4G Wild Weasel radar suppression aircraft (foreground) flies formation on a Fairchild A-10 Thunderbolt II (centre), and an RF-4C reconnaissance aircraft. USAF

ABOVE: A Boeing E-3 Sentry airborne warning and control system (AWACS) viewed from a KC-135 tanker. E-3s played a central role in Desert Storm, flying 7314 combat hours controlling 20,421 tanker operations. USAF

ABOVE: *The General Dynamics EF-111F Raven carried out electronic warfare operations similar to those conducted during the Vietnam Wear but with more advanced and sophisticated electronic equipment.* USAF

ABOVE: *The A-10 Thunderbolt II provided a unique ground air support service aiding ground forces, plinking tanks and heavy artillery, destroying vehicles and digging out soft targets in infantry positions.* USAF

unified command under American leadership, assured that this was to be a military operation and one devoid of national political meddling.

From the outset, generals Schwarzkopf and Horner accepted a plan with four objectives, the first of which was to disable utility supplies and to disconnect Iraqi government forces from communications with their command centres and between themselves. This was to be achieved through predawn air strikes to disable electricity grid lines, communication centres, telecommunications lines and radio communication nodes. It was also important to completely shut down transport routes and to disengage the political leadership from its people.

The second objective was to gain total air superiority by destroying as much as possible of the Iraqi Air Force on the ground, digging up its runways and air base facilities, and engaging it in the air if it dared to fly. For these two, AWACS would be vital elements in coordinating aircraft in the air, this being in the days before intralinks connecting individual aircraft with each other. The third objective involved a feint attack in a different area to the main force, comprising the fourth objective, which was expected to endure several weeks and require extensive air support. Air superiority was essential, as was the preparation of the battlefield, and for these air power was the only enabling force.

These individual objectives meshed in with a four-phase strategy. Phase I would mount a strategic air offensive against Iraq; Phase II would be total suppression of all enemy air defences in the Kuwait Theatre of Operations (KTO); Phase III was preparation of the battlefield; Phase IV would comprise the ground campaign, to evict Iraqi forces from Kuwait and to destroy the Republican Guard to prevent it reasserting itself.

Other Air Force elements were to support the US Army which would use helicopters to land munitions and supplies at pre-chosen locations, some distance inside Iraq itself but in remote desert locations of which the Iraqi government would have no knowledge. These locations would serve as rendezvous points for the invasion forces and for subversive actions

as the initial shield against such a move.

The only US forces immediately available in the area were two KC-135 tankers, a carrier battle group and a mobile operations carrier deployed to Abu Dhabi at the request of the United Arab Emirates, plus six Navy ships of Central Command. Saudi F-15Cs and AWACS aircraft ran a continuous defensive patrol across the Arabian Peninsula as the 1st Tactical Fighter Wing and E-3 AWACS arrived from the US and troops from the 82nd Airborne Division flew in to secure the airfields. By the end of August, Britain's RAF had two fighter squadrons in place and 14 US tactical fighter squadrons had arrived along with a B-52 squadron, four tactical airlift squadrons, seven Army and Navy brigades, each with attack helicopters, and Patriot missiles and three carrier battle groups.

General Schwarzkopf had been back in the United States for most of August but when he returned at the end of the month the political processes were already under way with the United Nations, crafting resolutions to legalise the impending war. In the broader military picture, the commander-in-chief of 9th AF, General Charles A. 'Chuck' Horner had been placed in command of all allied air operations for Desert Shield and for the impending Desert Storm, the eviction of Iraqi forces from Kuwait. A total of 32 countries had initially pledged unity behind the coalition and all accepted the need for a single

SELECTED MUNITIONS EMPLOYED IN DESERT STORM

Munition	Air Force	Army	Navy	Marines	Total
General purpose bombs:					
Mk-82 (500lb)	59,884		10,941	6828	77,653
Mk-83 (1000lb)			10,125	8893	19,081
Mk-84 (2000lb)	10,467		971	751	12,289
Mk-117 (B-52)	43,435				43,435
CBU-52 (Frag')	17,831			17,831	
CBU-87 (Comb')	10,035			10,035	
CBU-89/78 (Gator)	1105		148	61	1314
Mk-20 (Rockeye)	5345		6814	15,828	27,987
Laser-guided bombs:					
GBU-12	4086		205	202	4493
Air-to-surface missiles:					
AGM-114 (Hellfire)		2876	30	159	3065
AGM-65 (Maverick)	5255			41	5296
Grand total:					**222,479**

ABOVE: The Lockheed F-117A stealth strike aircraft carried out the first combat raids on Baghdad during Operation Desert Storm in January 1991, without experiencing a single loss. USAF

ABOVE: General Charles H. Horner commanded all coalition air operations and provided much of the initial planning for Desert Shield and Desert Storm. USAF

by commandos and special forces. There was no defined end objective but it was assumed that the Air Force would pursue the evicted forces all the way back through Basra and up the road to Baghdad, a distance of 280 miles.

Moving the necessary amount of material across a distance of some 7000 miles required a massive airlift as C-5, C-141, KC-10 and aircraft from the Civil Air Reserve Fleet (CARF) brought in 99% of the personnel. This 'aluminium bridge' between America and the Arabian Peninsula called for 50-65 strategic airlift missions per day in the initial phase before settling on an average of 36 a day by late October. When President Bush approved a major increase in US forces on November 8, the rates for C-141 and C-5 flights ramped up to an unprecedented average of 100 per day throughout December and January.

A total of 65 civil and military aircraft were employed delivering 8000 troops to 16 different airfields daily. But moving them around to various points of debarkation in the theatre required almost 17,000 C-130 tactical airlift sorties, logging 21,000 flying hours delivering

159,000 tons of freight and 184,000 personnel. The strategic airlift alone involved 15,402 sorties freighting 544,000 tons of cargo a distance of more than 7000 miles in 206 days. Supporting these and combat deployments, 17,285 air refuelling sorties were flown.

As the coalition forces assembled in Saudi Arabia, Riyadh became a focus for planning, hosting a specially constructed library, briefing rooms, analysts and planners, with staff officers liaising with their opposite numbers in coalition air forces. In all, some 680,000 men and women, including 540,000 ground troops, assembled along with 1800 aircraft from 12 countries and a large naval force in the Persian Gulf and the Red Sea. Throughout, there had been concern expressed by Islamic partners that there must be no attempt to overthrow the Iraqi government itself, or to depose Saddam Hussein, as that was not considered acceptable in a force led by Christian soldiers in an Islamic country.

Countering this, the US Defense Intelligence Agency estimated in January 1991 that Iraq had mobilised 540,000 troops, 4200 tanks,

2800 armoured personnel carriers and 3100 artillery pieces. In addition, Iraq had 700 combat aircraft, a multi-layered air defence system, missile-firing patrol boats and Silkworm surface-to-surface missiles for coastal defence. Post-war analysis indicated that some 84,000 troops were either on leave or had deserted when the air war began, bringing close to 336,000 troops actually in theatre.

DESERT STORM
H-hour was set at 3am local time on January 17, 1991, but long before then aircraft were in the air positioning for a coordinated series of strikes at targets across Kuwait and Iraq, focused on achieving air superiority and severing power and communications. Just 21 minutes prior to H-hour three HH-53J Pave Low helicopters hugged the desert floor providing navigational direction for nine AH-64 Apache attack helicopters heading for Iraqi early-warning sites.

Peeling away just short of the target, the Pave Lows left it to the Apaches to destroy the radar sites, allowing 19 F-15E Strike Eagles through to bomb Scud missile sites in western

BELOW: A conventional air launched cruise missile (CACM) heads inland after being released from a B-52. BOEING

U.S. AIR FORCE

ABOVE: Twenty-two F-117A bombers with the 37th Tactical Fighter Wing line up prior to Operation Desert Storm. *USAF*

ABOVE: F-15E Strike Eagles during Desert Storm, deployed ready for combined sorties providing a heavy punch with guided munitions and iron bombs. *USAF*

ABOVE: An F-117A drops a 5000lb GBU-28 guided bomb, nicknamed the 'Saddomiser', which augments laser-guidance with inertial navigation and GPS guidance. *USAF*

Iraq, followed through in turn by three EF-111As providing electronic countermeasures for a group of F-117s from the 37th Tactical Fighter Wing destined for Baghdad itself.

Nine minutes before H-hour, a single F-117A planted two 2000lb Paveway III laser-guided bombs on the Nukhayb Sector Air Defense Sector southwest of Baghdad and the air defence and command and control system began disintegrating. Firing blind, downtown Baghdad lit up with tracers and anti-aircraft fire, flailing the sky at unseen targets before the F-117s arrived overhead and put laser-guided bombs directly on to the main military communications centre and on the General Staff's wartime headquarters. As the CNN screens went blank in General Horner's headquarters, a loud cheer went up.

As bombs and precisely guided weapons sent blasts reverberating through the Iraqi capital, swarms of BGM-109C Tomahawk missiles launched from ships in the Persian Gulf and the Red Sea 90 minutes earlier slammed into their precisely selected targets, flying up main street to take out the electrical grid by releasing coiled copper wire spools that wrapped themselves around the overhead electrical wires, shorting out the power grid.

Shortly thereafter, seven B-52Gs from the 2nd Bomb Wing based at Barksdale Air Force Base, Louisiana, completed a 17-hour flight when they released the new AGM-86C cruise missile equipped with conventional warheads and returned to base concluding a 35-hour mission involving four aerial refuelling sessions, the longest combat mission in air warfare. On that first day alone, the coalition flew 2759 sorties including 432 by refuelling tankers.

During the war the 68 B-52s comprised a mere 3% of the aircraft employed but delivered 30% of all munitions dropped during the conflict, flying from bases in England, Spain, Diego Garcia and other locations. In 1600 sorties they delivered 72,000 individual pieces of munition weighting more than 27,000 tons.

Early on in the war, the Iraqis decided to place their aircraft in hardened shelters and ride out the attacks and the coalition air forces made a specific targeting objective on these locations, destroying some 375 hardened shelters on 44 airfields including three in Kuwait. The campaign against the shelters began on the night of the January 22/23 with attacks by F-111Fs with

McDonnell Douglas F-15 Eagle

Failures immediately before and during the Vietnam War to find an aircraft common to both Air Force and Navy applications stimulated development of a new lightweight tactical fighter. The appearance of Russia's MiG-25 Foxbat Mach 2.5 interceptor encouraged a rethink and in September 1968 the Air Force issued a requirement that resulted in McDonnell Douglas getting the contract in December 1969 to build the F-15. NASA carried out preliminary wind tunnel studies of the large area fixed wing and twin tail fins, the fuselage carrying two engines and conformal carriage of four Sparrow missiles similar to the configuration of the Phantom II. The large, shoulder mounted wing is a cropped delta with a 45° leading edge sweep.

The F-15B was delivered to the Air Force on November 13, 1974, and with excellent export sales a wide range of variants quickly evolved. F-15C, D, and E variants were deployed to the Gulf War in 1990 with a confirmed 34 'kills' against Russian aircraft with the Iraqi air force, including MiG-23, MiG-25 and MiG-29 types. The F-15E Strike Eagle, specified below, was adapted as an all-weather multi-role strike aircraft and was also deployed to the Gulf, attacking a variety of heavily defended targets and Scud sites. It can carry a weapons load of 23,000lb on two underwing pylons and racks. The F-15E is powered by two 29,000lb thrust Pratt & Whitney F100-PW-229 afterburning turbofan engines. Some 1619 have been built.

LENGTH	63.8ft
WING SPAN	42.8ft
HEIGHT	18.5ft
MAXIMUM TAKEOFF WEIGHT	81,000lb
MAXIMUM SPEED	1875mph
CEILING	60,000ft
COMBAT RADIUS	790 miles

ABOVE: *An Iraqi Scud missile brought down by a Patriot air defence missile.* DOD

ABOVE: *Three F-15s flanked by two F-16s patrol the airspace over burning oil fields set alight as Iraqi forces retreat.* USAF

laser-guided munitions. After this the Iraqis began flying aircraft to Iran, eventually sending a total of 132 which were expropriated, some not being returned for more than 20 years. The Iraqi air force lost more than 400 of its 700 combat aircraft to attack by coalition forces, mostly to hard-target penetrators delivered by the F-117A, the only type capable of launching these weapons at the time.

Another and potentially more sinister threat was that of the Scud missiles, which were used by Saddam Hussein against coalition targets and also against Israel in an attempt to draw them in to the war through reciprocation; the agreement placing many Arab states within the collation was contingent on Israel not being part of the international force. The Israelis held their nerve and the coalition remained intact. More than 80% of mobile Scud launches occurred at night, when the sites were hard to detect. Some 88 extended range Scuds were fired at Israel, Saudi Arabia, and Bahrein. Nevertheless, over the 43 days of Desert Storm, around 1500 strikes were made on Scud-related targets, including 215 on the missiles proper, not a large percentage of the 42,000 combat strikes overall.

Coalition ground forces comprising SAS units moved into Iraq in late January to gather intelligence about Scud missile deployments and on February 24 British and American armoured forces stormed across the border. Two days later Iraqi forces began a retreat from Kuwait and, as part of a scorched earth policy, set light to 737 oil wells. Coalition forces moved faster than anyone had expected and on February 28, 100 hours after the ground campaign had begun, President Bush declared a ceasefire, with much of the Republican Guard intact despite a massive attack on units fleeing back from Kuwait, deep into Iraq. The air campaign had worked – air power had come of age and a war had been dramatically shortened because of it.

STOCKTAKING
During the war of liberation, the 10 principal coalition members and associated air forces flew a total of 118,661 sorties of which the US Air Force contributed 69,406, or 58.5%, during the period January 16 to February 28, 1991, an average of 2697 sorties per day. Peak day for the coalition was February 24 when 3280 sorties

were logged. The greatest number of USAF sorties was logged by tanker/transport aircraft, an aggregate of 27,841 of which 50% were flown by the C-130, 34% by the KC-135 and 6.3% by the C-141. Of combat aircraft, the most flown was 13,087 sorties by the F-16, 8084 by the A-10, 7857 by the F-15, 3985 by the F-111 and 2687 by the F-4 Phantom II. The B-52 flew 1741 sorties while the F-117A flew 1299. A total 68,337 tons of bombs was dropped by USAF strike aircraft, an average of almost 1600 tons per day.

For several types it was a swansong. The variable-geometry F-111, flying in its strike and electronic warfare versions, spanned the two eras of Air Force engagement with enemy forces. Developed as a dual-purpose Navy/ Air Force strike fighter and regarded as another McNamara folly, it had its baptism in Vietnam after being rejected by the Navy, yet made a highly significant contribution in the Gulf War. And the F-117A was about to be succeeded by a new generation of stealthy aircraft but it played a central role in laying the foundation for evicting the invader from Kuwait.

A further signpost to the future was the extensive and highly successful application of precision-guided munitions. Of the 156,846 general purpose and guided bombs dropped by the USAF, only 5.4% were PGMs yet in the decade to the end of the century, guided bombs would come to form the core of assigned munitions in the new conflicts of the modern era, as we will see in the next chapter. And behind it all the logistical and supply requirements for the more than 500,000 men and women engaged through Desert Storm amounted to consumption of 1272 million gallons of fuel. The transport of men and materiel was greater in the given time than at any other similar in the history of US military aviation.

It was a turning point in many ways. Because only the F-117A stealth attack aircraft could carry certain types of precision hard-target munitions, expanded capability was a vital factor for the post-Gulf War Air Force. And because 25-30% of the original 336,000 personnel in the Iraqi armed forces deserted, the 222,000 remaining after the conflict implies a drastically reduced number of casualties to the enemy forces than would be expected from the severity of the strikes by coalition forces, not to mention the ground war. Despite Iraq's lack of reporting on the number of casualties, from these figures as few as 15,000 Iraqi personnel were killed.

Without stealth and using conventional bombs a standard strike package would consist of 32 bomb droppers, 16 escort fighters, eight air defence suppression strikes and 15 tanker aircraft, a procurement and 20-year life operations cost of $6.5 billion. Using precision guided munitions, only 16 bomb droppers would be needed, with the same number of escorts and air defence suppression strikes, but only 11 tankers for an equivalent cost of $5.5 billion. With precision and stealth combined, the package consists of eight aircraft and two tankers, a cost of $1.5 billion. Of the 2040 bombs dropped by the F-117A, 1659 hit their targets with a miss distance 5ft to 540ft, an unprecedented 81%.

At the end of the Second World War, General Eisenhower and his staff identified five key technologies without which they believed the war could not have been won: the amphibious DUKW or 'Duck'; the bulldozer; the Jeep; the 2½ ton ➤

ABOVE: *Demolished civilian and military vehicles caught on the road out of Kuwait.* DOD

ABOVE: *Denied the ability to pursue Iraqi forces up to Baghdad, due to a prior agreement with the Arabs not to unseat another Islamic state, air strikes destroy as much of the Republican Guard as possible.* DOD

STRATEGIC AIRLIFT OPERATIONS

Operation	No of missions	Tonnage	Distance (miles)	Duration (days)
Berlin	277,000	2,300,000	300	463
Vietnam (May '73)	8750	42,200	7500	30
1973 Yom Kippur	560	21,190	6450	33
Gulf War	15,402	544,000	7000	206

truck; and the C-47 aircraft. None were designed for combat. Similarly, the five key technologies vital for the success of the Gulf War were: stealth/ Low Observables; laser-guided bombs; aerial refuelling; High-speed Anti-Radiation Missiles (HARM); and the STU-III, a secure telephone.

The F-117A single-seat bomber flew only 2% of combat missions but accounted for almost 40% of strategic targets and remained at the centre of the air campaign. Two unpiloted platforms used as stealth weapons, the Tomahawk Land Attack Missile (TLAM) and the Conventional Air-Launched Cruise Missile (CALCM), were never contemplated in the pre-war planning yet came to play a highly significant role.

Of the 288 TLAMs fired during the war, 64% were launched during the first two days and all 35 CALCMs launched from B-52's were fired in the first 24 hours. LO weapons were at the very heart of strikes against Iraqi air defences, from which they never recovered. The stealth systems were the only weapons fired against downtown Baghdad, the F-117As by night and the TLAMs by day.

The laser-guided bombs comprised only a small fraction of weapons deployed and were merely adapted general-purpose bombs fitted with guidance kits and laser detection equipment – the true age of the precision-guided bomb had yet to arrive. Nevertheless, LGBs in the Gulf War were crucial in accurately placing munitions on hardened shelters and buildings, although their dramatic visual effect so loved by the media represented only 7.5% of the total munitions dropped.

Aerial refuelling was vital for extending the range of the F-117A, F-15E, F/A-18 and B-52G, all of which required range-extension to reach their targets. The HARM weapons too were essential for the role they played in destroying radar emitters, launched from a range of aircraft including most prominently, the F-4G Wild Weasel. The Air Force accounted for 54% of all HARMs dropped, ensuring an attrition rate per sortie unparalleled in air warfare, only 14 aircraft being lost to combat operations, 0.4 per thousand sorties, an average loss rate of 0.04% per sortie, or 0.4% of the attrition rate in the Second World War.

This was largely achieved through extensive planning, meticulous preparation, adequate training and high operability levels. But the success of the entire campaign had been possible because the mistakes of the past were recognised and the military leadership was granted complete freedom by the political, civilian executive. It changed the way the Air Force was seen by the government and the population at large and was a great step forward, a renewal of applied independence.

In one other aspect the Gulf War changed the way the Air Force embraced new technologies and enhanced operational modes; it was the first conflict in which space-based operations had played a critical role and enhanced mission success. That would become embedded and only grow over the next several decades until today it is an integrated and highly important arm of the Air Force. Established as Air Force Space Command on September 1, 1982, it now has more than 38,000 people operating through 88 locations around the globe and manages and operates satellites, launch vehicles and missile warning radars. ✪

Chapter 16: 21st Century Air Force

ABOVE: Aircraft of the USAF 379th Air Expeditionary Wing and UK and Australian counterparts stationed together at Al Udeid Air Base, Qatar. Aircraft include KC-135 Stratotanker, F-15E Strike Eagle, F-117A Nighthawk, F-16CJ Falcon, RAF GR-4 Tornado, and Australian F/A-18 Hornet. USAF

ABOVE: Begun in April 2006, Operation Mountain Lion was designed to find enemy fighters in remote regions of Afghanistan and to destroy their camps. USAF

For the first time in the history of aviation, in the Gulf War of 1991, air power was the clear deciding factor in a major conflict involving land, sea and air forces – and the US Air Force provided the key to evicting Saddam Hussein from Kuwait. The preparation of the battlefield had been complete and the ground war progressed with lightning speed because of that.

The strategic assault on Iraq's infrastructure had proven to be a vital element in bringing Iraq to its knees and allowing the coalition to proceed in a way that would have been impossible without stealthy weapons and smart munitions.

In a war that lasted 44 days, the ground campaign was over in just 100 hours because of air power. The USAF flew 60% of coalition air sorties and executed a leadership commanding adequate resources and unimpeded with political meddling in how the campaign was managed. But the conflict was not over. Along with Britain, France and Italy, the role of the Air Force continued in Provide Comfort, the protection of refugees and Kurds hunted down inside Iraq by Saddam Hussein. Armed A-10s pursued ground forces carrying out ethnic cleansing and F-16s and F-15s patrolled the skies looking for enemy aircraft, policing a no-fly zone in the north.

The struggle to establish peace in Iraq was sustained by a succession of internal crises, beginning with the Shi'ite rebellion in southern Iraq and by Iranian incursions into the country watched by US forces. Beginning on August 27, 1992, Operation Southern Watch supported the intent of a UN resolution calling on Saddam Hussein to stop bombing and strafing the Shi'ites. US aircraft were kept constantly busy in a sustained counter-air operation against Iraqi aircraft which soon scuttled away whenever American fighters were sighted. And so it went on until President George W. Bush began a more aggressive policy toward Saddam Hussein, seeking to enact a policy of regime change which had been an official US objective since October 1998.

Worsening tension on the world scene followed the September 11, 2001, attacks on New York and Washington by Al-Qaeda terrorists, causing the deaths of 2996 people. With the Air Force committed to hunting down Al Qaeda fighters in Afghanistan, the US Air Force was once again conducting operations across the globe, resources stretched by sustained operations in Iraq. These were applied also to the invasion of Iraq itself in March 2003 with the successful removal of Saddam Hussein where air support was crucial, albeit on a much reduced scale to the eviction of Iraqi forces from Kuwait in 1991. ➤

ABOVE: F-15E Strike Eagles drop 2000lb JBU-31 guided bombs on Afghan positions in 2009. The aircraft proved spectacularly successful in dropping precision guided munitions in the campaign against Afghan rebels. USAF

of Air Force organisation dated May 31, 1992, dissolved the once-proud SAC as well as Tactical Air Command and Military Airlift Command and absorbed those assets in the new Air Combat Command, also responsible for all ICBMs.

After the inactivation of SAC, all strategic nuclear forces formerly controlled by the Air Force and the Navy were transferred to United States Strategic Command, activated at Offutt Air Force Base, Omaha, Nebraska, the former SAC headquarters. In 2009, the ICBM force and the B-1B and B-2 strategic nuclear delivery systems were transferred to Air Force Global Strike Command (GSC), essentially SAC by another name, headquartered now at Barksdale Air Force Base, Louisiana, and consisting of the 8th AF and the 20th AF, an historic assemblage of elite forces.

Currently, the GSC has 62 B-1B and 20 B-2A aircraft in its inventory together with 450 ICBMs: a total strategic nuclear force of 532 airborne and missile delivery platforms. Added to these are the 336 Trident II missiles in 14 US Navy Ohio-class nuclear-powered submarines making a total strategic strike force of 868 delivery systems for the 4018 nuclear weapons presently deployed or

Further involvement of the US Air Force was called for after the domino effect of revolutions breaking out in North Africa, where America supported a campaign to depose Muammar Gaddafi, accomplished in October 2011. But here the involvement of the Air Force was in a support role. The radical overthrow of national leaders by rebels frequently associated with terrorist organisations, a trend which had ignited conflict across the region, came to Syria in March 2011 but escalated as radical and extremist groups flared to prominence over the following three years.

A new and more sadistic element of Islamic extremism emerged with Daesh and the Americans were involved once again. Under Operation Inherent Resolve, led by the US Air Force, UN nations had been fighting Daesh since President Barack Obama ordered the first air strike on August 7, 2014.

By the end of 2015 some 15,000 air strikes had been launched. And by the end of 2016, more than 30,700 strikes had been mounted against this brutal and inhuman regime in the previous 12 months. The more robust and determined approach taken by President Donald Trump, formally declared at a Joint Session of Congress on February 28, 2017, will increase considerably the role the US Air Force plays in the assault on Daesh.

A NEW ORGANISATION

Over time, the structure of the US Air Force has changed with evolving needs and responsibilities. No longer a service dominated by strategic nuclear deterrence, with secondary attention paid to tactical air requirements, the Air Force has been reshaped by a succession of geopolitical events, not least the changing international arena. And from that has come a greater emphasis on tactical and multi-purpose combat aircraft.

With the collapse of the Soviet Union and the end of the Gulf War in 1991, the role of America's nuclear airborne deterrent began to evolve toward a different structure. Strategic Air Command appeared superfluous to the evolving political landscape and a redirection

ABOVE: An Air Force Special Operations Command HC-130P refuels an HH-60 Pavehawk during training at Randolph Air Force Base, Texas. USAF

ABOVE: Loaders arm a B-1B with 2000lb GBU-31 precision guided munitions for a bombing raid on Afghanistan. USAF

in storage. Thus the Air Force remains a crucial element in the national strategic nuclear deterrent.

Air Combat Command consists of elements formerly under Strategic Air Command, Tactical Air Command, and Military Airlift Command. When it formed it was to be the service provider for non-global strike combat aircraft, supporting the unified combat commands and to organise and maintain combat-ready units. To achieve that it assumed control of all fighter assets, bombers, reconnaissance platforms, ICBMs and battle management resources. As indicated above, ICBMs were eventually shifted to Global Strike Command.

Inevitably, changes arose where experience demonstrated a need for readjustments and the first was to assume responsibility for the combat search and rescue mission (CSAR), formerly with Air Mobility Command, and that transfer was activated on February 1, 1993. On July 1 that year, the F-15 and F-16 training units (58th and 325th Fighter Wings) were moved out of ACC and into Air Education and Training Command (AETC). In October 1993 all the C-130s with Military Airlift Command were moved to Air Combat Command, with the exception of cargo and tankers specifically assigned to United States Air Forces in Europe (USAFE) and Pacific Air Forces (PAF).

USAFE was formed back in 1945 to dismantle the air power of the Third Reich but on April 20, 2012, it was re-designated United States Air Forces Europe – Air Forces Africa (USAFE-AFAFRICA) when the 17th AF was inactivated, leaving the core 3rd AF. With 38,000 personnel it supports NATO objectives and operations across the European continent and Africa and has air bases in the UK, Italy, Portugal, Germany, Turkey and Djibouti.

In the UK, over the next few years operational wings at RAF Mildenhall will deactivate and remove to Germany and the base will be shut down, leaving RAF Lakenheath as the UK's primary USAF combat base.

Pacific Air Command (PAC) is headquartered at Joint Base Pearl Harbor-Hickham (renamed from Hickam AFB) and is one of two major commands outside the continental United States, with 45,000 personnel. Responsibility extends from the west coast of the United States to the east coast of Asia and from the Arctic to the Antarctic, an area containing 44 countries and two billion people.

With political tension between China and the United States, two successive US presidents have chosen to make a stand in South-East Asia over territorial claims to contested islands in the South China Sea and have increased force levels in Japan and South Korea, the former maintaining a close watch on China's ambitions regarding Taiwan, and the latter specifically regarding the military aspirations of North Korea.

Formed on September 1, 1982, USAF Space Command is headquartered at Peterson Air Force Base, Colorado, and has responsibility for expendable launch vehicles, satellites and space operations, supporting not only the Air Force but the Army, the Navy and the Marine Corps. It provides weather information, communications via satellite, missile warning and navigation through the Navstar Global Positioning System (GPS) series of satellites.

While it is true to say that the USAF had been 'in space' since the 1960s, it is only within the last 35 years that space-based assets have assumed such an important role in defence activity, in the

securing of vital services for all US forces and in managing their procurement and launch. The USAF is largely out of the business of developing and launching reconnaissance and surveillance satellites, which are primarily the prerogative of the National Reconnaissance Office, which serves all armed services, and the Central Intelligence Agency, with images and electronic information including signals intelligence.

Quite recently though, US Air Force Space Command has assumed responsibility for cyberspace operations and for network integration, net-centric warfare and space innovation and development. New systems are continually being developed in conjunction with other Air Force commands and units and with other armed services and civilian organisations responsible for the national defence. USAFSC operates integrated programmes generated and evolved with different commands and with other services. One such example is the Boeing X-37B spaceplane which is a classified project under the responsibility of the USAF Rapid Capabilities Office.

Developed from a NASA-funded project in the 1990s when there was a plan to develop a satellite repair vehicle which could be carried to space inside the Shuttle orbiter, it was taken over by the Defence Advanced Projects Agency and adapted as a systems development vehicle powered by deployable solar arrays. The vehicle borrows its aerodynamic shaping from the NASA Shuttle orbiter design and is equipped with propulsion systems for changing orbit and for retro-fire prior to return to Earth.

First launched on April 22, 2010, for a flight lasting 224 days it was returned to a runway landing at Edwards Air Force Base, California. A second X-37B was launched on March 5, 2011 and remained in orbit for 468 days before returning to a controlled landing, followed by the return to space of the first flight model on December 11, 2012. It returned after 674 days in space and was followed by the launch of the second X-37B for the second time on May 20, 2015 – which was still in orbit as of March 2017.

Formed through the same restructuring

ABOVE: Maintenance training on a C-130 by technicians with the Air National Guard, a vital component of the Air Force in peace and in war. USAF

AIR FORCE PERSONNEL STRENGTH 1995-2015

Year	Strength
1995	400,409
2000	355,654
2010	334,196
2015	311,357

which saw the establishment of ACC and GSC, with headquarters at Scott Air Force Base, Illinois Air Mobility Command (AMC) carries the heavy responsibility of strategic movement and repositioning of personnel and material around the globe, supporting every other command to varying degrees. Its existing fleet of C-141 Starlifters was replaced from 1993 with the C-17 Globemaster III, the third generation cargo-lifter of that name, while presiding over the modification and upgrading of the C-5B and C-5M Super Galaxy. AMC has 170 C-17s, 34 C-5 Galaxy variants, and 97 C-130 variants among aircraft in its total inventory of 381 transport types.

AMC also has responsibility for special missions, aerial refuelling, aeromedical evacuation and provides alert refuelling for United States Strategic Command as well as supporting VIP flights with a variety of aircraft including Air Force One and Two. AMC has a large fleet of 159 KC-135 tankers comprising

ABOVE: The lower deck battle station on a B-52H. With an average age of more than 50 years, the B-52 has received frequent upgrades as the aircraft continues to play a unique role in air operations as a bomb truck with unparalleled warload capacity. USAF

ABOVE: A KC-135 from the 100th Air Refueling Wing, RAF Mildenhall, England, tops up a pair of F-16s from Spangdahlem Air Base, Germany, during a multinational exercise. The 100th ARW Stratotanker fleet bears the 'Box D' tail marking, the only unit in the USAF authorised to display its Second World War tail insignia. USAF

ABOVE: Women have access to every job in the modern Air Force. Here, Senior Airman Nayibe Ramos of the 2nd Space Operations Squadron at Schriever AFB, Colorado, runs through a checklist during GPS satellite operations. USAF

ABOVE: The fifth-generation Lockheed Martin F-22A has advanced open-architecture avionics and intralinks allowing formations of Raptors to exchange target and weapon load designations for coordinated attack beyond visual range and beyond detection by enemy fighters. USAF

when the F-15 was introduced as a successor to the F-4 Phantom II, that it was far too expensive and could never be afforded, continue to reverberate. The issue of cost continues to be hotly debated today whenever the procurement of replacement aircraft is proposed. The issue remains highly relevant too – because at present the Air Force has a rapidly ageing inventory and little money to do much about it.

Skewed perhaps by the aged B-52 force (airframes being 53 years old on average among the 76 G and H variants), the average age of the bomber force is 39 years, but even the B-1B/B-2A force has an average age of 24 years, which is the same for the fighter and attack inventory where 543 F-15 variants have an average age of almost 28 years. Across the grand total of 5472 aircraft in the US Air Force inventory, a number of which types are non-operational, the average age is close to 30 years.

The size and resource base of the Air Force today is in decline due to eight years of reduced funding, the total number of active aircraft falling by 9% from a peak of 6013 in 2006. Reduced funding has also cut the number of tactical flying hours per crew per month, from 16 in 2006 to 13 in 2017. That 19% reduction is having a debilitating effect on the training, on combat effectiveness and on the ability of pilots and air crew to maintain peak readiness and achieve optimum performance.

Overall, the Air Force gets 28% of the total defence budget, the Army receives a little more than 23%, while the Navy and the Marine Corps gets more than 30%. Between 2007 and 2013, funding for the Air Force fell by almost 10% and only modest reductions in the level of that decline have been granted in the last four years. However, the USAF remains home to the world's most advanced aircraft.

The Advanced Tactical Fighter programme, launched in 1981 to develop a new air superiority fighter possessing advanced stealth and low-observable technology, resulted in the Lockheed Martin F-22 which entered service in 2005. As a fifth-generation combat aircraft it incorporates a wide range of radar, thermal, acoustic and visual suppression technologies, many of which emerged through the A-12, F-117A and B-2A programmes.

The highly sensitive nature of those processes, materials and applications has meant that the F-22 has never been made available for sale to any other government and because of that it is unable to take advantage of volume sales to lower the unit cost for the American armed

66% of the tanker force, others comprising 59 KC-10A and 21 HC-130 variants.

Other major commands of the US Air Force are Air Education and Training Command, Air Force Materiel Command, Air Force Reserve Command, Air Force Special Operations Command, and the Air National Guard.

NEW WEAPONS

The Gulf War had a successful outcome thanks to quantitative and qualitative superiority and that would become the doctrine for the 21st century, where new weapons and demanding requirements would engage assets with unpredictable enemies in asymmetric warfare. In net-centric warfare which grew during the 1990s, the opposition can be overwhelmed with

minimum force based on enhanced computer networking through dispersed elements.

That is allowing the Air Force to maintain access to disproportionate response – always necessary for the enemy to know that its adversary has that capability – while minimising collateral damage and holding in reserve the option for deploying overwhelming force. But it requires an entirely new type of aircraft – one which is designed from the outset for integrated operations involving several different platforms focused on to a single mission objective, but with spectrum options to take in a wide variety of situational changes during a single sortie.

The desire to acquire the very latest technology and the very best designs comes at a high price and arguments that were raised even

services – unlike previous generations in this class such as the F-86, F-104, F-4, F-15 and F-16 combat aircraft since the Second World War, which sold very well abroad. Moreover, constraints on the overall defence budget, and the cost of foreign wars, prevented the Air Force receiving the number of aircraft it wanted.

When the projected number of F-22 that the Air Force could afford fell, the price per aircraft went up. When the production run was assessed at 750 the unit price was an estimated $140 million, rising to $200 million when the run was cut back to 341, and $370 million when the buy dropped to 187. Opponents of lower quotas said that with a full procurement of 750 aircraft the total bill would amount to $105 billion, compared to less than $69 billion for an F-22 force of only 187 aircraft, which was the final total the Air Force received. The unit cost would be very much higher but the overall cost would be lower.

Unfortunately, the operating cost of the F-22 has remained higher than originally projected and despite efforts to reduce the operating expenditure per aircraft, it remains high. Nevertheless, maintenance requires 43 man/hours per flight hour while the cost per flight is over $67,000 per flight hour. This is almost four times the cost per flight of an F-16. However, assessments of a combat aircraft's true value must also take into account levels of flight readiness. When the F-22 was introduced it had a mission availability level of 62% and this increased to 70% within five years. However, changes to procedures and technical problems have set this back again down to 63% at present.

Pricing and costs must be set against the overall advantage to be had from an aircraft of the calibre of the F-22 as a means of maximising the type's value per-dollar which, while much more costly to buy, might be more effective and in itself reduce the overall cost of the package otherwise required to complete mission objectives in the long term. But there is one further element in the equation – smart weapons, and particularly laser-guided bombs – as force multipliers.

LGB procurement seemed a logical way to cut overall munitions costs, reduce the number of aircraft required to achieve a

ABOVE: A GBU-24 Paveway III with a 2000lb BLU-109 warhead for penetration strikes demonstrating pinpoint accuracy and effectiveness in opening buried bunkers. *USAF*

F-22 Raptor

The Air Force set out its requirement for a fifth-generation fighter in 1981 through the Advanced Tactical Fighter programme. Designed to replace the F-15 and F-16 and as a counter to emerging Russian threats such as the Su-27 and the MiG-29, the ATF resulted in a competition between the Lockheed Martin YF-22 and the Northrop YF-23, with a decision to buy the F-22 announced on April 23, 1991. The aircraft featured a large truncated trapezoidal wing, twin vertical fins canted outward, tailerons on the aft fuselage and two engines with super-cruise capability ensuring supersonic cruising speed with afterburner and two-dimensional thrust vectoring capability for high levels of manoeuvrability. The Air Force wanted 750 F-22s with a first flight in 1994 but the type was compromised in that its high cost due to stealthy design and exotic materials for low radar cross-section, plus the inability to sell such a sophisticated aircraft to foreign countries, made it very expensive for the US Air Force to buy and operate.

The Air Force received only 187 F-22s, with production ending in December 2011. The F-22 became operational in 2005 and got its combat debut in September 2014 during the intervention in Syria. While combat operations are anticipated, the aircraft's primary role is on intelligence, surveillance and reconnaissance (ISR) gathering missions. The F-22 is powered by two Pratt & Whitney F119-PW-100 turbofan engines with a thrust of 26,000lb or 35,000lb on afterburner. The Raptor has a single 20mm six-barrel Vulcan rotary cannon in the starboard wing root and can carry six AIM-120 AMRAAM and two AIM-9 Sidewinder missiles. In air-to-ground mode it can carry two 1000lb JDAM or eight 250lb GBU-39 small-diameter bombs, with four AMRAAM and two Sidewinders.

LENGTH	62.1ft
WING SPAN	44.5ft
HEIGHT	16.7ft
MAXIMUM TAKEOFF WEIGHT	83,500lb
MAXIMUM SPEED	1500mph
SUPERCRUISE	1220mph
CEILING	greater than 65,000ft
COMBAT RADIUS	529 miles

ABOVE: A Block 20 F-22A Raptor with two large 600 gallon external fuel tanks. The aircraft has four underwing stores points each with a 5000lb capacity. *USAF*

ABOVE: The USAF launches a military satellite for the National Reconnaissance Office on a Delta 4 Heavy at Cape Canaveral, Florida, November 6, 2016. *USAF*

in conflict management around the world.

While LGBs were used during daylight in the Vietnam War because the pilots had to visually acquire their targets, during the Gulf War operations could be conducted around the clock because the aircraft carried forward-looking infrared radar (FLIR) target sensors such as Pace Tack fitted to the F-111F and the F-117A. But the clear-air requirement which still restricted its use was solved with the Joint Direct Attack Munitions (JDAM) guided by Navstar GPS satellites transforming this into a truly all-weather weapon.

JDAMs were first employed by the B-2 against Serbian targets during Operation Allied Force in 1999 and while the munition's initial design error distance was 43ft, accuracy when dropped by the B-2 was improved by using the aircraft's radar. Because of this, JDAMs dropped by the B-2 have a proven average miss radius of less than 20ft. The lessons learned here were applied to an Air Force of the future, one which could live within constrained budgets using technology to get much greater value than ever before. It was to be a signpost on the road to the Air Force of tomorrow. ✪

specific objective and lower the attrition rate through placing fewer aircraft in harm's way. First used in the Vietnam War during 1968, Paveway laser-guided bombs started the long and evolutionary journey from industrial age air warfare, where most ordnance missed its target, to one in which they either hit them or came close enough to do the job required.

Operational use of LGBs demonstrated an average miss radius of 9.8ft and they became the first to be employed in significant numbers and proved highly effective in combat, achieving 50% hit rates. In the period from 1991 to 2003, they accounted for 52% of the nearly 54,000 guided munitions deployed by fixed-wing aircraft

USAF AIRCRAFT INVENTORY BY TYPE 2017

	Active	ANG	AFRC	Total
Bomber	140	0	18	158
Fighter/attack	1312	611	111	2034
Special operations	144	4	0	148
ISR/C3	437	91	10	538
Tanker	239	184	68	491
Transport	381	207	139	727
Helicopter	157	17	15	189
Trainer	1,187	0	0	1,187
Grand Total	**3997**	**1114**	**361**	**5472**

Note: ANG denotes Air National Guard and AFRC denotes the Air Force Reserve Command. These figures denote operational quantities.

ABOVE: An F-22 from the 1st Tactical Fighter Wing, displaying the box-shaped air inlet and shaped fuselage, external design features of which maximise stealth characteristics that give the aircraft high levels of survivability in a hostile environment. *USAF*

Chapter 17: Future Force

The US Air Force has come a very long way since President Woodrow Wilson sent American airmen to the Western Front in 1917 and, since the Gulf War of 1991, it has faced many demands, challenges and responsibilities – most recently supporting an alliance of nations against the terrorist organisation known as Daesh (or ISIL).

Yet today there is a new awareness of the value placed in the combined assets of stealthy, low-observable, design features matched to smart bombs, guided weapons that have an incomparably better accuracy than anything that could have been imaged when the Air Force was formed 70 years ago. No surprise then that those who count the very real price of new and exotic weapon systems like to draw comparisons to show the logic of their path to the future.

Comparisons always gain traction from parallel experiences at the same place but separated by different generations of equipment and strategies, the latter made possible through transformative technology. On April 15, 1986, the US Air Force mounted a strike mission to attack targets in Libya in response to terrorist activities and the bombing of a nightclub in West Berlin ordered by Muammar Gaddafi. Known as Operation Eldorado Canyon, 18 F-111F medium bombers of the 48th Tactical Fighter Wing flew from Upper Heyford, UK, in a combined attack involving 15 carrier-based aircraft off two carriers in the Mediterranean.

Overflight denial by France, Spain and Italy forced the formation to fly a circuitous route involving 28 KC-135A refuelling tankers and 16 electronic warfare aircraft, including four EF-111s, to suppress Libyan air defences. The 33 strike aircraft dropped 48 guided and 252 unguided bombs on five designated targets, with the loss of one F-111F and its two-man crew. Fast forward 31 years to January 19, 2017, and a strike on Libya where B-52s from Whiteman Air Force Base, Missouri, dropped 108 precision guided bombs that destroyed two

ABOVE: B-2As at Whiteman Air Force Base after returning from a long duration strike. USAF

ABOVE: A B-2A Spirit drops 32 JDAM bombs during a capabilities test. USAF

terrorist camps and killed 108 Daesh terrorists.

The 2017 attack was accomplished with just two B-2s and four crewmembers placed in harm's way plus 15 tankers out of area, a result more decisive than the 77 aircraft in the 1986 raid which dropped 300 bombs. And on a measure of cost, the 2017 raid was much more economical, despite the fact that the B-2 support costs run at $110,000 a day. The total strike package on Libya in 2017 cost $600,000 for the aircraft and $2 million for the munitions, compared with around $15 million for the 1986 raid on the basis that each of the two US carriers

cost about $6.5 million a day, notwithstanding the cost of the land-based aircraft.

But the lessons were being learned long before January 2017. The operational debut of the B-2 Spirit occurred during the Kosovo war and a bombing campaign which lasted from March 24 to June 11, 1999. The NATO operation brought in more than 1000 NATO aircraft and provided an opportunity to evaluate the stealthy bomber under operational conditions. Full operating capability had only been achieved on January 1, 1997, and the 50 sorties carried out by the B-2 accounted for one-third of all selected ➤

ABOVE: An MQ-1 Predator carries four Hellfire missiles on pursuit of a mocked-up target during an evaluation flight. *USAF*

ABOVE: MQ-1 Predator pilots at Balad Air Base, Iraq, controlling the Remotely Piloted Aircraft before the US departed in November 2011. *USAF*

Serbian targets in just eight weeks, despite dropping only 11% of all bombs. Operationally too, it was a demonstration of long-range strike, six aircraft flying from Whiteman Air Force Base on a round-trip lasting 30 hours.

Statistically, the B-2 carried out a mere 1.7% of all NATO sorties in the Kosovo campaign, and while many of those were not bombing runs the overall performance of the aircraft was exceptionally high and displayed the ability of this type to carry out conventional operations in addition to its design role of nuclear deterrence. The missions also allowed the B-2 to boast first-use of GPS-guided JDAM munitions, ushering in a new era of precise targeting and a more efficient use of assets at much lower cost per target.

As confidence grew, the aircraft was employed on targets in Afghanistan during Operation Enduring Freedom, flying nonstop from Whiteman and back. In 2003 confidence had grown sufficiently high to base B-2s in the Middle East beginning in 2003, shortly after full operational capability had been declared. Support for foreign deployments included special environmental hangars at RAF Fairford, UK, and at Diego Garcia in the Indian Ocean, in spite of which very long distance raids have been conducted requiring the aircraft to be in the air for more than 44 hours.

Half the B-2 sorties flown in support of combat operations have been from non-US locations and a test of the aircraft's penetration survivability came when it was assigned a strike on Libya in 2011, a similar strike to that conducted by non-stealthy aircraft in 1986 but this time alone and without any support aircraft for radar suppression tasks. In fact, the reason the B-2 had been assigned to these raids on Libya was because it could fly direct from the US without overflight permissions requiring diplomatic discussions for which there was always a risk of prior warning being passed to the enemy.

B-2 operations in several theatres in which it has flown with impunity point the way toward an emphasis on very long-range strike from the continental United States, avoiding the need for overflight permissions or support at foreign bases where terrorist attack is always a threat. This had always been the driving imperative behind the Cold War search for a very long-range strategic bomber and some had imaged that a supersonic strike package was the way ahead. The high fuel consumption demanded by conventional

turbojet engines for supersonic flight continues to prevent that. But promising technologies for hypersonic flight, speeds in excess of Mach 5, are now being considered, about which more anon.

A WAY FORWARD?

Strategists and planners in the Air Force and among civilian think-tanks alike, recognise that the future for the Air Force lies not only in these assets, even combined in a single stealthy package capable of providing highly accurate and precise results using smart weapons at a fraction of the cost of operations to achieve similar objectives just a few years ago. Most recently the focus has been on a mixed fleet of piloted and pilotless air vehicles. These today are already synonymous with effective combat operations and go largely unpublicised whenever piloted aircraft are quoted in the media.

The January 2017 strike on Daesh camps in Libya was set up on detailed intelligence obtained from the MQ-9 Reaper Remotely Piloted Aircraft (RPA). Today the Air Force has three RPAs in its inventory (MQ-1 Predator, RQ-4 Global Hawk and MQ-9 Reaper), and a fourth (RQ-170 Sentinel) silently in the mix.

The MQ-1 is a weaponised platform carrying out a multi-mission role and made its first flight in July 1994 and was delivered to the Air Force as the RQ-1 in 1996. Now capable of carrying two AGM-114 Hellfire missiles, four AIM-92 Stinger or six AIM-176 missiles, the fleet is currently being phased out and will be replaced with the MQ-9 in 2018. The MQ-1 is powered by a single 115hp Rotax 914F turbocharged four-cylinder engine.

The RQ-4 Global Hawk is a large, 32,000lb long range endurance sensor platform which made its first flight on February 28, 1998, and is currently based at Beale Air Force Base, California. It is powered by a single Rolls-Royce F137-RR-100 turbofan engine providing a speed of 356mph and a range of 10,000 miles. New payloads including an optical bar camera similar to that previously flown in the U-2, first flown on the RQ-4 on October 6, 2016, and enhanced weather survivability for synthetic aperture radar applicable to poor atmospheric conditions.

The MQ-9 reaper is a high-altitude, long endurance, RPA capable of supporting a wide range of missions through an adaptable payload capability, tailoring it to specific objectives. It has a persistent hunter-killer role, for which it can carry external propellant tanks for its single 900shp Honeywell TPE331-10GD turboprop engine. First flown in 2001, this is a highly flexible weapons platform in operation with the Air Force since 2007. With seven hard points it is capable of carrying 2300lb of ordnance, options including four Hellfire missiles, two 500lb

ABOVE: Setting its bulky proportions in scale, technicians attend an RQ-4 Global Hawk at Beale Air Force base. *USAF*

ABOVE: Carrying four Hellfire missiles, the MQ-9 Reaper has already paid back its development cost many times over through the saved flight costs of piloted aircraft. *USAF*

ABOVE: The RQ-170 is a highly classified platform which has already played a significant role in covert intelligence gathering. *TRUTHDOWSER*

ABOVE: The Lockheed Martin F-35A will replace large numbers of F-16 fighters in service with the Air Force and eventually carry out roles presently performed by the A-10. *USAF*

Paveway II LGBs and the 500lb GBU-38 JDAM. It can also carry the AIM-9 Stinger air-to-air missile and the RAF has successfully conducted tests with the Brimstone missile, a 'fire-and-forget' ground-attack weapon with a range of 12 miles.

The classified operational use of the very stealthy Lockheed Martin RQ-170 Sentinel testifies to its sophisticated capabilities, applied already during operations in Afghanistan, Iran, Pakistan and other places where covert intelligence gathering is required. Operated by the Air Force for the CIA, the RQ-170 is powered by a single turbofan engine and is part of a family of RPAs and unmanned aerial vehicles, including the mysterious RQ-180, which is another stealthy surveillance aircraft for operation in heavily contested airspace. The RQ-170/RQ-180 series are quietly retiring ageing types such as the RQ-4.

Integrated intelligence gathering and exploitation of long-range strike with stealthy aircraft is already firmly entrenched in Air Force operations but the economics of combined stealth/RPA is driving planning toward a successor to the B-2A Spirit in a programme designated B-21. The origin of the B-21 rests within the Next-Generation Bomber programme, a series of studies between 2004 and 2009 examining options for a successor to the existing fleet of manned bombers, anticipating deployment by 2018. That was cancelled, itself succeeded by the Long-Range Strike studies programme with priority on affordability and quantity production.

HEMISPHERIC STRIKE

Examples of high-tech response to emerging threats and world challenges had driven the cost of solutions to such a high level that they became unaffordable, the B-2A and the F-22A Raptor being examples quoted here already. In each example, the production runs had dropped dramatically, the B-2A from 132 to 21 and in the case of the F-22A from 750 to 187. The levelling of expectations and the integration of mission roles now applied to the new generation placed greater emphasis on lower procurement cost, higher production runs and enhanced flexibility in systems configuration, so that the B-21, like the F-22A, will have an open-architecture avionics and electronic weapons suite.

Only vague ideas about what the B-21 will look like have been hinted at, despite the relatively rapid pace of programme development. Although contested by the losing bidder Boeing, the Northrop Grumman long-range strike aircraft is expected to be in operation by the late 2020s and to keep it affordable the Air Force pledges a unit procurement cost of $500 million, a quarter that of the B-2A, for the 100-200 aircraft it intends to buy.

The B-21 represents a truly transformational path to the future, an evolved configuration marrying clear and distinct features from the piloted B-2A and the unpiloted RQ-170/RQ-180 series, in external shape and adaptability. It is quite likely that the B-21 could be operated unmanned, although that is not the prime design function. But the pilot-heritage is there and was demonstrated on September 19, 2016, when the aircraft was officially named Raider, after the Doolittle raid of 1942, at a ceremony attended by the last surviving Doolittle raider, Lieutenant Colonel Richard E. Cole.

Operations with the B-21 will be selective and applicable to unique mission requirements

REMOTELY PILOTED AIRCRAFT

	MQ-1 Predator	MQ-9 Reaper	RQ-4 Global Hawk
Length	27ft	36ft	47.6ft
Span	55ft	66ft	130.9ft
Height	6.9ft	12.5ft	15.3ft
Maximum weight	2,250lb	10,250lb	32,500lb
Speed	84-135mph	230mph	356mph
Ceiling	25,000ft	50,000ft	60,000ft
Range	770 miles	1150 miles	10,000 miles
Endurance	40 hours	14+ hours	32+ hours

but the large bulk of conventional tactical aircraft in today's inventory will be replaced by the F-35A Lightning II, of which the Air Force has a requirement for 1763. The F-35 emerged from the Joint Strike Fighter programme which began in the early 1990s seeking a common, affordable, fighter for the Air Force, Navy and Marine Corps. It was to replace a wide range of existing types in US service including the F-16, A-10, F/A-18 and AV-8B, and provide a replacement aircraft for export to NATO countries, much like the F-16 had been marketed in the 1970s.

What emerged from a competitive fly-off where Boeing lost to Lockheed Martin, was a single design configuration for three solutions: the F-35A for the Air Force, the F-35B short-takeoff/vertical landing variant for the Marine Corps, and the F-35C carrier-based variant for the Navy. Despite the attempt at commonality, there is wide variation in the detailed configuration of each variant, especially with the vectored thrust engines for the F-35B, a type which the Air Force once considered as a replacement for the VSTOL AV-8B but has now declined.

Beyond the immediate deployment of the F-35A throughout this decade and the B-21A in the next, the third decade of this century should see the appearance of a hypersonic strike system, complementing the new stealthy bomber as a truly hemispheric weapon capable of hitting targets anywhere in the world within three hours of launch. Such a system will almost certainly be pilotless, a further extension of the role played by subsonic RPAs in today's air war.

Still further into the future is the Prompt Global Strike concept bringing that response down to within one hour, merging the acquisition of real-time intelligence and the arrival on site of a response package fired from the continental United States. It may well be that these two concepts will merge, perhaps have merged already, and that the B-21 will be the more conventional response blending search, surveillance and strike within a single aircraft, no longer a package requiring multiple assets.

While the Air Force continues to remain

ABOVE: An F-35A Lightning II from the 58th Fighter Squadron, 33rd Fighter Wing lines up for a refuelling operation. USAF

flexible, adapting, responding and shaping its organisational structure to evolving requirements it will remain a bedrock of national defence for the United States and, through partnership agreements and the 'coalition of the willing', for its allies too, a strident force for security in a dangerous and troubled world.

Covering a broad spectrum, from nuclear deterrence to famine and aid relief, from humanitarian missions to providing shelters after natural disasters, the US Air Force is the world's largest military air power. It has won the right to be that through 100 years of air combat experience and 70 years of independence. It will continue to be so. ✪

F-35A Lightning II

The F-35 programme evolved from the Joint Strike Fighter studies which specified a common airframe for three separate variants replacing existing types with the Air Force, the Navy and the Marine Corps. The Air Force variant is a fifth-generation combat aircraft for ground-attack and air defence. It is the cheapest of all three variants and, when in full scale production, unit costs are expected to stabilise at an affordable $85 million, a figure reduced by export sales and high volume production for several air forces. Extracting considerable engineering and design detail from the much more costly F-22A Raptor, the F-35A is a stealthy aircraft with exportable technology evolved from previous experience on other stealth projects.

It is required by specification to match the F-16 in manoeuvrability and high performance agility while providing greater range, payload and survivability. The type has some operational limitations and is not considered to be an air superiority fighter like the F-22A but many of the duties carried out by the F-15 will be shared between the Raptor and the Lightning II. The F-35A first flew on December 15, 2006, and by the end of 2016 the aircraft had been declared as 'basic' combat ready with the 34th Fighter Squadron at Hill Air Force Base, Utah.

The F-35A is powered by a single Pratt & Whitney F135 turbofan engine with a dry thrust of 28,000lb and 43,000lb with afterburner. It carries a single 25mm GAU-22/A-4 rotary cannon with 180 rounds and a total munitions capacity of 18,000lb, accommodated in two internal bomb bays, with a capacity of 1500lb each, and six underwing stores pylons, each with a capacity for 2500lb.

LENGTH	50.5ft
WING SPAN	35ft
HEIGHT	14.2ft
MAXIMUM TAKEOFF WEIGHT	70,000lb
MAXIMUM SPEED	1200mph
CEILING	50,000ft
RANGE	1380 miles

ABOVE: The X-51A Waverider is an air-breathing hypersonic development programme, a successor to which may provide the Air Force with a global strike capability. USAF